Curriculum Confidential 9

by Jim Sweetman

COURSEWARE PUBLICATIONS 1999

This book is dedicated to Jessica Sweetman.

Index

Education Update...5

Curriculum Development.. 22

The 3-16 Curriculum... 27

The 14-19 Curriculum 37

Schools 49

Computers in Schools 72

OFSTED & Inspection 75

Literacy and Numeracy... 86

Raising Standards... 92

English 1999 99

Mathematics 1999.. 106

Science 1999 114

Design & Technology 1999 122

I.C.T 1999.. 125

Modern Foreign Language 1999... 127

Humanities 1999 129

Art & Music 1999... 133

Physical Education 1999.. 136

Religious Education 1999... 138

Sex and Drug Education 139

Addresses 140

Introduction

Dear Colleagues,

Welcome to **Curriculum Confidential 9**, your essential guide to the national curriculum and much, much more. After the heady months following the 1997 election, the last year has brought slower, but perhaps more lasting, change. The introduction of fair funding, the publication of the government's Green Paper on teaching and appraisal and the implementation of the School Standards and Framework Act are all likely to have a substantial impact on the way that schools are managed in the future. The arrival of the National Literacy Strategy in primary schools has also had a significant impact on the curriculum there. Alongside these major changes, a raft of lesser changes has been launched and new money for buildings, books and ICT is filtering slowly into schools.

Stephen Byers has moved on after a brief spell at the DfEE but Chris Woodhead remains in place with his influence almost undiminished. With his enduring capacity to reinvent himself, he has subtly realigned OFSTED to match the new standards mentality and the concern for improvement rather than monitoring. However, the Qualifications and Curriculum Authority and the Teacher Training Agency have struggled to make the same impact. The former has been tied up with a massive review of vocational courses and the latter has been caught between a desire to make its headship qualification sufficiently rigorous and the difficulty for deputy headteachers in finding the time to complete it.

The Standards Task Force and the National Grid for Learning are two innovations which have yet to make an impact but their influence will increase as value-added measures of school improvement develop and the ITC teacher retraining exercise gets into gear from September.

There is more on all of these developments in the following pages which try, as usual, to bring some sense of history and insight to what is taking place in education. The infomatic revolution is threatening to bury schools under a deluge of facts and statistics but that is not the same as standing back and taking stock. For example, will the people who bring in new methods of appraisal from September really try to find out why the last appraisal system was - ultimately - made so anodyne by those who had to implement it? And, how certain is it that the immensely well-funded training in new technology for teachers will not end up as a pile of videotapes and CD-ROMS on the shelves of people in schools who cannot find the time - or a spare machine - to view them?

As always, **Curriculum Confidential 9** sets out to do more than report on what has happened. Because it is an annual publication, I always welcome comments, corrections and amendments and your ideas on how it can be improved.

With best wishes,

Jim Sweetman

April 1999

Education Update

Institutionalised Racism

The fall out from the Stephen Lawrence inquiry raised the issue of institutionalised racism in English society and that has to include its schools. Exclusions for black pupils are still too high (around three times as many as for white pupils), the proportion of teachers from ethnic minorities remains stubbornly low, OFSTED does not monitor antiracist policies in schools and Herman Ouseley, the chair of the Commission for Racial Equality, accused the Teacher Training Agency of 'sticking two fingers up at antiracism' in 1998 and claimed that British education was 'institutionally racist' in 1999.

If institutionalised racism refers to access, opportunities, glass ceilings and locked doors then English schools are racist for both teachers and pupils. As just one example, a 1999 survey showed that three-quarters of all teachers admitted to overhearing racist language in use but fewer than 10% of schools logged racist incidents. It should not be forgotten, however, that schools are also biased against the poor and socially disadvantaged, against children with special needs and against the other low attaining pupils in the system who do not fall into these groups.

Whether schools are racist or supremacist in their cultural perspectives is a more difficult issue. As well as the truism that schools reflect society they also shape its future, and it is arguable that living harmoniously is as important as a sound grasp of phonics and should be equally valued. It is also worth noting that the compulsory curriculum does carry a surprising amount of cultural baggage. It would be pleasing to be able to report that preparation for adult life in the revised curriculum says more about multiracial Britain than the old history (few famous people are black), geography (black people are poor), English (black people write colourful poems about markets) or music (black people love rhythm) curriculum documents but it will need a sea-change to deliver that.

Furthermore, it is not only the case that schools have never taken a lead in antiracism but, oddly enough, no-one has ever come up with a clear picture of exactly what such a lead might entail. Most headteachers with predominantly white Anglo-Saxon staff and pupils, make the appropriate noises, say the correct things in policy documents, are impressed with the studiousness of Asian girls without thinking overmuch about the quality of their lives and suspend pupils without thinking about their colour. But, whether they address antiracist issues forcefully and regularly is less certain.

The current fashion - see the Education Development Plan of almost any London borough - is to address black underachievement, yet this is always couched as a remedial programme where extra literacy, numeracy and basic skills and a multi-agency focus on attendance will bring black boys into line and stop them wanting to join gangs and abuse drugs. The bigger issue, of course, is what schools and society do to black boys (and to poor white boys to a lesser extent) to turn them from bright-eyed hopefuls at age five into problem cases. It looks from the existing evidence that it is primary education that does the damage; secondary schools stir the unstable mix and light the fuses.

So, what goes wrong? Parental links are one possibility. Working parents, single parents and fathers who are poor, unemployed, disadvantaged or who had bad experiences in schools themselves, can disappear through home-school links that appear to any cursory evaluation to be flourishing.

The curriculum is another suspect. What children do in school may appear to be futile or numbingly boring without the sense of progression that makes learning fun for those who accomplish it successfully. Being in the top 20% target group for literacy and numeracy, having your hand up constantly and being rewarded by the teacher is fine but sitting there for two hours a day wondering what is going on because you don't quite understand the teacher is another matter - so is differentiated group work when you are in the bottom group!

School ethos also raises some questions. Adults who travel know that it is only the English who get on without asking questions even if they make mistakes, who chose to work quietly, to form queues and to eat what is on their plates out of politeness but such taken-for-granted assumptions permeate primary school life and the judgements made by teachers.

Government and Politics

In the first government reshuffle, Stephen Byers was promoted to the Treasury as Chief Secretary. Charles Clarke became Junior Schools Minister behind Estelle Morris, George Mudie was given responsibility for lifelong learning and Margaret Hodge came into the government as a junior employment minister with responsibility for equal opportunities and childcare (these last two replacing Alan Howarth and Kim Howells). Tessa Blackstone and Andrew Smith stayed where they were. As the ex-chair of the Commons Education Select Committee, Margaret Hodge is a rising star and could yet, if things turn out well for her, be a future secretary of state for education. Estelle Morris deserved her promotion for some sound work on exclusions and special needs policies and it was certainly in the interests of teachers to have someone who was previously a teacher in a comprehensive school in an area of genuine social deprivation (Sydney Stringer Community School, Coventry) at the heart of government. With responsibility for standards she was set to work more closely with Chris Woodhead with whom, one suspects, she does not have a great deal in common but there have been no indications of clashes thus far. The move of Stephen Byers to the Treasury may also benefit education where it is clearly helpful to have a sympathetic hand on the public purse.

For the opposition, David Willetts replaced the uninterested Stephen Dorrell. Known as 'two brains' for his reputation as a thinker on the Conservative right, Willetts lost his job as paymaster general in the John Major government after the 'cash for questions' affair. He is now rehabilitated and his presence may keep the DfEE on its toes - something that his predecessor failed miserably to achieve.

The Liberal Democrats have an effective spokesman in Don Foster but found themselves in difficult waters over an annual conference proposal to allow local communities to form trusts to run schools. This was defeated but is not a million miles away from what Labour is now encouraging for the next round of education action zones. It does, however, seem to have the support both of the outgoing leader, Paddy Ashdown and of Don Foster. There has also been talk of a community led action zone bid in Liverpool with the support of the Liberal Democrats who control Liverpool Council. The party is also uncertain of where it stands on grammar school abolition.

Since Labour came to office the influence of political advisers - rather than career civil servants - has increased. The School Standards and Effectiveness Unit (SEU), headed by Michael Barber rather than a civil servant, has a staff of over one hundred as well as a team of specialist advisers while the DfEE's communications are handled by David Blunkett's old press officer. However, it would be easy to make too much of this. After OFSTED took away the HMI function from the DfEE, it lacked the sound of expert voices for a number of years and the changes may simply be a means of finding a better balance.

The work of the Standards Task Force (STF) behind the scenes is interesting. It has, for example, a sub-group led by Carol Adams, Chief Education Officer (CEO) for Shropshire, which is responsible for disseminating professional good practice by making use of the internet and the National Grid for Learning (NGfL). The membership of this group includes John Macbeath, David Hargreaves, Stephen Heppell and Nick Tate and it could be the work of this powerful little committee which has led David Blunkett to develop such a sour view of the worth of the Teacher Training Agency (TTA).

As policy emerges, it is interesting how Labour has adopted a stick and carrot policy with teachers. Fast-track dismissal, the Byers-Woodhead power axis, 'naming and shaming', and intervention in the curriculum with the literacy and numeracy strategies were all designed to keep teachers and education in their place but they can be balanced against the 1997 Education White Paper moves to improve the status of the profession and the shift to 'acclaiming' the work of schools. There is an element of what might be termed 'googly-doctoring' in this, where the initial spin satisfies the right-wing traditionalists but there is an additional twist to the ball which reassures teachers that education is still the great concern of the government.

It is a precarious path but one that has been followed successfully thus far, perhaps partly as a result of the extensive - and increasing - representation of the education sector within government. Charles Clarke once worked as a mathematics teacher, Margaret Hodge taught children with special needs, Estelle Morris was a full-time career teacher and Alan Michael was a youth worker. Gordon Brown, Robin Cook, Mo Mowlem, Tessa Blackstone, Stephen Byers and Ann Taylor have all worked at some time or other as lecturers in further education or in universities. Cynics may yet suggest that those who can't teach go into politics! As a measure of comparison, John Major's last cabinet included only three people with education experience or affiliations.

Not many people know about them but the DfEE has performance targets to meet just as they exist elsewhere in education. As one might expect they incorporate the National Advisory Council for Education and Training (NACETT) targets, those relating to class size and the literacy and numeracy targets for key stage 2 but they also include the ambition of reducing truancy by one-third, doubling the percentage of nursery places for 3-year-olds by 2002 and getting 250,000 under 25-year-olds off state benefits by 2002.

The Third Way

If there is one thing the government is keen to introduce it is the third way but few people have a clear understanding of what it means. It is posited on the assumption that society has tried the first and second ways which have been unsuccessful!

The first way is where wealth is concentrated in a few hands and the rich own everything. The free market shapes the world, public spending is limited and taxation is low. Education in such circumstances is highly differentiated by wealth and aptitude and the poor are offered the occasional philanthropic gesture to make them better workers or to stop insurrection. The second way, not in truth very convincingly espoused by socialist governments, redistributes wealth through high public spending, public ownership and high taxation coupled with legislation. It creates a bureaucracy of identical schools delivering national policies and, in theory, will do away with differentiated education for the wealthy or the clever. It may be associated with the voice of 'old' Labour but it has never been enacted in English schools.

The third way involves shared ownership and no increase in personal taxation. Here, the self-interested philanthropy of the Victorian era is transformed into sponsorship and partnership in education and the differentiation on the basis of wealth and ability is covered over with a new stress on diversity on the basis of aptitudes and interests.

The third way is based in two key principles. The first is mutualism based in the utilitarian notion that individual well-being is only attainable through collective interdependence. Applied to schools it creates the stakeholder mentality, where teachers, pupils, parents, governors and the community all have an interest in the success of the school. It also supports visions of lifelong learning and the idea of the school as being at the heart of community education in its relationships with the community it is part of. This notion of interdependence also underlines a shift from the public or private dichotomy to mixed ownership, makes education outcomes more important than resourcing and inputs, and puts the consumers in education on a level with the providers.

Pragmatism is the second key principle because it provides the means by which mutualism can be made to work. In the sense that it is used today, it is opposed most specifically to ideology. Ideology means working by principles but pragmatism is doing what works best in the circumstances. That is why a battle over selection or parental choice is not worth fighting in a particular local area - it is better to develop the system as a whole.

Taken as a whole, this is the way forward espoused by new Labour. To its critics it is wishy-washy and unprincipled but its supporters see it as a genuine means of breaking the mould of society. It remains to be seen who is right.

Social Inclusion and Exclusion

Tackling what the government defines as social exclusion on a broad front is a priority in which schools are bound to be involved. The definition of social exclusion is vague but overwhelmingly negative. It is essentially a euphemism for the group of people described by the last government as 'welfare scroungers'. It covers areas and households characterised by poverty, long-term unemployment, benefit dependency and shattered relationships. Schools which have sometimes in the past been the only organisations to attempt to pick up the pieces should welcome any new initiative in this area.

The policies include neighbourhood renewal, where the problems are tackled on a geographical basis. This involves improving amenities, the environment and increasing community participation in local affairs and, where this has been carried through, there is no doubt that the achievements have been impressive. In September 1998, seventeen local authority areas were identified as Path Finder areas and will be able to bid for extra cash to find out what works best in tackling problems on the ground. The areas were chosen for high rates of adult unemployment, a preponderance of one-parent families and for notable levels of drug use and high rates of truancy in schools. Schools are involved with the new policies on exclusion in many ways. To begin with, there are two specific targets to be met with which schools will be involved. The first is that permanent exclusions and days lost to truancy are to be cut by 30% by 2002, and the second is that those permanently excluded will receive an alternative full-time education by the same date. In addition, under the Crime and Disorder Act (1998), the police now have the power to take truants back to school - previously they could only act if the pupil was in danger or committing a crime - and courts can impose parenting orders which could require the parents of truants to deliver their children to school each day in person or to attend classes in parenting.

A related initiative is the Sure Start programme which will target the children of the poorest families in Britain, rather as Head Start programmes have done in the USA. With around £500 million of funding, the scheme will operate through nurseries and playgroups in areas of social disadvantage. The idea is that the family is visited within three months of birth by someone from the project who can talk about constructive play and offer parenting classes and then monitor the child as a family 'friend' rather than a social worker. Education Action Zones will be obvious early candidates for the money which has generally been welcomed although a few of the voluntary agencies working in these areas have warned the government about the dangers of moralising to, and patronising their clients.

Political Publishing

One of the most important publications of the year was OFSTED's review of secondary education in the first cycle of secondary school inspections (*Secondary Education 1993-97*, OFSTED/ Stationery Office, 1998). Most of the statistical information was relegated to an annex but many of the facts about schools were fascinating for teachers. The tone of the book was occasionally self-congratulatory and anecdotal but it presented a clear vision of where OFSTED believes that schools should be heading in the next millennium.

More interesting was Philip Gould's 'kiss for cash' book about the emergence of new Labour. *The Unfinished Revolution* claimed that the Blairite reformers were horrified by Harriet Harman's decision to send her son to a grammar school in 1996. They thought she was in the wrong but felt that if she resigned it would be a victory for the old guard. So, she was supported in public but isolated by the party machine. Gould also claims that Labour changed its education policy as far back as the summer of 1994, deciding then to evade the clutches of the teacher unions and the local authorities by focusing on standards and improvement.

Peter Clark, the man sent in to save The Ridings School in Halifax, published his account of the first months spent in the job. It was generally considered to be a colourful story and Karen Stansfield, the former head of the school, disassociated herself from the way that she was described. The controversy over the on-screen gestures that were carried on television

news behind the first reports from the troubled school flared up again with Clark's claim that a magazine photographer or cameraman had asked the pupils to 'flick some Vs'. The BBC, which brought in an outside broadcast camera on a hoist on day two of the inspection and borrowed a pensioner's flat that overlooked the school to film for *Panorama*, carried the pictures but said the event was nothing to do with its staff.

Another person in the news was Tom Bentley whose new book, *Learning Beyond the Classroom*, argued that the focus of education must become the learner not the school, and that learning must be for life and take place in a range of contexts. Along the way, Tom came up with the mind-boggling insight that teachers only exceptionally 'transform' pupils' lives and that to expect major change to come from an emphasis on classrooms and teaching is optimistic. Of course, some people might think that a twenty-something Oxford graduate who looks about fourteen and only got noticed because he won an essay writing competition has some cheek telling those who have been at it for years how to reform the education system but, if you work for the think-tank Demos and write the odd speech for David Blunkett, it is apparently okay.

New Legislation

After Labour came to power, there were 'broad-brush' statements of policy in 1997 but 1998 saw the enactment of the necessary legislation. The two flagship acts took over two hundred and fifty hours of parliamentary discussion to achieve agreement and, when tuition fees for university students were discussed, almost led to precipitous constitutional change. Education is now in a phase where circulars and guidance interpret the intentions of the legislation and some of the chickens start coming home to roost!

The Teaching and Higher Education Act

The Teaching and Higher Education Act (1998) was a key piece of legislation that introduced a raft of changes. The establishment of the General Teaching Council (GTC) is a major event in education and while its long-term significance remains uncertain teachers will soon notice that they are paying for this extension to their career structures. Amendments to the legislation as it went through Parliament ensured that the GTC would have a majority of serving teachers and take over teacher registration (and deregistration) from the DfEE. There is more detail on the constitution of the GTC in the *Teachers and Pupils* section.

THE TEACHING AND HIGHER EDUCATION ACT (1998)

This act provides the legislative framework for:

- The General Teaching Council

- OFSTED inspection of local authorities

- Means-tested tuition fees for students

- Professional qualifications for headship

- An induction year for all new teachers

for candidates and the transferability of their skills into the school setting but the principle is undoubtedly important.

Similarly, the induction year for new teachers is a much-needed development but schools will find that it places additional responsibilities on senior staff as the government Green Paper indicated at the end of 1998. And, finally, this was the legislation that empowered OFSTED to inspect local education authorities which could yet turn out to be the agency's Achilles' heel. The effects of the Act have hardly been felt by teachers in schools but they will undoubtedly be significant and may be controversial in the longer term. As one example, the ruling that failing schools cannot take on teachers in their induction years is one that has already been alleged to have harmful and, perhaps, unanticipated consequences.

Equally important is the introduction of a compulsory qualification for new headteachers. Of course, the extent and quality of change that this brings about will be judged by the quality of the experiences provided

THE SCHOOL STANDARDS AND FRAMEWORK ACT (1998)

New powers for central government:

- Fresh start policies for failing schools

- The right to take over failing local authorities

- The allocation of specialist school status

- The introduction of Education Action Zones

- The right to set class size limits

- The abolition of the Funding Agency for Schools (FAS)

New requirements for local authorities:

- Local Education Authority development plans

- Admission procedures based on school organisation committees and local adjudication

- Monitoring of school status framework

- Local Education Authority Code of Practice defining relationships with schools

- Regulations to ban local 'assisted-places' schemes

- Rules to enable more parental representation on governing bodies and LEAs

- Early-years development plans

New requirements for schools:

- School truancy targets

- Ballots to abolish selection and grammar schools

- Nutritional standards for school midday meals

The School Standards and Framework Act

The School Standards and Framework Act (!998) is likely to have an extensive impact on schools. Apart from setting up the new categories of school (community, aided and foundation) and consigning the grant-maintained sector to history, the local education authority code of practice and the mechanism for local ballots over the status of grammar schools will give local politicians and bureaucrats plenty to argue over.

Meanwhile, the establishment of education action zones (EAZs) will maintain the tensions between local authorities and schools. The legislation on class sizes (a maximum of thirty for infant classes) was politically astute but it will provide a lever that local authorities can use to manipulate primary school places in ways that teachers and parents may not like. The Act also banned corporal punishment in independent education, courtesy of the Liberal Democrats. Anyone who thinks that this was anachronistic nonsense should remember that there was a police inquiry into the use of corporal punishment at an independent school in Essex in 1997 after which several teachers were suspended.

These two mammoth pieces of legislation dwarfed one that could also have a significant effect on schools. The National Lottery Act (1998) added the New (National) Opportunities Fund to the five good causes (The Arts, Heritage, Charity, Sport and the Millennium) on which lottery profits can be spent and speeded up the procedures by which the money is distributed. Change was probably necessary but nobody noticed how a fundamental principle of the national lottery - that its profits would not replace government funding - was discarded with indecent haste.

There is now £800 million to spend by September 2001. A huge sum will go to homework and after-school clubs and about as much to the retraining of teachers and librarians in Information and Communication Technology (ICT) skills. One innovation in the law is to allow the good causes to give out vouchers for spending which will, in theory at least, enable local beneficiaries to have more control over what they purchase.

County Council Changes

The government is consulting on changes to the organisation of county councils which could have a significant influence on how education is supported by local government. One popular proposal is for a cabinet style government which would take power back from committees such as the typical education committee to a smaller - and largely policy-making - centralised body. For good or bad, this could reverse the flow of decision-making within local authorities where, currently, it is usually a committee's proposals that go on to be confirmed by the full council.

Fairness at Work

The government's White Paper on proposed employment legislation could have some effects on schools if all of the proposals are implemented. Reducing the qualifying period for maternity leave from two years to one would give teachers forty weeks of maternity leave after only one year in post. The proposals for parental leave would allow all teachers to take up to three months unpaid leave in their child's first eight years of life and those for 'urgent family leave' could require a revamp of the cover system.

Reducing the qualifying period for protection from unfair dismissal claims from two years to one is likely to see the end of short-term teaching contracts which currently end with a form of non-renewal that is tantamount, legally at least, to dismissal. School managers might also note that an unfair dismissal case involving an application to job-share was won in 1998. The tribunal affirmed that job-sharing is an acceptable way to work and cannot serve as the grounds for dismissal.

The next phase of the Data Protection Act legislation will give workers the right to see almost all of the information about them that a school holds - not only that held on computers. The rights are being introduced gradually but it would make sense for schools to implement an open filing system before then and to ensure that old references, comments on incidents involving members of staff and unsubstantiated allegations about them are cleared out well in advance.

Educational Finance

The government has developed a tendency to announce good news several times over, so barely a week goes by without the media carrying a new story about more money for hospitals and schools. In July 1998, as part of the annual comprehensive spending review, Gordon Brown announced an extra £19 billion for education to reduce primary classes to fewer than thirty pupils more quickly, speed up the rebuilding programme, fund six thousand new teachers and provide almost 200,000 new places in education for 3 to 5-year-olds.

Around £17 billion of the money was allocated by the end of the year which was slightly unfortunate since this was intended to be a three year programme. However, much of the money is paying for initiatives that run for several years. Over £7 billion has gone to local education authorities to cover teachers' salaries but also including a slight increase in the standard spending assessments (SSA) for 1999-2000. A review of these, self-evidently unfair, calculations is to take place over the next couple of years to bring schools in different parts of the country into line but the government has not been rushed into action that could be locally controversial and particularly so in the South-East of England.

Of the rest, £3 billion has gone to Scotland and Northern Ireland, nearly the same amount to further and higher education, £0.5 billion for the early years strategy and just over £2 billion for capital spending projects (including the class size reduction initiative). That leaves £1.63 billion sloshing about at the DfEE for a range of improvement initiatives, special needs and drug education.

Further education has been the big winner in percentage terms but schools should still feel better off. There is no doubt that the government, having taken a strong line with the local authorities about ring-fencing new money for education, has since been irritated by their unwillingness to devolve it. Advisory teams, teachers centres and central services have all benefited. There was also evidence in early 1999 that some councils were going to re-route the new money whatever David Blunkett said to them. Wiltshire, for example, was planning to put £7.2 million out of an additional £10 million into schools, siphoning £1.3 million into social services and highways while retaining the balance for central services.

While there is undoubtedly more money for education under Labour, economists wrangle over exactly how much. The magical £19 billion, for example, covered a three year period and once salaries and inflation are taken into account it is a much smaller, but still significant, sum. As a reference point, the annual budget for all of education in 1998-99 was £38 billion. There is also a government tendency to announce the global figure for one set of headlines and then to

trumpet each element additionally as it is allocated, so that the DfEE sometimes appears to be giving more away than ever reaches schools. However, for 1999-2000, all schools should see an increase of around 5% under one heading or another.

The top people continue to do well. The news that Chris Woodhead's new contract would see his annual salary rise to £115,000 was greeted with incredulity in staff-rooms. He is now £25,000 ahead of David Blunkett (£90,000) and slightly further ahead of Nicholas Tate of the QCA (£89,000) and Anthea Millett of the TTA (£78,000). Payments to the general secretaries of the teacher unions go up to around £80,000. A teacher's starting salary in 1998 was £15,012 rising to £22,410 at the top of the main professional scale without additional responsibilities. Teachers at this level work for around 55 hours a week.

An interesting piece of research showed that after the abolition of the Inner London Education Authority (ILEA) in 1990 the, then, Conservative government pumped up the standard spending assessments for the inner London boroughs by almost £200 million over and above what was being spent by ILEA. The aim was to make an organisation which the government branded as overtly politicised, inefficient and extravagant look as if its central spending had been out of control. It is only fair to say that the strategy was a complete success and most schools felt better off after ILEA - now they know why!

Devolved Funding

Devolved funding is the key term set to replace budget delegation. It is a framework which gives schools the power to control their own spending on services like school meals, buildings and maintenance, payrolls, and cleaning and ancillary staff. They can also opt into or out of curriculum support, school library services and

---

DEVOLVED FUNDING (1999 ONWARDS)

Local authority non-school spending:

■ Adult education

■ Student grants and awards

■ Youth services

Local authority retained funding:

■ Strategic management

■ Access (transport and admissions)

■ School improvement

■ SEN provision

Individual School Budget spending:

■ Buildings, repairs and maintenance

■ Minor capital works

■ School meals

Central support:

■ Ancillary services (payroll, cleaning and catering)

■ Curriculum, advisory and training

■ School libraries

⬅ **BUY BACK FROM LEA IF REQUIRED**

supply cover arrangements. Local authorities are to be left with strategic management and education development plans, admissions, school transport and SEN provision. The proposals were outlined in *Fair Funding: Improving Delegation for Schools* (DfEE, 1998), a consultative document which attracted wide support initially but which also raised some doubts. The essentials of the new scheme should be in place by April 1999 with the exercise completed in April 2000. Around £1 billion will change hands in the exercise.

One view about devolved funding is that it is a sop to grant-maintained schools designed to make them feel at home in the educational mainstream. Another is that it is an admission that, in financial management at least, the grant-maintained sector has scored a considerable success. However, moving from the principle of devolving finance, which most people in education agree is a good idea to the practice raises some uncomfortable questions.

Among the most pressing are the formulae to be adopted by local education authorities in distributing cash to schools for their individual school budgets (ISB). The first grant-maintained schools were endowed with a massive injection of new cash over and above what they would have received from any local authority delegation. This allowed them to appoint bursars, develop their premises budgets and staff development plans, and do all this with the protection of a financial safety net for the first few years. The situation in 1999 will be rather different and small secondary schools and most primaries are likely to find their budgets disappointing, while being unable to achieve any economies through working on a different scale. As examples, staff services and payroll services only come into their own in organisations with around fifty staff - with smaller numbers they are simply an expense and a worry. The local authority formulae are largely driven by pupil numbers but there are enough exceptions to make space for either flexibility or argument.

From the local education authority side, the same problems will emerge as happened in the early 1990s in those authorities with a large number of grant-maintained secondary schools. Advisory teams fell apart, there was no continuity of provision as schools opted in or out of services, and functions like school meals, cleaning and catering lost the large scale economies which made them viable in the first place. There is also certain to be a tension between the local authority's overall responsibility for school improvement, its lack of resources to monitor it and the school's control over the budget that delivers it. And, somewhere along the line, the differential spending on pupils from one authority to another will have to be challenged.

School meals and library services will be two immediate battle grounds. Many local authorities additionally subsidise school lunches as part of their social responsibility but if this subsidy is handed to schools it cannot be ring-fenced for spending on meals. Logically, therefore, it will not be passed on where schools 'take the cash' but may remain as a hidden factor for those schools that stick with the authority. Unison, the main trade union represented in this area has vigorously opposed the transfer.

Library services which have considerable emotional support among the public also cannot function as stopcocks to be turned on and off as spending fluctuates year by year and in this area there is a danger that schools will try to take over functions which overload staff. A modern integrated library and ICT resources area sounds inviting but if it takes a teacher at the top of the salary spine and with allowances to run it, then it may not be economic and may quickly become a drain on resources. The lesson from the grant-maintained revolution is that many schools will be attracted by the control over cash that devolved funding offers and the local education authority provision will be damaged as a result. And, as happened before, it is the peripheral services - welfare or non-school education, for example - where the damage will be greatest.

The best advice for schools is to plan carefully and to allocate resources to change rather than simply taking the money. Payroll management proved a real challenge for the grant-maintained schools because so many factors - apart from the money - are involved in taking on responsibility for staffing. Primary schools may not need a bursar but they do need someone with a clear grasp of accounting, as well as a site manager and someone with personnel responsibilities. In even a medium sized primary school these people will be hard to find and resource.

But, having sounded a cautionary note, it is worth stressing that there are real advantages for schools in having their own cheque books and earning interest on their balances. It can make staff more aware of the need to get a return on investment and can make financial planning - as part of school development - into a genuine exercise. Getting the Parent-Teacher committee into school to repaint the entrance makes better sense when the school has a facility to buy the paint, the beer and sandwiches to deliver a cheaper and quicker result than the local authority.

The DfEE has also said that it will publish league-tables showing which authorities are laggards when it comes to devolving their budgets. These will be interesting because the increasing number of appointments of literacy and numeracy co-ordinators and of advisory staff is clearly having the effect of increasing central spending within local authorities at the moment. Perhaps the plan is to build this to a peak so that after April 1999, any downturn will look like devolved funding in action!

The removal of more powers from the local authorities through devolved funding has reopened the debate about what kind of future the bodies are entitled to. There is a view that local education authorities are - almost inescapably - politically motivated, monopolistic and financially careless because they are not genuinely accountable. While it is understood that there has to be a bridge between national policy and local implementation the argument is that this could be provided - locally - by national companies working in competition. So, Asda or Tesco might compete to run services for a group of schools in a local way but under a national framework much more efficiently than a local education authority can.

The argument against this is that education does not need a layer of profit-taking between schools and government, and that the education service relies on local democratic accountability and the links between all the other aspects of local government - social services, museums and libraries to name but a few. It may be the case that the government likes to keep the argument on the boil so as to keep local authorities in line rather than that it possesses any real desire to do away with them.

Rebuilding Schools

Improving the fabric of the maintained school stock has been a key priority for Labour. In April 1998, the government announced a further £500 million for school renovation projects involving four thousand schools nation-wide. This was in addition to £115 million allocated in September 1998 which led to work in two thousand schools and the 1998 Budget announcement of money to replace outside toilets.

Most of the total was drawn from the 1998 New Deal allocation of funding but it included some private money introduced as part of public-private partnership schemes. Education authority projects benefited by sums ranging from £50,000 to almost £7 million.

Public-private partnerships where projects are completed with private money and then leased back to public organisations have worked well for the odd toll-bridge but have been less effective in education. Colfox School in Bridport where a leisure centre has been developed along with the school's new buildings is one of the few examples but a 1998 analysis of the costs involved suggested that over the thirty years of the contract the saving to the local education authority would be minimal.

However, the government is still prepared to experiment with this kind of collaboration. Ten schemes are underway and another five pilot schemes were announced in April 1998, to rebuild, repair or develop schools in Cornwall, Tower Hamlets, Stoke-on-Trent, Kirklees and Sheffield. Just under two hundred schools could be involved in these projects which involve the setting up of Joint Venture companies to undertake the work rather than selling long term leasing arrangements to the private sector as happened with the PFI initiative. The government is prepared to invest £12 million in these over the life of

this parliament. Westminster is also still toying with the idea of similar funding for the renovation of the main buildings at Pimlico School.

The Bid Culture

In every aspect of education, headteachers and governors are now routinely involved in bidding for cash. Headteachers have to bid for the money to address class size problems and to provide new buildings, as well as for music provision and for after school initiatives. The Thatcherite notion which underpins bidding procedures is that value-for-money is defined by those making the bids working in competition with one another and not by those who administer the funds.

There is increasing evidence that some local authorities are clearly better at making bids than others. The *Times Educational Supplement* undertook an analysis of bid funding in 1998 which revealed wide disparities between areas over and above what one would expect from a government emphasis on areas of social deprivation. Newcastle, at £309 per pupil, topped the list but the first authority in the north-west, Salford, only came in at £140 per pupil behind Barnet and North Somerset!

As the process is devolved, schools also have to bid for money from their local authorities. Again, there would appear to be inequalities, so that a school which has successfully bid for one slice of funding and delivered the building or improvement on time seems to have a better chance of attracting further funds. This may be a consequence of a good track record in introducing innovation or it may simply mean that someone in the school has the time, inclination and skill to prepare bids that catch the eye of fundholders.

The lesson is that making effective, well-presented bids can attract spending and being thought of as an innovative organisation can help as well. The education departments in City of London, Doncaster, Enfield, Havering and Lincolnshire which all attracted less than £50 per pupil extra in the period surveyed might be thought to have some explaining to do by the headteachers and governors in their schools.

Section 11 Funding

Section 11 funding, currently administered by the Home Office and placed under threat in 1997, is to be delivered in future through the DfEE. This should mean that more of the cash is devolved to schools but it could threaten the specific units and peripatetic staff in urban authorities. There are some complicated issues involved. In many urban schools with problems of social deprivation, there is money coming through for literacy and numeracy support and for SEN pupils which sits uneasily with the Section 11 funding. In the worst cases, pupils find themselves withdrawn from additionally-funded literacy classes to go to Section 11 lessons with peripatetic teachers! However, full devolution of the cash to schools could appear to be racist in its effects - if not in its intentions - especially if existing Section 11 funded-teachers lost their jobs or responsibilities.

That explains why the government has popped the money into the standards budget at the DfEE, promised to maintain support to the local authorities at current levels for 1999-2000 and to sort out and consult on new proposals for the following years.

The Government Agencies

The QCA, Food and Classics

The Qualifications and Curriculum Authority (QCA), the offspring of the forced union between SCAA and NCVQ, has had a difficult year. This culminated in a financial crisis after the debacle over the contract for the computer processing of national test results which cost the agency an alleged £2 million and the overspend on the furnishing of its extravagant new headquarters in Piccadilly. With more experts in the DfEE in key advisory and policy roles, OFSTED's continuing hegemony over schools, standards and improvement, and a lack of control or influence over primary literacy and numeracy, QCA has appeared to outsiders to have been excluded from the heart of educational policy-making in 1998. Its current role seems humdrum, more concerned with monitoring and maintenance rather than innovation. So, it accredits qualifications (including hundreds of trivial vocational qualifications with tiny candidate numbers), monitors examinations and sets national tests without much apparent sense of ambition. Even in a key area like national curriculum revision, there is a strong sense that the agenda is being driven from elsewhere. Where QCA does good work - auditing NVQ providers or developing new qualifications for childcare workers, for example - it does not catch the public eye.

There is no doubt that some of the past year's work has been particularly challenging and it is arguable that the authority's more proactive projects have suffered from a lack of self-belief. As an example, the new criteria for A and AS Level courses after the year 2000 are based on a model that was espoused and hardened by a right-wing conservative government and the subjects, while experiencing the indignity of bolt-on key skills, have not been modified for the new millennium in terms of their appropriateness and value to society. It is quite surprising - if not shocking - that no-one has dared to think about what sort of history, geography or modern language is appropriate to be

taught and tested in a world where information handling and processing, media and communications have so fundamentally changed since these syllabuses were first laid out in the 1950s and 1960s. A 1997 initiative to separate responsibilities for academic and vocational subjects so as to avoid syllabus overlaps particularly at GCSE level also fizzled out in 1998.

For the primary sector, QCA published schemes of work for key stages 1 and 2 in response to the government's curriculum changes. The schemes of work covered science and ICT initially but geography, history and design & technology followed later in the year. The problem for the authority lay in the status of the schemes which were simply advice produced in response to a change the authority was caught on the hop by and which seemed to have a shelf life of only a couple of years. The DfEE Standards and Effectiveness Unit (SEU) also seemed intent on taking most of the credit for them.

Elsewhere, the accreditation of thousands of NVQ certifications, launched as indicative of a new rigour in the merged organisation, has turned out to be simply onerous and pointless. Many certifications are too specific to particular spheres of employment or exist on too small a scale to justify the work that has been involved in putting them through new bureaucratic hoops. Another initiative involved working with publishers to identify weaknesses in print and CD-ROM resources for schools. Understandably, the publishers did not rush to confess to these, especially around the table with their commercial competitors and the enterprise fell rather flat.

Worse still, and for perhaps the past three years, QCA - previously as SCAA - has shown an embarrassing tendency to explore blind alleys. John Patten set in train the lengthy discussions of the spiritual and moral curriculum which, with the personal support of Nick Tate, ended with mountains of paper and some undignified public wrestling between the churches. But this is now simply something to feed into the DfEE discussions of the new agendas on citizenship and preparation for adult life. Conservative politicians - or the manoeuvres to please them - were also behind the preparation of *Classics in the Curriculum*, a document designed to support the teaching of Latin, Greek and classical studies and with a nod in the direction of the history curriculum. As a promotional newsletter for the Association of Classical Teachers, the publication of the document in February 1998 was interesting but it was questionable whether this was either appropriate work for QCA or of particular interest to new Labour!

Another 1998 initiative saw the establishment of expert committees to monitor standards over time and to receive the results from QCA monitoring of public examinations. While it makes sense to have such a group in the interests of transparency and accountability, choosing the membership and maintaining more than an illusion of separate status is a challenge. What is more, QCA noted how the new body's judgements would be 'informed and impartial' almost as if its own conclusions might not be. There again, if the body does not exist simply to rubber stamp QCA findings, what will happen when it takes a different line from the authority?

And also in 1998, while the DfEE was trailblazing action zones and OFSTED was getting its teeth into the local authorities, QCA was considering 'opportunities for enriching pupils' experiences of food'. The Food in Schools Project was largely sponsored by the food industry but was hosted by QCA. It eventually turned up a series of classroom ideas and projects to make young people think about family values, nutrition and the idea that learning could be fun. However, the ideas were expounded with missionary zeal in a style which made it appear that the pupils were simply there for the ride while the curriculum links to history and technology were tenuous. In contrast to literacy and numeracy or to standards and target-setting the whole endeavour appeared rather frivolous. In the end, however, perhaps QCA was right. A MORI poll showed that 93% of a sample of 7 to 15-year-olds thought they could play computer games competently but only 38% reckoned they could make a baked potato.

QCA did claim one other victory in 1998. It stopped the examining boards from rationalising their syllabuses in minority languages. Publicised plans to abandon unprofitable syllabuses in subjects such as Dutch, Modern Hebrew and Polish were put on the shelf after QCA's intervention.

The next big test for QCA will come with the completion of the national curriculum review. There are three challenges here. The first is to make sense of the elements of the primary curriculum outside of literacy and numeracy and to do so in such a way that they lie comfortably alongside those in terms of appropriateness and status. The second is to produce a curriculum that is responsive to outside pressures without caving in to them. There are currently demands for more citizenship and preparation for adult life, more key skills and literacy at key stages 3 and 4 and more freedom for action zone schools to develop work-related education. The third and final challenge is to produce a curriculum for the new millennium, a framework of useful knowledge and skills which will reflect and take account of what young learners are going on to do with their continued lifelong education, their careers and their lives.

The Teacher Training Agency in Trouble

The Teacher Training Agency has promised much over the course of its existence but has delivered less. Most of its work on teacher standards lives in some advisory limbo-land, the headship qualification is not doing as well as hoped and is unlikely to be able to certificate all incoming headteachers by 2002, and the

rigorous work on initial teacher training which, with OFSTED's help has had the effects both of antagonising the providers and cutting provision, has irritated government ministers.

There are three challenges for the TTA in the coming year. The first is to get a handle on the appraisal system outlined in the Government Green Paper. If that exercise sidelines the agency and leaves the framework to the SEU, then the TTA is in trouble. However, its problems will be even worse if it cannot find a proper accommodation with the new General Teaching Council - the second challenge. If that body starts to make a bid for the new teacher accreditation business, then people may begin to argue that the TTA no longer justifies its budget. And, finally - the third challenge - the agency now has responsibility for the teacher training budget inherited from the Higher Education Funding Council (HEFC). If it fails to bring consensus and leadership to this area there will be few people left to support its work in the future.

The fundamental weakness of the TTA has always been that it has failed to carry the profession along with its proposals. Very early in its life, it went down the competence route to accrediting performance, turning out more fragmented statements about what teachers and headteachers should do or be able to do than even OFSTED would dare to. This approach has often obscured some sound analytical work. For example, in setting out the Special Educational Needs Co-ordinator (SENCO) standard, the agency delivered a first rate job description and a good argument for greater status for SENCOs but somehow managed to alienate even this hard working group in the small print by appearing to police them rather than offer support.

It has also been blinkered in terms of its direction. The developers of the headteacher qualification started off with the comfortable view that they knew what good headteachers should be like - lots of policies, schools run as tight-ships, management plans, ICT in the office - and then manufactured an induction course which patronised its clients and insulted their skills by gratuitous needs assessment, shabby delivery and underfunding. Then, they wondered why potential headteachers would prefer an MBA certification - international accreditation, individually focused, research based, self-directed - rather than their bit of paper to stick on the office wall.

The OFSTED Empire

The renewal of Chris Woodhead's contract for a further four years in 1998 and a 34% increase in salary to £115,000 (a little more with performance bonuses) was the icing on the cake for the school inspection agency. Surviving a change of government and a move to shorter and six-yearly inspections, OFSTED has gone outside its remit of inspecting schools to ravage or cultivate - depending on the point of view of the natives - vast areas of the educational landscape.

OFSTED took QCA to the cleaners in 1998 over the primary curriculum and the imposition of the literacy and numeracy strategies but Chris Woodhead has also spoken publicly in the last year about the inadequacies of national testing, and the need, as he sees it, to slim the curriculum further at key stages 3 and 4.

His interventions into the inspection of initial teacher training courses have posed a direct challenge to the authority of the TTA which has sometimes been reduced to following in his wake. The inspection of the local authorities seemed in 1997 to depend on a good understanding with Stephen Byers but, at the end of 1998, OFSTED was asked by David Blunkett to extend the programme to include all of the local authorities in spite of the antagonism engendered by the inspection reports on Birmingham and Manchester.

The beacon school initiative and school-based teacher training in selected primary schools was another slap in the face for the TTA and the higher education institutions while the report on educational research - also aimed at higher education - even annoyed the DfEE as it overshadowed their work in the same area. Meanwhile, some of the forays into the finances of local authorities upset the Audit Commission.

If, apart from the Audit Commission, Chris Woodhead has upset the universities, the TTA, the QCA and elements of the DfEE by his abrasive intrusions into their fields of influence, the question has to be asked of how he has survived let alone prospered. The answer is complex. First of all, Chris Woodhead is a highly astute thinker and manager and OFSTED is a relatively small organisation which makes it relatively easy to steer. OFSTED is far better than QCA, for example, at scenting the directions in which ministers are headed. Secondly, Chris Woodhead has a vision - sometimes categorised as anti-progressive but, in practice, far more complex - of educational management and leadership which many of his peers lack. Metaphorically expressed, it is concerned with fitness, work-rate, muscularity and energy in response to a system that is slightly overweight, flabby and easy-going. Thirdly, as an independent agency, OFSTED is responsible to Downing Street rather than the DfEE. It is said, for example, that Chris Woodhead personally sold John Major the idea of the literacy and numeracy strategies without involving the DfEE. This gives OFSTED a unique freedom of action. Fourth, the agency is adroit strategically. There are many areas where OFSTED acts as both initiator and evaluator. So the monitoring of the national literacy strategy is undertaken by OFSTED but the agency also designed the scheme and the documentation. The same is broadly true of the work on initial training.

And, finally, all of this would be as nothing without contacts and influences. The beacon school scheme

was launched at Highgrove, the home of Prince Charles and it is somewhere from within the Highgrove coterie - Jonathan Dimbleby, Melanie Phillips, the *Sunday Times* columnist, Penny Junor to name but a few - that Chris Woodhead's power base is sustained and supplied with the levers that enable him to be confident of his position, at ease with the right-wing press and able to open the doors at Downing Street and beyond.

There was a good example of this patronage in operation when Chris Woodhead was in difficulties early in 1999 after an 'off the cuff' comment to trainee teachers that sexual relationships between teachers and students (over the age of consent) might be 'educative'. His subsequent apology said that he was trying to be reassuring to someone who he felt might have been personally involved in such a relationship.

It is likely - but not certain - that he was set up after his acknowledged relationship with an ex-pupil, Amanda Johnston, came back into the public gaze because of the legislation which will make relationships between teachers and under 18-year-old pupils illegal. However, more damage was done when his, then, wife claimed in a Sunday newspaper that the relationship started when the girl was at school and that the soon to be HMCI had suggested a *menage a trois* as a way of resolving it.

What is odd about this old and relatively trivial story is the way that it never took off in the media - compare what happened to Robin Cook. Also, Tony Blair took the time to let it be known that he had every confidence in Chris Woodhead, the DfEE kept quiet and Melanie Philips - who is rarely tolerant of anything that reeks of moral equivocation - wrote a vituperative defence in *The Sunday Times* which implied that the whole exercise was a plot hatched by left-wing educationalists.

There has also been evidence in 1999 of OFSTED's capacity to change course in tricky waters. The Education Select Committee of the House of Commons was hearing some damning evidence before Christmas 1998 about the overwhelmingly critical nature of OFSTED inspection reports on a number of local authorities. However, what might easily have become a threatening situation was luckily averted in early 1999 with the coincidental publication of glowing reports on three authorities - one of them was the London borough of Brent!

The Examination System

The merger between NEAB, SEG and the City and Guilds vocational awarder was referred to the Office of Fair Trading as potentially monopolistic when it was realised that the combined organisation, the Assessment and Qualifications Authority (AQA), would have over half of the examinations market at 16+ and 18+.

The procedure is that the new organisation is first asked whether it trades fairly under the terms of the 1973 legislation to stop monopolies and, following its response, can be referred to the Monopolies and Mergers Commission. As far as the DfEE was concerned this was a formality and unlikely to lead to any action. However, in the future, AQA may have to tread carefully in promoting its courses to schools and colleges.

Another of the new confederacies was in the news when Oxford, Cambridge and RSA Examinations (OCR) research director, Alastair Pollitt, was featured in *The Daily Telegraph* over a story stating that he had claimed that public examinations were 'getting easier'. In fact, he was talking about one mathematics course but he made things worse later by suggesting that syllabus change could lead to lowered standards in almost all subjects.

His argument is that when a syllabus is changed, examining teams make allowances in the first year of the award but this dispensation then becomes part of the practice in subsequent years. There is little doubt that this feature - in the sense that standards of performance rise after syllabus changes - is detectable in examination awards since the mid-1980s but it might be explained by other aspects of the changed assessments which allowed candidates to 'do better'.

Appeals Against Results

The Independent Appeals Authority for School Examinations (IAASE) was in the news in 1998 for more than its adjudications. Firstly, it was taken more closely under the wing of the QCA, then it faced replacement by a new and more powerful independent organisation and was, finally, criticised for not dealing with appeals fast enough. Several appeals against 1997 examinations were still trundling through the appeals process in October 1998 and, where these involved A Level results, the potential for damage to the careers and higher education choices of the pupils involved was obvious.

However, while the IAASE got the flak, the problems in these cases often lie with the examining boards and their procedures which move very slowly and which have to be fully exhausted before a case can go to the IAASE. It is also possible that, after a string of defeats and with their futures more secure, the examining boards had already decided between them to take IAASE on. Several of the cases that went to appeal in 1998 were closed without genuine agreement and the examination boards, which are not bound by IAASE findings, proved unusually intransigent on some occasions. This new attitude - as much as anything else - caused the appeals system to crash.

That said, schools did win some victories in 1998. Marlborough College appealed successfully against SEG which was found to have handled the original appeal poorly by sending a chief examiner only five scripts to remark and sharing a remarking exercise between two examiners. NEAB was in trouble for managing to destroy a batch of English scripts that formed the basis for an appeal in the November following the 1997 examination and promised to review its procedures. The same board was also in the dock for a 1996 GCSE Accounting examination where the arithmetical grade boundary for A* was a mark of 201 out of 200! The school won this case and its candidate, who scored 195 out of 200, was given the higher grade.

However, other cases were settled less easily. One was the concluding of an appeal where the parents of a home-educated child appealed against NEAB over ten GCSE subjects sat by their daughter in 1996. The parents alleged that the board had caused their daughter stress by wasting time in processing her entries so that coursework and examination revision coincided. The IAASE agreed and asked NEAB to reconsider, whereupon the board made different adjustments to the examination marks in different subjects. The board may have had some logical argument for taking this action but to outsiders it simply appeared to be incompetent and the whole episode ended rather unpleasantly. The parents issued their own statement in May 1998, once the IAASE had closed the case, accusing NEAB of going back on agreements made with the IAASE and taking arbitrary and secretive actions.

But the greatest trouble occurred in the context of continued arguments with OCEAC (The Oxford and Cambridge Examinations and Assessment Council). The first was over its English A Level examination in 1996. This was the examination where the chief examiner and five examiners were sacked for alleged cronyism after a SCAA scrutiny team observed them at work. However, they later won a victory when the examining board settled with them before an industrial tribunal hearing took place, paying compensation and recognising that the team was following established procedures. The fallout from this award - which must have been chaotic - has led to a number of appeals the best known of which involved King Edward VI Grammar School in Chelmsford. The discrepancy between the schools 1996 and 1997 results was massive so the school appealed. As the process unravelled, OCEAC, admitted that two-thirds of the marking of a sample inspected was flawed and the board was criticised by IAASE for delays and poor communication. Appeals rose from 13 per 1000 in 1996 to 48 per thousand in 1997.

The other case involving OCEAC was first reported on in *Curriculum Confidential 8* and involved an appeal over a modular A Level in Theology where the standards for one module were out of line with other modules and with the achievements of the same candidates when they sat the module test again three months later. The school involved seemed to have a strong case. The aberrant module produced low marks nationally, the same pupils did much better on modules that were assessed against similar criteria and the candidates did considerably better the second time. However, on reviewing the marks, OCEAC made few changes and was adamant that its procedures were not at fault. It called an extraordinary meeting of its Grading Advisory Committee to look at the evidence and agree with its view and took what might be seen as a fairly strident attitude towards the IAASE recommendations.

The use of the heavy artillery by the examining board was understandable. If an appeal could be allowed on the basis of discrepancies between module marks then the whole basis of modular schemes would be called into doubt which would damage government policy as well as questioning the basis of an area ripe for lucrative examination development. The end result was a stalemate and the IAASE closed its case. OCEAC is now subsumed into OCR (Oxford, Cambridge and RSA Examinations).

All of this left a stale taste in the mouth as the work of the IAASE came to an end. It was set up in 1990 as part of the Parents' Charter and did some good work even if its procedures were slow to deliver results. As one of its last acts, it is worth recording that the authority appealed successfully to Tessa Blackstone on behalf of a handful of students who took a year out after receiving A Level results which were later judged to be unfair. Tessa Blackstone agreed that these students entering higher education in 1998, a year later than would have been the case, could be excused tuition fees for the full duration of their courses and receive maintenance grants on the old basis.

The new system for hearing appeals - the Examination Appeals Board (EAB) will be introduced in time for the 1999 examination cycle but IAASE will deal with outstanding cases from 1998. The EAB will be independent allowing open access to scripts and marking which are the subject of an appeal. There will be performance targets for concluding appeals and a parallel system for managing those made against GNVQ results. QCA has developed recommendations on the implementation of the EAB framework and these include the establishment of a number of pilot schemes in 1999 where GCSE scripts in selected subjects will be returned to schools.

Access to Examination Scripts

As noted above, one aspect of the new Examination Appeals Board (EAB) procedures will be that schools - and presumably parents - will be allowed to see the marked scripts that are the basis of an appeal once the case reaches review level. This is a significant change. Its introduction at key stage 3 has reduced script annotation to a minimum which, ironically, makes the

appeal process there less reliable because there is no indication on a script of exactly how the original marker came to his or her decision.

Currently, script marking at GCSE and A Level requires the standardisation of an examiner by attendance at a meeting where scripts and standards are discussed. Once initiated in this way, the marker's work (annotation and assessment) is then best thought of as a private correspondence between the script, the marker and other members of the marking team. This correspondence can use shorthand for shared understandings and include criterial and other references to the mark scheme as well as comments - usually expressions of admiration, amusement or despair!

The advantage of this system is that if a script is revisited for the purposes of an appeal, the train of thought leading up to the awarding of an eventual mark is evident. And, in reviewing a number of scripts it is relatively easy for a senior examiner to identify whether a colleague has been diligent and thorough and whether he or she is severe or lenient in making judgements.

However, once marking becomes a public exercise, this sense of correspondence breaks down. The marker has to write for a public audience, be exact in his or her observations, refrain from negative comment and has to make judgements that are explicit and supported by reference. There is an argument that this would be no bad thing but it would make examinations prohibitively expensive and would, perhaps oddly, not make the examiner's judgement any clearer to his or her colleague. So, what happens instead is that annotation all but disappears from the marked script which contains only the odd tick or reference to criteria and a final mark.

In this process, however, the value of the script as far as an appeal is concerned is diminished. The train of thought that led to the original mark is obscured and so the script is simply remarked by another examiner - a different procedure from following the logic of a colleague to the same or a different conclusion.

Where this happens at key stage 3 it has two consequences. The first is that most 'second' examiners, where they make a change, inflate the original mark slightly. They know that there is a concern about the script, they know what the original mark was and so it is human nature to look for additional credit in the pursuit of fairness. The second is that, when this happens, it is a misconception to imagine that the second marking is somehow more 'accurate'. The likely truth, or the most reliable judgement possible, is that the deserved mark is somewhere in the area covered by the two marks. Also, when there is an appeal and the blank script is presented, its relevance to the appeal is reduced. It is only possible to disagree with the original marker not to see what he or she was thinking.

The other point to consider is that, at key stages 2 and 3, the criteria are generally very clear. Where they are most abstract, as in the Shakespeare test for English at key stage 3, there is the most concern expressed about the unreliability of the judgements. Now, if there is substantive disagreement about something as transparent as what Brutus is up to in *Julius Caesar*, the possibilities for uncertainty must increase in GCSE and A Level subjects where the set material is more complex and the questions that much more demanding.

Computerised Marking

A new piece of software from the United States, the Intelligent Essay Assessor, was claimed in 1998 to be able to mark a student's work within seconds. There are several other developments underway in this area, most of which are programmed with a range of answers to which a candidate's work is compared. Some offer feedback as well. Experiments suggest that the software's reliability is almost as good as that achieved by different teachers and that, for standardised testing, computer programs have a genuine future in marking and assessing written answers. The benefit for the student is that the feedback is almost immediate which encourages formative redrafting. It should be possible to harness this technology to the examination system within the next five years or so.

Further Education

As usual, further education continues to show a capacity for irregularity and criminality that schools seem unable to match. There were allegations in 1998 that senior lecturers at a private business college in Oxford were requiring some of their staff to leak questions to students and to draft their answers. In one instance, the whistle-blower saw an invigilator and student change places during an examination. In other cases, it was alleged that college funds went on foreign junkets, the exotic refurbishment of a principal's office and the establishment of private profit-making companies run from college premises. It will be interesting to see whether the introduction of national devolved funding leads to a similar level of corruption and fraud allegations in schools.

However, funding for further education is increasing more rapidly than anywhere else in education with the government's emphasis on lifelong learning and re-skilling the workforce. Partnership is the key to attracting funding with Training and Enterprise Councils (TECs), local authorities, colleges and local industry and business working together on new projects which will fit neatly into the strategies of the

new regional development agencies (RDA). City Pride, based in Manchester, is a typical example pulling together a rang of agencies that have previously worked in the same field without talking to one another. The indications are that the colleges which do not enter into partnerships and fail to explore these emergent relationships are likely to lose out on funding.

Training and Enterprise Councils

The government is intent on changing the role of the regional Training and Enterprise Councils (TECs) but, currently, their involvement in mainstream education is growing. A 1998 consultation paper, *TECs: Meeting the Challenge of the Millennium*, proposed objectives for TECs that included the promotion of lifelong learning and raising standards in education. TECs are currently involved with training credits and national traineeships for 16 to 18-year-olds (linked to qualifications at NVQ Level 2), and modern apprenticeships for 16 to 22-year-olds (linked to qualifications at NVQ Level 3) as well as with the Investors in People (IiP) scheme.

From 1999, the TECs will have to work with the new regional development agencies (RDAs) and eventually they will probably be funded through them. Schools that have little to do with their local TECs need to build closer relationships because TECs have a key role to play in action zones, work-related learning and the development of careers education.

The University for Industry

A pilot phase in the North East of England has been completed and the new University for Industry will operate as a national institution from 2000 onwards. Gordon Brown is credited with the idea for an organisation that operates as a broker for education and training courses, taking education opportunities into the workplace, putting people in touch with distance learning opportunities and establishing drop-in centres where people can use research facilities.

The aim is that over two million people will be making use of the university each year when it goes national with the help of the BBC and the media to promote opportunities. In the pilot phase, there has been a stress on ICT qualifications but the aim is to offer a whole range of vocational avenues from a single telephone call. While the pilot has been a success, and the idea is sound, sustaining the momentum of a national institution will be harder. One proposal, supported by the TUC, is for the university to fund learning representatives in major companies so that on-the-spot advice is available to employees.

Youth Workers

In November 1998, OFSTED reported on the training and qualifications of part-time youth workers. This report is of particular interest to schools with community facilities attached or for those which are thinking of using part-time youth workers in after-school clubs. The report found the qualifications framework to be diverse if not actually anarchic, supervision and teaching to vary from one region to another and quality assurance to be limited. This was unsurprising given the way that the National Youth Agency accredits regional accreditation and moderation panels (RAMPS) that then, in turn, approve courses from NVQ providers, other bodies and maintained youth services. Clearly, OFSTED was undertaking the spadework for a new national certification in youth work with specific criteria and, at the minimum, a code of practice for providers. If nothing else, the report spells out the need for one.

Current Issues

Educational Research

The right-wing academic, James Tooley, whose views include the belief that IQ tests could replace national assessments and that the school-leaving age should be fourteen, published a scathing attack on the failings of educational research with the help of OFSTED. His conclusion that much educational research was partisan and made use of flawed methodologies was not unexpected, given that Chris Woodhead used his annual HMCI lecture in 1998 to berate educational academics for their lack of rigour and their failure to pursue higher standards. Tooley's research was followed up by a DfEE commissioned report which said much the same things and by the onslaught on Peter Mortimore of the London Institute of Education for his book, *The Road to Improvement*, which came in for the same kind of disparaging treatment as Harvey Goldstein received in 1997.

There has been a whiff of unpleasantness about this entire issue and it is hard to believe that the attack on educational research has not been an orchestrated one. The conspiracy theory is that OFSTED's pride was hurt by the constant attacks on its procedures and performance emanating from a broad group of 'liberal' academics, many of whom contributed to Mortimore's book. Salt was then rubbed into these wounds by the TTA's comments on research in 1997 which OFSTED must have felt did not go far enough. Perhaps, OFSTED also perceived the TTA's support for practitioner research and research that focused on teaching and learning in classrooms as a threat. So, allegedly, a plan was hatched to 'go after' the TTA's findings. Tooley was funded to take its observations apart while, to keep the issue warm, Chris Woodhead

used the - possibly inappropriate - opportunity of his annual lecture to launch more criticism. For conspiracy theorists, the sight of the columnist Melanie Phillips going after Peter Mortimore in *The Sunday Times* as if he was public enemy of the week simply proved their point, since on occasions she has appeared to be the public mouthpiece of the chief inspector. The involvement of the DfEE was less clear but Michael Barber did have a disagreement with Harvey Goldstein in 1997, so maybe he was in on the plan as well!

Money For Music

Another new initiative for 1998 and beyond was a new emphasis on music in schools. The resources are coming from the national lottery through the Youth Music Trust (YMT) set up by the Culture Secretary, Chris Smith. This worthy move should rescue peripatetic teaching, and school and regional youth orchestras from the brink of extinction. The first wave of bids were invited in December 1998 and the changes should be felt in successful local authorities by September 1999. Around forty councils have been hampered in making bids because they have either disbanded their provision for music entirely or have previously privatised it either to benefit from charitable status or to avoid having to devolve the funding to schools. Those that start a new music service from scratch will have to match any grant from the YMT with local money which may be hard to find in this year's budget.

School Security

School security continued to be big business in 1998. The trend is for new primary schools to have either secure boundaries - wire-mesh fences with mobile CCTV cameras - or to be bricked on the outside with shuttered windows. Door-entry systems are common and some nursery schools are tagging children. The costs are high but the situation is fast approaching where primary schools with unmonitored doors will be considered to be failing the children in their care. The other problem that teachers need to be aware of is fire - simply locking outside doors can replace one threat with another. Incidentally, it is important when installing security to make sure that parents do not get the impression that they have been locked out!

Dyslexia and the Courts

The woman who won £46,000 damages from a local education authority in 1997 for its failure to diagnose and treat her dyslexia saw the award taken from her by the Court of Appeal in November 1998. This was an important case since it appeared to have established the precedent - equally applicable to self-governing schools - that the local education authority owed

Pamela Phelps, a duty of care that included identifying her condition. Following the original decision, there were several hundred cases pending and they may have only been the tip of a much larger iceberg. The Court of Appeal has now ruled that the dyslexia was not congenital and that, therefore, the failure to respond to it could not be considered a dereliction of care. In principle, had the precedent been established it would have been possible to claim for poor teaching, in a school under special measures, or for bullying and victimisation by other pupils. These latter claims in particular, many of which have been settled out of court in recent years, would now appear to have less chance of success. While one sympathises with the dyslexic woman, school insurance premiums would have rocketed had her award been confirmed.

Other News

- 1998 saw the death of Ted Hughes, the Poet Laureate. For English teachers, reared, or often blooded, in the classroom on collections like *The Hawk In The Rain* and *Lupercal*, it was like the passing of an age where, against all the odds, poetry had remained on the syllabus. That this happened at all was largely to the credit of Hughes who invented the 'comprehensive' school of poetry - not clever, funny or wry but accessible to a wide spectrum of pupils through its deep roots in the darker side of nature. Many teachers also benefited indirectly from his work through the 'battery recharging' effects of the Arvon Foundation courses he sponsored in Devon.

- Hughes was also instrumental in establishing the post of children's laureate - the first post-holder will be announced in May 1999. One problem with the short-listing has proved to be that many children's writers, if not quite in the 'weirdo' category, appear not to be too keen on mingling with children as the job requires. Others whose works fall into the 'jolly doggerel' category could upset the cultural cognoscenti.

- Ashley Bramall, one time leader of ILEA also died in 1998. He was with the ILEA throughout the 1970s and steered the organisation to the position of political influence that caused Margaret Thatcher to determine its destruction.

- The National Confederation of Parent Teacher Associations which has been beset by internal rifts for several years attempted to re-establish itself. The Charity Commissioners appointed a new trustee to put the organisation back on track but, at the private annual general meeting in 1998, only 180 out of 11,000 members turned up and the old divisions resurfaced in bureaucratic squabbling. The main concern was whether the organisation could discuss a resolution to dissolve itself!

- Nord Anglia, the services to schools provider has seen its share price fluctuate between £4.50 and £1.30 in the last year, showing the volatility in this sector of education. The company failed to win a contract to lead an action zone and lost out in the bidding to run King's Manor School in Guildford. It needs an action zone, or perhaps an ailing local authority to take over, in 1999.

- New transport policies could see the introduction of workplace parking charges which could effect any plans that schools have to develop parking spaces. However, government plans to deliver children to schools more economically were broadly welcomed and it is possible that some bright spark will soon come up with the idea of having a publicly-funded free bus service!

- Schools that failed inspections in 1998 included St George's, Westminster where the headteacher, Philip Lawrence was murdered in 1997.

- Twenty-eight teachers, a caretaker and a school maintenance worker from St Thomas Aquinas School in Chorlton shared a £9 million lottery jackpot at the end of the year. The school had a teaching staff of forty-two before the event. Other school syndicates that were successful included twelve teachers from a Banbury primary school (£2 million), eighteen teachers from a Manchester primary (£3.5 million) and seven dinner ladies from Bristol (£100,000).

- Whatever Chris Woodhead may have been accused of doing with ex-pupils, was outdone by Mary Kay Letourneau, the American teacher who was sentenced to seven years in prison for raping a 13-year-old boy in her class. She also thought that no damage had been done by the event.

- An unknown number of teachers applied for jobs advertised at a school in Botswana which did not exist. Those who made applications were asked for $100 to cover work permits and visa checks. It is reckoned by Interpol that the organisers of the scam may have made over £100,000.

Curriculum Development

A curriculum is the experiences, opportunities and activities that you offer in your educational programme to help children learn and develop.
An Introduction to Curriculum Planning for Under-Fives, QCA, 1998.

Curriculum cut to side of A4

Headline in the *Times Educational Supplement.*

One lesson we learned from the first version of the current curriculum is that unless there is a shared understanding of why changes are being made, and a commitment to them, they are unlikely to succeed.

Dr Nick Tate, QCA.

THE CURRICULUM REVIEW PROCESS			
Phase 1	*May-Aug 1998*	*Preparation*	
Phase 2	*Sept-Dec 1998*	*Development*	
Phase 3	*Jan-March 1999*	*Informal Consultation*	QCA circulates draft proposals and submits recommendations to the secretary of state.
Phase 4	*April-Aug 1999*	*Formal Consultation*	QCA canvasses responses to statutory proposals and finalises them.
Phase 5	*Sept 1999- Sept 2000*	*Publication and Dissemination*	Revised curriculum orders sent to school and guidance published.
	September 2000	*Implementation*	New curriculum introduced in schools. New A and AS Levels introduced.
	September 2001	*Assessment*	New or revised GCSE / GNVQ syllabuses commence where appropriate.

Curriculum Review

QCA's ongoing curriculum review was strait-jacketed by the government in May 1998. Although the QCA's consultative processes were already underway, David Blunkett stressed that there should be minimal and evolutionary change so as not to add to teachers' workloads and asked that the government's primary literacy and numeracy targets should be made the priorities. This was an odd move, probably motivated by the recognition that QCA's corporate nose had been put out of joint by the January 1998 changes - slimming the primary curriculum and making space for work-related learning. David Blunkett therefore designed a pre-emptive strike to ensure that curriculum review did not mean longer documents and a return to compulsion in the primary sector. There was a whiff of OFSTED's handiwork in the timing and substance of what was said.

Obliged to comply, Nick Tate argued that evolution should include a review which gave the curriculum a clearer rationale and purpose, drew clearer links between subjects, provided more flexibility and yet maintained the breadth and balance teachers had come to expect. He agreed that QCA would align the key stage 1 and 2 orders for English and mathematics with the national strategies, that there would be an effort to reduce prescription and that the orders for the disapplied key stage 1 subjects would be simpler.

It is arguable that, from this point forward, QCA lost control of the process of review. Instead OFSTED's agenda came to dominate discussion with that agency's demands for a more limited curriculum with fewer subjects and no programmes of study at key stage 4, plus an extension of the literacy and numeracy strategies into key stage 3. By December 1998, QCA had intended to publish a discussion document on aims and priorities and have revised subject orders ready for consultation but these were delayed. Draft versions of the new curriculum for each subject were finally disseminated in early 1999. The drafts came with questions relating to non-statutory guidance, access statements and the best way to publish the materials for teachers to consider at local conferences.

One new feature was a lengthy statement on the values and aims of the curriculum organised under the two broad headings of opportunities to learn and preparation for adult life. Meanwhile, the curriculum purposes were reduced to four slogans: Entitlement, Standards, Continuity and coherence, and Public understanding.

Where the core subjects were concerned the aim was - as noted above - to make minimal changes to the English and mathematics orders so as not to disrupt the work of schools working towards government targets. The proposed changes were largely designed to bring the orders into line with the strategies and, where possible, to lighten their requirements as well.

For other subjects, the aim was brevity and flexibility to be achieved through fewer options, more choice for teachers and subject linking. In the draft version, each subject now begins with a statement about its contribution to the aims of the curriculum and is presented in a common format that covers learning experiences and skills. It works better in some subjects than others. There are a few adjustments - renaming mostly - to the attainment targets and some fine tuning of level statements. QCA is also consulting on whether art, music and PE should have an eight-point scale - something which may make little sense in subject terms but could assist with the measurement of added value.

Disapplication remains an issue. There is a growing belief that, in secondary schools, the modern language and design & technology will join the humanities, art and music on the list of optional subjects at key stage 4. However, both subjects have key stage 4 programmes of study in the drafts. Taking them away

- perhaps the simplest option - would leave a core of English, mathematics, science, ICT, RE and PE but doing this leaves another anomaly, because there are GNVQ options for ICT (and there may yet be for science) which do not directly relate to the key stage 4 programme of study.

The subject drafts show considerable uncertainty over how to treat key skills. There is agreement that there are six of these: communication, application of number, information technology, working with others, improving own learning and performance; and, problem solving. However, there is less confidence about how they should, firstly, be incorporated into the curriculum and, secondly, be assessed. The drafts suggest that communication, application of number and information technology skills will be predominantly addressed in English, mathematics and ICT lessons at key stages 1 to 3 but they may be separately assessed at key stage 4. The three non-assessed skills seem likely to float across all subjects.

It is important to stress that this is draft material. QCA has not yet drawn up final recommendations for the secretary of state or for formal consultations with interested bodies which will follow later in the year and its openness is to be applauded. Having said that, there is little in the proposals to excite teachers. By and large, the existing curriculum is being restated in new terminology and with a different house style. It may be more user-friendly in places, some statutory content may now be expressed as advice and there is less prescription in the non-core subjects at key stage 2 but this is not an ambitious realignment of schooling for a new century - that now seems to be OFSTED's mission.

While one can sympathise with the straitjacket that QCA was placed in by the DfEE, the requirements for ICT, for preparation for adult life and for the inclusion of the non-assessed key skill areas could have created at least a framework for substantive change even if not delivering it entirely on this occasion. Also, by playing a very cautious game, QCA has not yet found the means to deliver key skills in the way that Sir Ron Dearing envisioned them in his curriculum review. The agency has not succeeded in writing ICT skills firmly into the curriculum either and, underneath the new clothes, the skeleton of traditional, right-wing conservatism can still be seen in its proposed new model.

At key stage 4, there is an additional worry. The new curriculum - in draft form at least - does not appear to be integrated with GNVQ or confident of its status. It contains, for example, some statutory programmes for subjects which might be disapplied in schools which seems anomalous and the orders seem at times to work against the requirement for key skills for all. While it might be argued that the concept of entitlement at this key stage has already been abandoned, the review could lead to the re-imposition of two old curriculum models; the academic, grammar

school track and the vocational secondary modern route to sixth form and college / employment respectively. This is a dire prospect when the 16-19 curriculum is giving some indication that it is turning away, albeit slowly, from academic specialisation.

Preparation for Adult Life

Take Citizenship, and add Personal Social and Health Education (PSHE) and Spiritual, Moral, Social and Cultural Education (SMSC). Combine them together with a sprinkling of creativity and culture plus a spot of sustainable development and the end product is Preparation for Adult Life (PAL); a dish that sounds more appropriate for dogs than people.

1998 saw a whole range of initiatives designed to fit under the broad heading of making today's children into 'better' adults. Better in this sense means different things to different people but it revolves around participatory citizenship, a respect for family life and social institutions, and the rejection of social drugs and criminality. The determination to act in this area, even if the immediate direction is uncertain, comes directly from Downing Street and, as part of the curriculum review, there is a requirement to link preparation for adult life, under an appropriate label, with each curriculum subject.

The first proposals for this new curriculum element went to David Blunkett in December 1998 and he is said to have been not much impressed. Leaks from the other groups have suggested that the Citizenship committee was pulling all the strings and that the Culture and Creativity Group had lost its direction! There was evidently much groundwork still to be uncovered in delivering the concept.

The first big problem for a PAL curriculum is what to put in it and the second is how to fit it into the school week. The DfEE's mistake may have been to address the issues in that order. Asking what, of all the valuable things there are to tell young people about, you can convey in fifty minutes a week - about the length of an episode of the *X-Files* - is a more relevant challenge.

That said, the enterprise has to be worthwhile. Young people evidently lack adequate education about relationships, as teenage pregnancy rates reveal, and they clearly need advice on drugs and on how to bring up children. Then, as the icing on the cake, they need to be encouraged to participate in democratic structures and have an understanding of legal processes, obligation and rights. If, as well, they can learn to respect the world they live in and lead a rich cultural life, so much the better. Some of this can be explored outside the classroom, some is crosscurricular and some is subject based but a good part of it needs to be taught.

Of course, the sensible way to do this would be to realign the subject curriculum to deliver it. It is, for example, only a mixture of post-Victorian modesty and Thatcherite conservatism that stops biology from being almost entirely about people and sex as it should be and makes it deliver all that peripheral information about plants and frogs instead. Physics, which should be the most interesting curriculum subject, manages to be inexcusably dull and unconnected to life. History has no idea of what it is trying to achieve - or rather has any number of ideas - but it could be reformulated around a main thesis that it was about the emergence of the democratic nation state and the conflict between local and global interests. English could get away from all those dreadful nineteenth century short stories and discuss modern writing, films, theatre and music, and so on.

Would this really turn the curriculum into a form of social conditioning, as those whose perceptions are framed by the existing curriculum tend to claim, or could it, just possibly, make the knowledge that schools transmit interesting and appropriate to everyday life? And, is it also possible that the various PAL groups are actually coming up with the best definition thus far of what schools should be doing in the next century?

Citizenship

The move towards developing a citizenship curriculum started with the establishment of Professor Bernard Crick's advisory group on Education for Citizenship and the Teaching of Democracy in Schools in November 1997. This worthy group included Kenneth Baker, the ex-secretary of state for education, Stephen Tumin, ex-chief inspector of prisons, Michael Brunson from ITN and Tom Bentley. By March 1998, this group came up with the recommendation that three curriculum strands should be pursued: social and moral responsibility, community involvement; and political literacy. The group also recommended that there should be some kind of apolitical statutory body to oversee how the process was completed and sustained.

In its final report, in July 1998, the group suggested a curriculum framework broken down to include four aspects: key concepts; values and dispositions; skills and aptitudes; and knowledge and understanding. The key concepts, it was argued, should be based on a Blairite agenda and include items like 'democracy and autocracy', 'freedom and order' and 'rights and responsibilities'. Values and dispositions were to be a mixed bunch of moral virtues and assertions; the skills covered communication, the use of evidence and the perception of manipulation while knowledge and understanding included legal, moral and social rights. The report included an indication of what might be delivered at each key stage.

In the autumn of 1998, these somewhat elaborate proposals were fed into QCA's curriculum deliberations with a view to analysing where the different aspects of the proposed framework might be addressed in curriculum subjects.

Citizenship education is a difficult area where schools are concerned. It is easy to agree on the need for it but hard to find the time for it or to define the nuts and bolts of the syllabus. The Crick committee believes that citizenship should not be taught like civics or local government and politics but should be based in the discussion of real issues but that may be hard for teachers if the real issues are local racism and sexism or involve eco-warriors and extreme action on behalf of animal rights. Faced with reality it will be easy to retreat into formulaic improvisations and scenarios which will not provide any training for dealing with genuine controversies or disputes.

Also, the key concepts could suggest that a 'one-nation' perspective and plenty of social inclusion is the only approach on offer. While many teachers may warm to Tony Blair's notion of inclusion, they would probably not have liked to teach Margaret Thatcher's and values like 'working with others for sympathetic understanding', skills like 'appreciating the experience and perspective of others' and knowledge of the 'nature of diversity, dissent and social conflict' may sit uneasily with a discussion about zapping Iraq with uranium-tipped missiles. Nigel de Gruchy of the NASUWT has made the point that it is quite hard to teach children about democracy when their government says one thing to teachers when in opposition and then acts quite differently when it comes to power!

However, good teaching should be able to circumvent these difficulties and provide an interesting and meaningful educational programme. There are already some education initiatives underway. Birmingham has a First Citizen Scheme for example and other related developments such as the Millennium Volunteers Programme and Extending Opportunity, the framework for after-school study support, are increasingly impinging on schools.

Ultimately, the real challenge for citizenship education, as for PSHE, is whether it can make any inroads into the traditional curriculum. The lessons of the past indicate that cross-curricular initiatives are ignored and fragmented approaches quickly sink in the curriculum soup. QCA can easily indicate which aspects of citizenship should fall under English, history and science but, once the cat is taken apart, it may not purr in quite the same way!

Alongside the citizenship group, David Blunkett also established parallel groups on Sustainable Development and on Creative and Cultural Education. These last two have yet to report formally but it means that, with the addition of the PSHE group and the QCA Spiritual and Moral development project there

are five groups in total feeding into the Preparation for Adult Life curriculum.

Personal, Social and Health Education

Personal, Social and Health Education (PSHE), sometimes without the health aspect, has been part of education since the introduction of comprehensive schools but has never had a powerful influence on the curriculum. However, in May 1998, Estelle Morris announced the establishment of yet another advisory group, the National Advisory Group on Personal, Social and Health Education, to bring forward proposals in this area. Chaired by Estelle Morris and Tessa Jowell, the then health minister, the plan was to establish a framework against which curriculum proposals could be tested. In this sense, the PSHE Advisory Group would operate in a similar way to Bernard Crick's citizenship group. Its establishment was said to herald the start of an 'exciting new era' for PSHE. The membership was mixed but interesting, with more health professionals than on previous education quangos and an 'expert panel of advisers' representing many of the other groups that work in this area.

The group's terms of reference mentioned life skills, drug abuse, teenage pregnancies, sex, and financial literacy. It was asked to prepare some principles for QCA to consider and to work with various agencies including the Department of Health's task group on sex and relationships and the UK Anti-Drugs Co-ordinator. It is not clear yet where this group is heading, however, its initial findings have already been fed into QCA's curriculum development work. Its establishment may also have had the effect of putting SCAA and QCA's work on spiritual, moral, social and cultural development (see below) onto the back-burner.

The Spiritual and Moral

Only two years ago the spiritual and moral curriculum (SMSC) was in the ascendancy. The death of a headteacher in a violent attack outside his school and the death of a teenager from drugs were the linchpins of a moral reform movement with which SCAA and the churches were quickly bound up. Then, in December 1997, QCA published its guidance on the spiritual, moral, social and cultural (SMSC) curriculum only for it to disappear into a black hole of inaction - a chilling indication in some ways of how a government can manipulate the education agenda to suit itself. Instead, citizenship and personal, social and health education took the centre stage as the focus moved from the morally responsible individual - John Major's ideal - to the nanny state, guiding and saving its primitive citizens from their own savagery! On the way, Michael Barber was in trouble for suggesting that, in the absence of God and Marx, teachers might have to give pupils moral guidance.

The extent of the sea change can be measured by the publication in 1998 of a tract written by the Thatcherite academic David Marsland. This called for 'optional' military service for 16 to 18-year-olds and a curriculum permeated with clear moral instruction. In 1998, it looked like someone's grandad whinging but

two years earlier, or if the Conservatives had held on to power, it might have been government policy.

While SMSC education is now on the back-burner, its brief flaming at least ensured that the post-election legislation did not tamper with compulsory religious education in schools or with regular school assemblies of a religious nature.

The 3-16 Curriculum

Ministers are proposing a new curriculum for three, four and five-year-olds, nicknamed 'key stage zero'.

Times Educational Supplement, 1998.

Key Stage Zero

Section heading in *Curriculum Confidential 7*, 1997.

All the research suggests that overly formal education in the early years does not lead to successful learning later on.

Professor Kathy Slyva on the DfEE's continuing Early Years Study.

If you coach your child, the assessment may only give a snapshot of what they have learnt very recently.

QCA leaflet for parents on baseline assessment.

The contractor appointed to process the results has experienced a number of technical problems leading to slippages in the planned schedule.

QCA letter to schools, June 1998.

Slimming the Curriculum

The new slimline 3 - 16 curriculum came into effect in September 1998, since when some of the implications of wholesale change are coming to be more clearly understood. It is only fair to note that there was a period of consultation over the changes and the majority of primary schools, where the changes were most sweeping, came out in favour. Workload was the key factor here, but there was also a feeling that the looser framework gave schools an opportunity to innovate and to develop new ideas before the next curriculum revision. Now, reaction has set in and there is a growing feeling in some quarters that teachers and pupils will soon be heartily sick of the non-stop emphasis on literacy and numeracy and that complaints will soon be filtering down from secondary schools that pupils are ill-prepared for the full ten subject curriculum.

The slimline curriculum booklet for primary schools did fit each subject on one side of paper - quite easily in fact. Geography, history, design & technology, art, music and physical education are the subjects which are most specifically affected by what is technically a two-year suspension of aspects of the national curriculum. The inclusion of swimming at key stage 2 was protected. Government ministers were keen to stress that none of these subjects was being made optional and that all must still be taught - it was simply the depth and extent of this teaching which was to become negotiable and the document stressed the need to continue to offer a broad and balanced curriculum.

Looking at the implications for curriculum planning, the document claimed that there was no need for schools to unpick structures radically. However, planning should take notice of the literacy and numeracy strategy requirements, the total time devoted to English and mathematics and the school's needs and priorities. The document made clear that the starting point had to be the time allocations for the national strategies. QCA promised to monitor the situation so that the experience could feed in to the revised curriculum for 2000.

It is well-known that QCA's sidelining in the decision-making process that led up to the curriculum changes damaged the agency which, allegedly, had responsibility for the curriculum. Salt was rubbed into the wounds when Chris Woodhead warned against any attempts to bring back more detail and prescription in the next curriculum review when he appeared shortly after Nick Tate at the Keele University Education Conference. This underlined the impression that the format and style of the national literacy strategy documentation could turn out to provide the model for the next primary curriculum.

THE CURRICULUM - KEY STAGES 1-3 1998-2000

The Core Subjects - following agreed subject orders and compulsory in all schools

| ENGLISH | MATHEMATICS | SCIENCE | INFORMATION & COMMUNICATIONS TECHNOLOGY |

The Foundation Subjects - the subject orders do not apply at key stages 1 and 2 but each subject should be taught

| DESIGN & TECHNOLOGY | HISTORY | GEOGRAPHY | MODERN LANGUAGE |
| ART | MUSIC | PHYSICAL EDUCATION | |

Compulsory subjects which are outside the national curriculum

| RELIGIOUS EDUCATION | SEX EDUCATION |

The Collapse of National Testing

After all that some teachers have done to subvert the more worrying aspects of national testing, QCA's number crunching agency did the job for them in 1998. The national data collection agency failed to calculate or deliver test results to schools which were then left to do the job for themselves. The contractors blamed the markers and the markers blamed the forms but the truth was probably that the collation and crunching of 7.5 million scores was always going to be more complicated than anyone had predicted and should have been piloted more extensively. One primary school in London sent a bill to David Blunkett but his spokesperson suggested that they redirected it to QCA. Even without this request for £75, it is clear that the shambles was a severe, and extremely costly, embarrassment to QCA which had not budgeted for the additional costs (around £2 million) of sending extra materials to schools. The agency was still suffering at the end of the year when it was too poor to issue corporate Christmas cards!

In a show of confidence for 1999, the agency has offered schools the chance to submit key stage assessment registration information via the internet. The necessary form DC1 should be available on the QCA website.

Making Sense of Test Results

There is a growing level of dissatisfaction with the outcomes of national testing. The criticisms comes from various quarters. Those who believe that the purpose of the tests is to sample national performance are becoming increasingly frustrated at the shortcomings of the eight-level scale and the undulating standards of performance from year to year. Chris Woodhead used the opportunity of a lecture at the London School of Economics to put the boot into a sister organisation. He argued that key stage tests were unreliable for a number of reasons including the vagueness of the level scale, the year-on-year changes and the way that they were administered 'creatively' by schools. He raised his own flag on behalf of standardised tests in literacy and numeracy.

There have been similar calls for the same set of tests to be set for samples of candidates each year as a measure of national progress. However, such tests have their own inherent weaknesses. Changes in the culture can effect the results so that as a word like 'fishmongers' goes out of use, 'oasis' comes in. A classic example for geographers is the increasing tendency to misspell the word 'deserts' as 'desserts' as the latter have migrated from stately homes and restaurants into council houses. There are also obvious problems of security.

Key Stage Zero

The Early Years Strategy

The government has a commitment to offer nursery or pre-school places to all 4-year-olds and to add 190,000 places for 3-year-olds over the next three years as part of the Early Years Strategy which runs from birth to six years of age. If the government meets its targets there will be places for two-thirds of 3-year-olds in nursery schools by 2002. However, there are a number of strands to the strategy apart from increasing the number of places. They include giving QCA responsibility for the curriculum and the oversight of training, standards and qualifications while the DfEE will set targets and allocate resources. In the longer term, there will be a new early years qualification in teacher training and a career structure running from new NVQs for helpers to degree qualifications for specialists.

One of the main worries about the implementation of the policy is that there are very few qualified practitioners in the field but a lot of people with experience whose expertise needs to be retained. The new NVQ proposals should help to give them the accreditation to remain in the area. Another worry is over curriculum content. The Conservative government's nursery initiative and voucher scheme was predicated on an 'academic' basis but there is some evidence that early pressure to read and write may disadvantage boys whose motor skills are not sufficiently developed by age 3. Partly as a consequence of this, there is a feeling that the existing Desirable Learning Outcomes (DLOs) are overtly prescriptive and formal and are not leading to improvements in schools. Margaret Hodge, as the new face of the government in this area, would like to place a greater emphasis on sociability and play but the DfEE cannot be seen to be 'less academic' than its predecessors.

There is a suggestion that key stage zero should break down into two distinct phases; play and activity for 3 to 4-years-olds, and more emphasis on key stage 1 skills for 5 to 6-year-olds. International comparisons are not particularly helpful but where there is extensive nursery teaching elsewhere it does tend to be informal and based in the development of speaking and listening rather than writing. There is some evidence from international studies that children in European schools which start at six or seven years of age do better later at maths and science.

In the light of all this, QCA's latest review of the DLOs may have been slightly off target. The agency proposed changes in 1999 that would see a foundation stage running up to the end of the reception year with early learning goals rather than learning outcomes to cover social skills, speaking & listening, reading, writing and mathematics. Clearly QCA was trying to satisfy the minister and the literacy and numeracy

strategies but may be in danger of ending up with insufficient play for younger children and insufficient work for those who are older. The consultation period for the review runs from February to April 1999.

There is still one anomaly to resolve. Private nurseries are still registered and inspected by local authority social services but those that receive government funding are subject to OFSTED inspection against the Desirable Learning Outcomes criteria. OFSTED reported in June 1998 on its own progress and on standards in the sector. The report covered 10,000 inspections of classes for 4-year-olds and was generally complimentary about the introduction of the Desirable Learning Outcomes and the teaching seen. Somewhere along the line, the monitoring systems will have it be brought into line.

Baseline Assessment

Baseline assessment is a necessary part of any value-added calculation. Essentially, to know how far you have come you need to know where you started from, and if this maxim is applied to education then it makes sense to set the baseline at the point where children start school. There is an argument that - on closer analysis - this conclusion may be flawed. This suggests that while it is possible to relate performance at a pre-school baseline to performance at age 7, to take it on much further could lead to a contamination of the value-added measure by a plethora of other variables - curriculum changes, different teachers, more use of ICT and so forth.

However, it makes sense to the DfEE and, from September 1998, all children entering school have undergone a baseline assessment. The cost to the Standards Fund has been put at £9.4 million which pays for the schemes, supports training and provides some supply cover for schools. The assessment covers literacy, numeracy, personal and physical development, and creative and social skills and it has to be completed within seven weeks of a child starting school. The testing process is unthreatening and based on procedures that should not take longer than twenty minutes per child. Almost all of the approved schemes - some are local authority and some are commercially developed - involve checklisting a set of scaled items of increasing difficulty. Each local authority has to have an accredited scheme - not necessarily developed in house or in the public sector - but its schools do not have to use it.

Variation between the schemes is likely to be increasingly limited. The reason is that it is advantageous for them to relate to the national baseline scales developed in 1998 by QCA. These are based on results from the testing of 12,000 children and allow regional schemes to be calibrated and individual school performances evaluated in a national context. As an example of how the scales work in

TYPICAL BASELINE ASSESSMENT ITEMS

Reading for Meaning and Enjoyment	**1** Holds books appropriately while turning the pages and retelling the story from memory **2** Is able to predict words and phrases **3** Uses memory of familiar text to match some spoken and written words **4** Reads simple texts
Number	**1** Sorts sets of objects and explains the criteria used **2** Counts objects accurately **3** Shows awareness of using addition **4** Solves numerical problems using addition and subtraction
Personal and Social Development	**1** Plays collaboratively **2** Is independent and keen to contribute **3** Concentrates without supervision for ten minutes **4** Expresses own opinion with a range of adults
	This example is based on Baseline 98, a scheme operated by the Modbury Group.

practice, these national guidelines move - for writing - from 'distinguishing between print and pictures', writing 'letter shapes', writing 'own name' and writing 'discrete words'.

A typical approved scheme might have up to fifteen categories, each one with a four-point 'scale' like the example above. Completing a short task or a period of observation then enables the teacher to give up to four points in each category. Totalled, these points give the baseline assessment score for that pupil. In some schemes it is only possible to show if the item has been fully achieved but, in others, partial achievement can be recognised. The outcome has to be a numerical score. Parents should be informed about the test taking place and must receive details of their child's performance or be invited to discuss it. The chart shows some typical items.

The government was quickly in trouble over the introduction of the assessment in September 1998 when Charles Clarke, the new - and slightly green - schools minister, appeared to have suggested that baseline tests could be used to set or stream pupils in primary schools. He was forced into a hasty retreat about how his words had been misunderstood but the issue was particularly embarrassing because it came after the government had leafleted parents asking them not to train their children for the assessment.

Just how parents will react to the new assessment is a worry for the DfEE. It is quite possible to 'prepare'

children and, realistically, many parents will do just that, even though the government has asked them not to. Publishers will also be quick to see a possible market. There is some evidence from the United States that even very young children can perceive test situations and that, when they know that they are 'doing a test', children perform better. For an ambitious parent, therefore, the logic is to practise hard and raise the anxiety levels for a better result now, without thinking of any long-term consequences.

This might seem faintly absurd, but it becomes a genuine cause for anxiety if baseline assessment will be used to assign children to categories that could label them for life. How might this happen? Being broadly characterised as under-achieving, or below average for the class, could mean that a child works with a different group in literacy and numeracy lessons and, from September 1999, these will take up almost ten hours of the teaching week. Also, in 1999, the government introduces unique reference numbers for schoolchildren which means that a poor result will follow a child from school to school and be part of that individual's permanent record.

Another worry, for at least fifty per cent of parents, is that boys seem likely, on the preliminary evidence, to do worse than girls. Pilot schemes have shown that girls outstrip boys in almost all of the categories. In one study, there were 30% more girls than boys in the top category and in reading and letter knowledge, 25% of girls reached the top level and only 16% of boys -

about the same divide as seen in GCSE English! One outcome could be therefore that baseline assessment will have the effect of creating an underclass of boys at the onset of compulsory schooling. There are already hints that the current weaknesses in the academic performance of boys may be related to starting school early. Because of their different maturation rates and cultural influences, boys at age five tend to have less developed co-ordination and social skills and shorter attention spans than girls. They are more inclined to be active and are less emotionally stable. So, the argument goes, they are more likely to be told off by teachers and may well develop an early distaste for reading, if not for school in general.

Some mathematicians are also concerned about the focus on number which, it is claimed, will lead teachers to focus on counting and recognition rather than on games and activities which will lead to genuine understanding. There is a theory that children are getting better at slavish arithmetic but that they are doing so by improving their abilities at counting rather than understanding the relationships between numbers and the concepts involved.

And, finally, there are additional concerns for schools over the accuracy of the assessment and how it is used. The record sheets that depend on teacher observation are very approximate measures of a child's position but, once a number is attached to them, they appear to be 'accurate' scores and may be misused. Finally, there are two statistical effects to consider. 'Negative coupling' is what happens when a generous baseline assessment makes achievements at key stage 1 look worse than they really are. 'Gaming' is the ploy of making baseline assessments deliberately severe in order to make key stage 1 achievements look better. Regular OFSTED inspection and the frequent scrutiny of their work is likely to make most teachers aware of the dangers of negative coupling; individual contracts, payment 'by results' and threats of dismissal could make gaming into a real possibility!

Baseline assessment is not going to be solely the business of primary schools in the future. There is a growing market for secondary schemes which, it is claimed, will provide secondary schools with a better baseline than key stage 2 test results or the reports from a number of feeder schools. Carol FitzGibbon's unit, now at Durham University, which developed the YELLIS system for predicting GCSE results is now offering MidYIS, a new baseline for secondary schools.

Benchmarks

Benchmarking is the process which helps schools set the targets they can achieve and allows them to measure how effective they have been. In January 1998, QCA published guidance on how to set targets by working from benchmark measures for school performance. In this process, a series of tables categorise primary schools by reference to the percentage of pupils for whom English is an additional language (EAL) and the percentage of pupils who qualify for free school meals (FSM).

For primary schools, there are six tables for use at key stages 1 and 2. The first five are based on less than 50% EAL and school meal percentages of 8%, 9-20%, 21-35%, 36-50% and over 50%. The sixth is for schools with more than 50% EAL. There is a sense in which the introduction of the EAL figure is cosmetic since it only has an effect at above 50% and it may have been included so that the FSM figure was not the only discriminator.

Each table shows the percentage of pupils achieving level 2 and above in a number of areas. At key stage 1, there are six of these. They are the teacher assessment, the reading test and the writing test in English, the teacher assessment and test in mathematics and the teacher assessment in science. For comparison, the performances of pupils are grouped at four points - the 25th (lower quartile), the 50th (median), the 75th (upper quartile) and 95th percentile point. The school can then map its own performance onto the appropriate chart and find out which quartile or percentile its performance in each area falls into. Clearly, a performance in the median zone is in line with the national averages for this type of school while one in the lower quartile is below.

At key stage 2, there are again six measures, made up of the teacher assessments and test results in English, mathematics and science and the performances are grouped in the same way. Exactly the same criticisms apply so that the majority of the schools are covered by three tables and what appear to be significant differences in FSM numbers equal very small numbers of pupils in practice.

QCA has also published supporting guides for primary schools on the use of the statistical data. This emphasises that socio-economic data is an indicator of performance rather than a determinant and then goes into detail about medians, quartiles and the different ways of presenting school performance data. It suggests some additional ways of analysing school performance data by using histograms and scatter graphs and by gender, by trends over time and by different groups within the school.

COMPARISON OF 1998 TEST RESULTS AND TEACHER ASSESSMENTS (TA) AT KEY STAGE 1							
	READING		WRITING		SPELLING	MATHEMATICS	
	TEST	TA	TEST	TA	TEST	TEST	TA
Level 2 or above in 1998	80%	81%	81%	79%	66%	84%	85%
1997 figures	80%	80%	77%	78%	62%	84%	83%
1996 figures	78%	78%	79%	76%		82%	82%
1995 figures	78%	79%	80%	77%		78%	79%

Key Stage 1

The 1998 results revealed few surprises but confirmed the trend of improvement at a rate of around 1% a year across all subjects. The biggest increase was in spelling where there was a year-on-year improvement of 4%.

There are no significant changes to the assessment structure for 1999 but there are three new titles in each book-list and the section on reporting in the guidance booklet (*Key Stage 1: Assessment and Reporting Arrangements*, QCA, DfEE, 1998) has been substantially rewritten. Small schools can use the photocopiable report forms quite easily but a more stylish option is to download the forms from the QCA website and then to produce customised reports for each pupil. While targets are not statutory for year 3, if schools have set these it is worth referring to them

KEY STAGE 1 TASKS AND TESTS 1999			
ENGLISH		MATHEMATICS	
Individual reading	Levels 1-2 (A-C) 15 minutes per pupil	Mathematics task	Level 1 20 minutes per group
Level 2 Reading comprehension test	Level 2 (A-C) (for all pupils at level 2 on individual reading) 40 minutes per group		
Level 3 Reading comprehension test	Level 3 (for pupils at level 2A on both individual reading and reading comprehension) 45 minutes per group	Mathematics test (including five oral questions at start of test)	Levels 2 (A-C), Level 3 40 minutes per group
Writing task (including handwriting and spelling at level 1)	Levels 1, 2 A-C and 3 60 minutes		
Spelling test (to be reported separately)	Level 1 (optional), 2 A-C and 3 30 minutes per group		

at the time when teacher assessments are made as well as to the national value-added project documentation.

For 5-11 schools, there is a fine line to be walked between achieving improvement at key stage 1 and adding value by key stage 2! Mindful that David Blunkett's future rests on it, the QCA guidance also notes that a level 2B for reading is the best predictor of a level 4 score by the end of key stage 2. The 1999 key stage 1 assessments will give an early indication of whether the magical aim of 80% at level 4 for English is achievable in 2002. At present, it looks possible.

There was a further attack on the reliability of the reading assessment in 1998. Peter Tymms from the University of Durham found that children achieving fifty per cent in the reading comprehension test could have a true score - on a more detailed analysis - of between 17% and 79%. QCA argued that more time devoted to testing would be unwelcome and bad for the children concerned in other ways.

Key Stage 2

The 1998 results revealed slow but perceptible progress towards the government's targets for key stage 2 with an overall improvement of just about 2%, but with boys continuing to lag behind girls. A final figure of around 65%, with girls on 73% and boys on 57%, is a long way short of the 80% target for achievement at level 4. Putting a brave face on the figures, the DfEE noted that the schools which had piloted the National Literacy Strategy did better than those that had not. The government also has a trick up its sleeve. Around 7% of 11-year-olds go untested each year, split roughly between children in special education and those who are absent from school.

Taking both groups out of the sums, lifts the performance by a couple of percentage points.

It is difficult to report on the state of play where the key stage 2 test assessments are concerned. At one level, everything seems fine in the sense that appeals against marking run at a tiny percentage of the 600,000 entry and the changes to levels following appeals affect less than 1% of the entry. However, what people say about the tests is very different. A National Primary Headteachers Association survey in 1998 found that headteachers professed themselves to have little faith in the results, particularly in science and English. While small scale, this survey reflected the common view among primary headteachers that the tests are something of an irrelevance.

There have been allegations that the commonly reported 'gulf' between reading and writing scores may have been more apparent than real. Although 68% of 11-year-olds read at level 4, compared to 54% who write at this standard, there is no evidence to suggest that the demands of the reading and writing tasks are equivalent and, in fact, the persistence of this gap suggests to some researchers that they may not be.

OFSTED was critical of many primary school teacher assessments in 1998. A survey recommended that assessment should be linked to more closely to planning and that there should be teacher records and evidence to support judgements if they were reliably standardised. It suggested that, in many schools, teachers failed to build assessment into the planning phase of their work, assessments were not used for formative purposes, that there were too many tick-lists in use and that records are often inadequate. One sensible suggestion was that tasks to support teacher assessment could be spread throughout the year and that local secondary schools should be involved in the discussion of what constitutes useful assessment data.

COMPARISON OF 1998 TEST RESULTS AND TEACHER ASSESSMENTS (TA) AT KEY STAGE 2

	ENGLISH		MATHEMATICS		SCIENCE	
	TEST	TA	TEST	TA	TEST	TA
Percentages reaching level 4 or above in 1998	65%	65%	59%	65%	69%	71%
1997 figures	63%	63%	62%	64%	69%	69%
1996 figures	58%	60%	54%	60%	62%	65%
1995 figures	48%	56%	44%	54%	70%	64%

KEY STAGE 2 TESTS 1999

ENGLISH	MATHEMATICS	SCIENCE
Reading Comprehension Test Levels 3-5 45 minutes + 15 mins preparation Wednesday 12th May	**Test A** Levels 3-5 (non-calculator) 45 minutes (ATs 2-5) Monday 10th May	**Test A** Levels 3-5 45 minutes (ATs 2-4) Tuesday 11th May
Writing Test Levels 3-5 45 minutes + 15 mins preparation Thursday 13th May	**Test B** Levels 3-5 (calculator required) 45 minutes (ATs 2-5) Tuesday 11th May	**Test B** Levels 3-5 45 minutes (ATs 2-4) Friday 14th May
Spelling / Handwriting Test Levels 3-5 10 minutes / 5 minutes Wednesday 12th May	**Mental Arithmetic** Level 3 and above 20 minutes (taped test) Monday 10th May	**Test C: Science Extension Paper** Level 6 (optional additional test) 30 minutes (ATs 2-4) Friday 14th May
English Extension Test Level 6 (optional additional test) 60 minutes (ATs 2-3) Thursday 13th May	**Test C: Mathematics Extension Test** Level 6 (optional additional test) 30 minutes (ATs 2-5) Wednesday 12th May	

There have been a number of changes for 1999. As a result of concerns expressed in the evaluation of the 1998 tests, the test period will be contained within a single week (10th-14th May). Also, after the collapse of the data collection contract in 1998, results will come to schools through the completed marksheets from the external markers. It is worth checking these for clerical error - the main reason why the procedures were changed in 1998. A range of optional interim test papers for years 3, 4 and 5 are also now available. The statutory section on reporting in the *Key Stage 2 Assessment and Reporting Arrangements* booklet (QCA, DfEE, 1998) has been sensibly rewritten but the booklet also contains some odd - and rather patronising - advice on report writing, including a set of model comments on a pupil.

Target-setting is now statutory for this age group. It will, therefore, be advisable for headteachers to check the teacher assessments - submitted in July 1999 - against the targets set in December 1998 as an early indication of whether the school is making adequate progress in this area.

Key Stage 3

The results from this assessment in 1998 showed once again the reliability of the teacher assessment as opposed to an externally marked test. Taking all three subjects together, there has been an improvement in performance since 1995 of around 2% - a situation which is mirrored at other key stages. Also, the consistency of the marking over this period makes a mockery of the OFSTED assertion that teachers are not making accurate and effective assessments at key stage 3.

For some years now, Dr John Marks with the help of the right-wing Social Market Foundation, has been reworking national assessment data to suggest that the gaps between good and bad schools are wider than anyone believes. The 1998 story was that struggling pupils do not improve in poor schools and that the gap between the best and the worst pupils grows steadily between ages seven and fourteen. A mini-study of secondary schools in selective Buckinghamshire was used to suggest that the best means of countering this trend might be selective education. Basically, all of the doctor's work is flawed because it is predicated on the notion that the national curriculum level scale is age-related with two years allocated to each level. So, a greater spread of performance at key stage 3 in comparison to key stage 1 is taken as indicating that students at the former level are somehow 'more behind' their contemporaries than they were in primary schools, and this is then taken as the basis for making judgements about schools.

The assessment pattern for 1999 is unchanged. However, a new play, *Twelfth Night*, has replaced *A Midsummer Night's Dream* as one of the three Shakespeare texts. There has been some surprise that the reviled test of responses to Shakespeare has continued into 1999. Over and above the fact that English teachers dislike it, there is accumulating evidence that this paper is the weakest link in the English assessment chain. Since 1995, the marking has been erratic, levels of differentiation have been low and the reliability of the assessment has been questionable. Low differentiation plus low reliability over a number of years suggests that an assessment mechanism lacks validity. In simple terms, the testing of understanding of a Shakespeare play in a two hour examination for 14-year-olds is not, thus far, a format that provides useful information about the performance in reading and writing of a national cohort. The 1998 results with a sudden increase in level 6 awards in English was typically unpredictable. Given the size of the cohort, change should either occur across all of the levels or be moderate and this

8% leap is indicative of a flawed assessment not of improvement - as measures of added value may well prove in two years time!

There is little doubt that QCA would like to see the assessment altered and advised the DfEE accordingly in 1997 but David Blunkett clearly fears - almost certainly unnecessarily - a cultural backlash. The issue is likely to resurface in the autumn of 1999 because, in 2000, *Macbeth* will replace *Julius Caesar*. This is a momentous change because over half of all secondary schools currently study *Macbeth* for GCSE.

In practical terms, and to make the best use of resources, schools will have to use *Romeo and Juliet* as a GCSE text and *Macbeth* at key stage 3. However, they cannot simply swap the texts or the 1999 key stage 3 cohort will find themselves studying *Romeo and Juliet* twice. The outcome is that schools will need another cohort sized set of playscripts at considerable expense.

Curriculum Confidential 8 included teacher assessment figures for the non-core subjects: history, geography, design & technology, information technology and the modern foreign language. However, as a consequence of a move towards regional collection of results and the QCA breakdown, this information no longer appears to be available at national level.

Finally, teacher may wish to note that, in common with other key stage booklets, the reporting advice to schools has been rewritten (*Key Stage 3 Assessment and Reporting Arrangements*, QCA, DfEE, 1998).

KEY STAGE 3 TESTS 1999		
ENGLISH	**MATHEMATICS**	**SCIENCE**
Paper One Levels 4-7 90 minutes + 15 mins preparation *Tuesday 4th May AM*	**Paper One** Tiers 3-5, 4-6, 5-7, 6-8 (non-calculator) 60 minutes (ATs 2-5) *Thursday 6th May AM*	**Paper One** Tiers 3-6, 5-7 60 minutes (ATs 2-4) *Friday 7th May AM*
Paper Two Levels 4-7 (Shakespeare scenes) 75 minutes *Tuesday 4th May PM*	**Paper Two** Tiers 3-5, 4-6, 5-7, 6-8 (calculator) 60 minutes (ATs 2-5) *Thursday 6th May PM*	**Paper Two** Tiers 3-6, 5-7 60 minutes (ATs 2-4) *Friday 7th May PM*
	Mental Arithmetic Test 20 minutes Tests A & C: *Wednesday 5th May AM* Test B: *Thursday 6th May AM*	
Optional Extension Paper Levels 8-10 (Reading & Writing) 75 minutes + 15 mins preparation *Wednesday 5th May PM*	**Optional Extension Paper** Levels 9-10 90 minutes (ATs 2-5) *Monday 10th May AM*	**Optional Extension Paper** Levels 8-10 (in 3 sections) 90 minutes (ATs 2-4) *Monday 10th May PM*

The 14-19 Curriculum

34% of school leavers go into higher education compared with 45% in the USA, 65% in Germany and 70% in Japan.
The extent of the problem.

It doesn't make much sense to prolong the agony of failure that too many have experienced for too long.
Chris Woodhead at the 1998 Keele Conference talking about curriculum disapplication.

But if Latin and Greek are dead languages, then Mozart is dead music and Shakespeare is dead poetry, and are they not pretty useless too?
Dubious logic from QCA's *Classics in the Curriculum* publication.

Work-related Learning and Curriculum Change

The government's strategy for linking education to employment is taking shape on a number of fronts which include a revamping of careers education in schools, a new emphasis on work-related learning and on employment-related vocational qualifications, and a new sense of teamwork - as opposed to sponsorship - in the relationships between schools and employers.

At one level, the intention is to prise more money for education out of business but, in return, business is being offered unprecedented access to schools and an opportunity to shape what schools are doing. While some of the new initiatives are being developed within action zones, their influence is certain to increase and all schools - not just those with problems or in areas of social deprivation - need to be exploring the benefits of greater business links.

The most significant change in 1998 came with the introduction of arrangements for work-related learning and the disapplication of part of the key stage 4 curriculum. As long as a school has a structured curriculum and learning taking place in courses outside the school, it is permitted to drop two subjects from science, design & technology or the modern foreign language. English, mathematics, ICT, RE and PE remain compulsory. The aim is clear. It is to allow disaffected pupils to try a working environment for at least one full day a week with the intention of giving them some enthusiasm for applied learning.

Legally, the situation is made more complicated because there is apparently no statutory assessment order for key stage 4 in 1999 so, while national

curriculum subjects must be taught, there is not a legal requirement for them to be assessed. This is presumably to allow education action zones to develop without any legal hindrance and to allow subjects like ICT to be taught through a number of certifications. However, the DfEE has stated that it expects all pupils assessed at grade G or above to sit examinations unless a parent asks in writing that this should not be done.

The protocol leading up to a work-related placement is carefully prescribed. The pupil, or pupils, must have careers interviews, their own curriculum plans (maintaining consistency, breadth and balance as key concerns), an induction programme and there must be periodical progress checks and evaluation by the school. QCA will monitor the programme and must be informed when a school wishes to introduce work-related learning on this basis.

The question is whether this is going to become a rare way of treating individual problems or something more. QCA gives the impression that the curriculum is sacrosanct and so it is necessary to tread very carefully but it could be the case that subject disapplication becomes a major area for expansion. There are a number of reasons why.

The first is that OFSTED has been critical of what schools currently do as work experience and with work placements. In *Work-related Aspects of the Curriculum in Secondary Schools* (OFSTED 1998), the agency suggests the need for coherent programmes and more links between schools and businesses. This is an important document for secondary managers to read. In part, it represents OFSTED's view of where curriculum review should be going. It also leads to the clear conclusion that if work-related learning is worth doing then it needs to be done properly and resourced appropriately.

The second reason is that there is a significant group of pupils who could benefit. Nationally, GCSE results indicate that at least the bottom twenty percent of pupils in year 11 are taking very little from their courses. In most schools, it would be possible to identify a coherent group and it goes without saying that schools and teachers would not be sorry to see some of these pupils employed elsewhere. It is worth noting that the day in the working environment could be complimented with attendance at college for related NVQ courses for some other part of the week.

This leads to the third reason; the image of the school. A school that is tackling low achievement and attendance will be popular with parents as will one that is working closely with business and the local TEC. This kind of course holds out the possibility of genuine links rather than cosmetic politenesses and it is also worth making the point that a small local engineering firm or a local council would accrue some benefit from having two or three pupils for a whole year - something that does not happen with work experience. And, this kind of initiative tied into NVQ might tackle the challenging government requirements for better qualifications for low achievers. Faced with introducing entry level courses or flogging the dead horse of GCSE passes at the lowest grades, work-related learning starts to look like a very attractive opportunity.

Finally, it is worth remembering that work-related learning is part of wider strategy outside education to deal with social exclusion and long-term unemployment. So, the New Deal strategy and the DfEE responsibility for employment both overlap with mainstream education initiatives. Careers Clubs for 16 to 17-year-olds who have left school are typical examples. There are also a few work-related learning

initiatives involving persistent truants that take students out of school in year 11 and some action zone schools are testing similar initiatives.

14-16

GCSE in 1998

The oddest event surrounding the 1998 GCSE examinations was the government's climb-down on tiering. Rather than face the possibility of large numbers of candidates on the higher tier ending as ungraded because they failed to make the bottom of the tier at grade D, the government asked the GCSE Joint Forum to create a dispensation and an 'allowed grade E' for candidates who 'fell off' the tier. As a practical and pragmatic solution to a potential problem, this was a reasonable action but in terms of the probity of the system it seemed to be covering up some previously identified weaknesses. The decision was announced very late to avoid any last-minute rush of candidates between the tiers which might have thrown administrative systems into chaos. However, it annoyed many teachers whose advice to students at the borderlines was undercut by the change. There was additional discussion of exactly what status the 'allowed grade E' was entitled to because it was in the odd position of being simply calculated mathematically rather than linked qualitatively to the grade E on the foundation tier.

The dispensation did not help everyone. The 1998 results revealed a decrease in the number of pupils receiving a GCSE award in mathematics. Around 35,000 candidates were left without a grade in this important compulsory subject. Mathematics is unusual in having three tiers and the regulations meant

---

GCSE TIERING

GCSE grades run from A* (the best) to G (the minimum standard) and unqualified for those who fail to meet the standard required.

	FOUNDATION	INTERMEDIATE	HIGHER
ENGLISH DESIGN & TECHNOLOGY SCIENCE INFORMATION TECHNOLOGY MODERN LANGUAGES GEOGRAPHY	*Grades G-C*		*Grades D-A**
MATHEMATICS	*Grades G-D*	*Grades E-B*	*Grades C-A**
HISTORY	*One paper covers grades G-A**		
ART, MUSIC, PE	*One paper covers grades G-A**		
Most other academic subjects have two tiers, non-academic or vocational subjects tend to have one.			

YEAR-ON-YEAR GCSE RESULTS (% IN GRADES A*-C)					
	A*	**A**	**B**	**C**	**Total**
1998*	4.1	10.6	16.5	23.6	54.7
1997	3.6	10.5	18.1	22.3	54.6
1996	3.4	10.4	18.1	22.3	54.2

* Provisional figures, likely to rise by 0.2 after appeals.

that those who performed at grade D on the higher (grades A*-C) tier would be unclassified. Similarly, those who performed at grade F on the intermediate tier would meet the same fate. The problem was exacerbated because the pressure to be entered for the higher tier - as opposed to the intermediate - is raised when it comes with the possibility of a grade C pass that will register in the key performance table measure. In February 1999, It was announced that the same dispensation would operate for the 1999 examination cycle. And, in the longer term, there is a review of tiering in process under the auspices of QCA. It has to be said that while, at GCSE, almost everyone accepts that tiering is a nuisance, a similar divide works quite well for GNVQ which is not burdened with eight grades. And, of course, it is always important for the government not to be seen to be lowering standards.

It is unclear whether the 1998 increase in unqualified candidates - from 1.5% to 2.3% - was caused by candidates falling off the tiers, by awarding committees being more rigorous at the bottom of the ability range or by the raising of the school-leaving age to the end of the school year in July. Most of the evidence suggests that it was a mixture of all three factors. Elsewhere, in spite of an increase in the entry, the technology options lost candidates overall and a degree of compulsion did little for the most popular modern languages; French and German. The short courses (religious education, information technology and design & technology in particular) all showed gains and, with over 200,000 candidates nationally, the syllabuses are showing strong growth.

Other than this, the results were as expected and reflected the slowing down at A-C grades that was noted in 1997. The proportion of pupils achieving the magic figure of five GCSE A*-C grades rose from 44.5% to 46.1% and there was a similar increase (92.3% to 93.4%) in the numbers gaining at least one GCSE. There was, however, a decline in performance in mathematics on the crucial A*-C measure which will not have been welcome to a government which is setting higher targets for schools.

One reason for the much more limited change overall in the past two years is that the examining boards are keeping a tighter grip on the process. NEAB and

SEG, for example, which are currently merging as part of the new AQA, managed very complex statistics to tie their awards together but, as part of this, carried forward standards from 1997 to 1998 and resisted any suggestion from the examination evidence that standards had risen. This was an eminently sensible thing to do but it raises the question of how annually receding targets for schools at GCSE level connect to a process of awarding that is sometimes akin to norm referencing. NACETT wants to see 50% of students with five or more GCSE A*-C grades by 2002 but that will not be deliverable if the examining groups actively resist improvement over the next three years. On the other hand, if the boards actively seek out higher standards and improvement, they will quickly be accused of diluting standards. All in all, this is a difficult tightrope for the government, the boards and schools to walk.

The system crashed occasionally. A computer glitch at NEAB played havoc with the grades of candidates for modular science and humanities. The grades of 130,000 candidates were affected but the board detected the error and reissued the right results as soon as the appeals began to flood in.

Also, several groups of pupils in Ulster schools saw questions from their history paper in advance, in one case as a deliberate leak and in six others as a result of administrative confusion. However, a detailed statistical inquiry into the results showed that they did no better than those who engaged with the papers unseen. This was an irritation for the Council for the Curriculum, Assessment and Examinations (CCEA) - the Northern Ireland equivalent of QCA and an examining board rolled into one - which monitors and sets public examinations in the province and which has come in for criticism over many of its procedures in recent years. CCEA is facing a decline in candidate numbers with a corresponding drop of around 12% in subject entries since 1996 as schools choose mainland examining boards as an alternative to the local option. There has also been criticism that, in an effort to hold onto its centres, the percentages of A* and A grades has been allowed to rise - by about a percentage point each year over the past five years. This is unfounded. The real issue for the board is that it has had to link itself to SCAA and subsequently to QCA over the past three years and to align its GCSE results with those of the English boards. This has proved more difficult than anticipated and the board has faced problems in meeting the requirements of the codes of practice under which examinations in England operate.

Any headteacher who is feeling satisfied with his or her results might like to look at the gap between the state and the maintained sectors. Almost half (48%) of independent school entries are graded at A or A* against a national average for all schools of just under 15% and the average entry is over nine subjects. Gender remains an issue. The average points score for all boys in 1997 was 33.5 but for girls it was 38.3.

Part One GNVQ

1998 saw the second set of Part One results. Completions were slightly down at 60.3% (against a figure of 64.5% for 1997) but the numbers of candidates more than doubled to just over 10,000. Also it was the foundation level completions which were down; intermediate was unchanged. Art & Design, Information Technology and Leisure and Tourism were assessed for the first time.

Part One GNVQ turned out to be advantageous for schools in 1998. The two subject equivalence evidently allows average candidates to ratchet up their points scores with the result that, in performance tables, schools that use the qualification do very well. In a typical comprehensive school with between 30-35% gaining five or more GCSE A*-C grades, one might expect to see 40% or more earning the equivalent of two grade Cs or above on newly introduced GNVQ courses. Those schools that

squeeze a GNVQ into a single subject slot (a practice which is looked on more neutrally by QCA than it was by NCVQ) can do even better.

Entry Level Qualifications

The new framework for entry level qualifications came into place in September 1998. This will bring various certificate of achievement qualifications under one heading with clearly stated criteria for success in each course. The new qualifications sit under GCSE grade G, NVQ Level 1 and Foundation GNVQ and are aimed at children in special schools and in SEN groups in mainstream education. They have attracted some controversy, not least because they undercut the principle of the same national curriculum entitlement for all pupils at key stage 4. They also formally state that there are sheep and goats in the qualifications system. Once that is accepted, it is only fair to recognise that there have been considerable efforts to bolster the qualifications and they do possess the potential to bring a sense of order to a chaotic area. There is also an argument that doing well in an entry level course may stand students in better stead than a GCSE certificate containing only a handful of F and G grades.

CURRENT SUBJECT FRAMEWORK IN YEARS 10 AND 11			
SUBJECTS	**SHORT COURSE**	**COMBINED COURSES**	**SUBJECT LINKS**
COMPULSORY SUBJECTS AT GCSE LEVEL			
English	NO	Not permitted	
Mathematics	NO	Not permitted	
COMPULSORY COURSES THAT NEED NOT BE FOLLOWED TO GCSE LEVEL			
Information Technology	✓ YES (replaces certificates)	✓ YES (available as a subject options)	✓ YES May be accredited through GNVQ units)
Physical Education	✓ YES		
Religious Education	✓ YES		

'COMPULSORY' SUBJECTS - DISAPPLICATION PERMISSIBLE IN ANY TWO AREAS			
SUBJECTS	**SHORT COURSE**	**COMBINED COURSES**	**SUBJECT LINKS**
Science (available as single and double-awards and as three separate subjects)	NO	NO	✓ YES GNVQ Science is accredited as full course equivalent
Design & Technology (available as a range of subject options)	✓ YES	✓ YES with Art, IT and Business Studies	✓ YES Part One GNVQ Manufacturing and Engineering are accredited as short course equivalent
Modern Language (available as a range of subject options)	✓ YES	✓ YES with Business Studies	✓ YES Modified GNVQ/NVQ units meet short course requirement
GNVQ PART ONE FOUNDATION AND INTERMEDIATE SUBJECTS			
Business	NO	NO	✓ YES Possible to meet short course requirements for information technology
Health & Social Care	NO	NO	
Manufacturing	NO	NO	✓ YES Possible to meet short course requirements for design and technology
Art & Design	NO	NO	
Information Technology	NO	NO	✓ YES Possible to meet short course requirements for information technology
Leisure & Tourism	NO	NO	
Engineering	NO	NO	✓ YES Possible to meet short course requirements for design & technology
NATIONAL CURRICULUM SUBJECTS THAT ARE OPTIONAL at key stage 4			
History	✓ YES	✓ YES as Humanities	
Geography	✓ YES		
Art	✓ YES		✓ YES GNVQ Part One Art
Music	✓ YES		

16-19

Delivering the Revolution

The intention to reform radically the 16-19 curriculum goes back a long way but genuine change has been rare and has failed to make any impact on the system as a whole. For this reason alone, it is hard to be confident about the impact of the government's plans despite its desire for change.

The current plan is that by the spring of 2000, all of the new syllabuses - A Level, AS Level, full GNVQ (12-unit) and half GNVQ (6-unit) - will have been developed by three new massive certificating enterprises (EdExcel, OCR and AQA) and approved by QCA. There will have been a huge shake-out in the number of syllabuses and options and some inter-board rationalisation in subjects with small numbers of candidates. Where appropriate they will incorporate the key skills of literacy, numeracy and ICT, perhaps as the new three-unit part award equivalent to an AS Level. The teaching of courses under the new regime will commence in September 2000 and the first AS and half GNVQ awards will be made in 2001.

The diagram shows the shape of the qualifications proposed in the 1998 consultation document, *Qualifying for Success*. Teachers were pleased to see the choice between modular and linear assessments. The synoptic test, sometime called a coherence test, is an idea which started with GNVQ. The idea is that it assesses the application of skills outside of the context in which they were taught and, perhaps, at another point in the course. While such testing is clearly relevant to a work-related GNVQ, it may be harder to make it a logical part of an A Level course and there is

a danger that assessment regimes could give it an undue prominence.

In March 1999, the government made its long awaited announcement. This confirmed that the modular and linear options would be available in every subject, that there would be a new key skills qualification as an AS equivalent test and that synoptic testing would be compulsory. The announcement was bullish about AS Levels suggesting that four or five subjects would be followed in year 12 with the possibility of more in year 13 and about the new replacement for S Level. The new six unit GNVQ was described as the successor to Part One and would be graded on the A-E scale like an A Level. Coursework in all but practical subjects would be limited to 30%.

The announcement followed a long period of uncertainty in the last half of 1998 and the start of 1999. The suspicion has to be that the DfEE was worried about William Hague waiting in the wings to attack the dilution of the gold standard - he called for an A* grade in A Level at the start of 1999. That explains why the standards message was communicated so strongly in the presentation of the reforms.

However, while the framework was still fluid, the criteria for syllabus development were agreed for all major subjects. These are best described as conservative and designed, for the major A Level subjects at least, to mirror current provision as closely as possible. The range of single award GNVQs was extended from September 1998 to include Art & Design, Health & Social Care, Information Technology and Business. At full award level, there is a programme of piloting already underway.

So, what will happen next? One view is that the

THE NEW 16-19 SUBJECT MODEL					
Six separately assessed modules					
Advanced Subsidiary	1	2	3			
A Level (A2)	1	2	3	4	5	6
NEW GNVQ	1	2	3	4	5	6
Synoptic Assessment	Compulsory test of applied knowledge / understanding					
Coursework	1/6 at AS			2/6 at A2		
Key Skill assessment (integrated or separate)	Communicating	Application of Number		Information Technology	Study Skills	
Assessment	Modular or Linear (final examination) with compulsory synoptic testing					

majority of schools with sixth forms will continue to operate in accordance with traditional patterns so that they offer three academic A Levels, grouped in traditional ways - arts, mathematics and/or science, arts and humanities - as two year courses together with AS Levels for the one-year-sixth or 'remove' with a theoretical option of transfer to full A Level which is rarely taken up. In year 12, an AS Level Key Skills course will be followed.

If this is done, the chance to offer a five subject core in year 12 with opportunities for specialism in year 13 will be lost. The mix of the academic and vocational which was the major reason for change in the first place will be accidental rather than in-built and transferability and credit accumulation will be an exception rather than the norm.

When commentators ask why so little has changed, the answers will be as predictable as the curriculum pattern above. Headteachers will say, 'We think that higher education prefers three A Levels studied intensively, we do not have the staff and resources to offer GNVQ in the school, we can only offer a limited range of options and the ones we do at the moment seem to work and… yadda, yadda… parents prefer three A Levels'. And, of course, the dire truth is that the headteachers who say this will probably be absolutely right. Given half a chance, some representative of the HEIs will undoubtedly start bleating on about how three top grades at A Level is still the only route into medicine and law and everyone knows that the GNVQ does not have the status of A Level, and that change costs money and upsets people and is risky when schools are judged by parental perceptions and the meeting of targets.

Sir Ron Dearing knew this which was why his plans included the certificates and diplomas which would change the structure of post-16 study by a mixture of regulation and incentive but that concept - along with his requirement for attainment in the key skill areas as a condition of certification - has been watered down or postponed.

That leaves society with three reasons to be worried. The first is that the problems for industry caused by early specialisation, the rejection of engineering, manufacturing and technology and a lack of basic skills among entrants to industry will not be addressed by education. The second is that the whole process of revising vocational subjects has had the result of making them more academic. And, if these courses remain largely as study fodder for the middle third of the ability range, there will not only be a 'sheep and goats' curriculum at 16-19 but disenchantment and drop-out rates will increase and the number of completions will fall still further. And, finally, the concept of education for life will be damaged if accreditation through national certification, credit transfer and accumulation fall by the wayside.

For schools that want to do something more radical there are two issues to confront. The first is taught

time, where the government has realised that the typical 16 to 19-year-old student in England receives eighteen hours of tuition a week compared with thirty hours in countries like France and Germany. This suggests that there is space for new courses but the staffing and cost consequences of introducing them will be considerable.

The second is time-tabling where the provision of a broad set of options in year 12 - encouraging scientists to do arts and the possibility of an additional language or a craft - will sit uneasily alongside a traditional set of A Level subject combinations in year 13. Resolving these issues could spell the end of the small comprehensive school sixth form and make the case for centralised - and probably separate - facilities. Colleges will be quick to spot this opportunity and, if an education company wants to open a school, a sixth form college would be a good place to start.

Lastly, it is interesting to speculate on where the new S Level replacement is headed. Sir Ron Dearing's motive in raising the idea was to divert the criticisms of those who claimed that his new vocational innovations would dilute the qualification but, since then, the idea has quietly taken root among examination boards and QCA. The idea is that there would be an extension paper in major subjects setting harder tasks but requiring no additional study. The new qualification would be worth twelve points on the UCAS scale. As to whether there is a need for the qualification, the numbers sitting special papers - which do require additional work in the majority of subjects - have declined from almost 18,000 in 1989 to fewer than 10,000 in 1998. And, it is also worth noting that 86% of entrants to Cambridge in 1997 scored three straight A grades.

A Level in 1998

The 1998 A Level results showed that the sharply rising curve of the early 1990's has flattened with the smallest annual increase in ten years. This was generally welcomed as reasonable evidence of slightly improved standards and a larger cohort - there was a 2.7% rise in entrants linked to a similar increase in the population. However, there is an argument that the near static figures are the result of examination boards becoming more determined to hold the line and to refuse to approve grade recommendations that vary upwards from the previous year's.

In fact, it is possible that the 1998 examinations were severe and, in particular, were bearing down more harshly on modular courses since there was a larger increase in the numbers of candidates entered for these options and past experience suggests that this should have raised the percentage pass rate overall.

There is an increasing gap between pupils from state and maintained schools. An Independent Schools Information Service (ISIS) survey in 1998 showed that 33.5% of the candidates from a sample group of over five hundred independent schools gained grade A against a national average of just under 17%. There were also almost six thousand S Level entries from these schools suggesting that they dominate this area of qualifications. Such an imbalance is a problem for a government that wants closer links and a more level playing field between the sectors and for the top universities which are being asked by the government to take more students from the maintained sector.

GNVQ in 1998

1998 was another difficult year for the GNVQ system as a whole although the Part One school-based qualifications made progress. The problem for GNVQ is that the mainstream qualification has been revamped at the same time as schools have chosen to postpone curriculum change until the choices arising from the Dearing review are clearer - realistically this will be in September 2000. At the same time, the examining boards have been urging their new AS Level as the sensible choice for less academic sixth-formers. One outcome was that the total number of GNVQ candidates actually fell in 1998, from 104,000 to 92,000. The figures conceal a drop in foundation and intermediate entries and a slight increase in advanced. Completions also flattened out after rising for the past couple of years. At foundation level, for example, the completion rate is still below 40% of entries. As an example of how far GNVQ still has to go to catch up with A Level, its most popular subject, Business Studies, moved from 28,000 candidates in 1997 to 29,000 in 1998. However, the comparable A Level increased its numbers by over 3000 and has a candidature of 37,000.

The statistics for 1998 indicate two trends. The first is that 1999 and 2000 are likely to show little improvement in the figures because schools are not moving into GNVQ in increasing numbers. The reason is undoubtedly the introduction of the new

model, currently being piloted, which will eventually bring major change to all GNVQs. In the interim, there is little incentive for schools to get on board. The second is the fall in foundation and intermediate entries which suggests, as many have forecast, that GNVQ, in the process of being turned into a vocational alternative to A Level, is losing touch with the cohort for which it was designed.

All the recent commentary on GNVQ has been concerned with its lack of rigour - a word that means unyielding, strict and harsh in the dictionary - and the opposite of a belief in tailoring assessment to the purpose or the people. OFSTED reported -once again - on Advanced GNVQs in March 1998. This time the focus was on sixth forms and the main conclusions were that most work was satisfactory, the best of it matched A Level, and student attainment benefited. However, there was some evidence of generosity, quality assurance measures were occasionally unreliable and grading and verification procedures needed attention. In short, the qualification lacked rigour!

The new model (pilot) for GNVQ is seen as the answer. Trialed as a pilot since 1997 and modified along the way it offers two sharp contrasts with the old. The first, generally popular, is a new unit structure that has been greatly simplified. The assessment evidence required is stated clearly and unit grading gives students more information about what they have to do. However, the second change, in the form and style of the new unit tests, is universally disliked. Each GNVQ unit is now assessed through the portfolio (by the teacher), through a set (benchmark) assignment or by a test. Many are assessed using a portfolio and a test. The three key skill areas are also to be assessed by benchmark assignments and tests. The complaints are vociferous because the increased - and to many the superfluous - assessment burden comes with no compensation offered in teaching time for the hours to be spent on the preparation for benchmark assignments and key

GNVQ QUALIFICATIONS		
These are available at six levels:		
Level	**Equivalence**	**Typically ...**
Foundation	4 GCSE grades at D-G	One year as an FE college course post-16
Intermediate	4 GCSE grades at A*-C	One year as an FE college course post-16
Foundation Part One	2 GCSE grades at A*-C	Two years school-based 14-16
Intermediate Part One	2 GCSE grades at A*-C	Two years school-based 14-16
Advanced	2 A Levels	Two years school or FE-college based post-16
Passes are currently at PASS, MERIT or DISTINCTION level.		

GNVQ SUBJECT AREAS	
Art & Design	Leisure & Tourism
Business	Management Studies
Construction & The Built Environment	Manufacturing
Engineering	Media: Communication & Production
Health & Social Care	Performing Arts and Entertainment Industries
Hospitality & Catering	Retail & Distributive Services
Information Technology	Science
Land and Environment	

skill testing. Under the new regime GNVQ will, for the first time, be assessment led.

Along the way, the mergers between examining boards and GNVQ providers are bound to have had some impact. The new OCR which incorporates RSA is steeped in tradition and steered from Cambridge and the smaller GNVQ partner will struggle to maintain its habits of small-scale innovation. Similarly, City & Guilds has been swallowed by NEAB and SEG into AQA. Only EdExcel looks like a real partnership. The result may be that when national policy is written and organisational strategies are discussed within the new monoliths, that NVQ and GNVQ end up with the crumbs from the top table.

In the future, GNVQ has to decide what to do about its special status as a work-related qualification. On paper, there is no doubt that geography teachers can deliver the advanced GNVQ in Leisure & Tourism under the new model, almost without leaving the classroom. Business Studies teachers can certainly deliver the GNVQ in that subject but the question arises of what is lost in the process. Along with the close employment and workplace links there is a danger that GNVQ will also lose its emphasis on independent learning and its faith in contextualised assessment. And, if that happens at the same time as set assignments are introduced, then some candidates will drop out while others turn to AS and A Level alternatives. An indication of the sea-change in the GNVQ sector can be seen in the proliferation of expensive text books to replace individual research and enquiry.

Finally, as GNVQ becomes more academic - not by existing on a higher plane - but because of more directive teaching, the introduction of set tests as hurdles, an A Level grading system and deadlines for completion there is a danger that this will work against the government's social inclusion policy. GNVQ was originally introduced for students who took little from their academic study, who benefited from learning

skills in work-related contexts and who were most likely to go on to employment in that skill area immediately after completion. Since its inception in 1993, the process by which the qualification has been first denigrated and then hijacked by the powerful self-serving interests that dominate higher education is an interesting one. One might ask whether, if the overriding intention had always been to keep the 'oiks' in their place, the 'development' of GNVQ and the 're-organisation' of the awarding bodies would have been any different.

Relative Values

The introduction of A Level performance tables has steadily eroded the status of 'point scoring' at 16-19. Under the current system, devised by UCAS solely as a convenient way of describing university requirements for students, a grade A scores ten points and a grade E scores 2. AS Level grades score from 5 to 1. Performance tables give an average points per candidate score based on these. The criticism of the approach, when used for this purpose, is that it inflates the importance of higher grade scores. One bright pupil notching up thirty points in a sixth form with fifty entrants will have a possibly undeserved impact on the average performance of the school because his or her performances may be only twenty percent or so above those of a candidate who scores just twenty points. The other problem is that vocational courses have to be fitted into the calculation. For 1998, the government proposed that a GNVQ Distinction should earn 18 points, a merit 12 points and a pass 4 points.

The Key Skills Debate

If the broader Dearing curriculum at 16 to 19 is ever to be a reality or a success, then it will be essential to get the key skill element right. While there is general

KEY SKILLS		
Communication	Information Technology	Application of Number
Personal Skills - Working with others*	Personal Skills - Improving own learning and performance*	Problem Solving*
* *Within the NVQ model these skills have traditionally been assessed by centres.*		

support for a key skills element in the curriculum and for the principle of accreditation, there is still a lot to argue over in terms of certification.

The latest problems have emerged with the pilots of the new model GNVQ where the key skills of communication, application of number and information technology are buried under an absurdly complicated assessment regime. This model requires a teacher assessment of the key skills' contribution to teacher assessed units, three externally set assignments taken under examination conditions and a separate test of number. The IT assignments require each candidate to have access to a computer but their form requires that all candidates sit them together - something that would simply be impossible on a national level. The number test - basically mental arithmetic against the clock - is probably the most blatant example of an utter disregard for the contextualised learning supposed to be at the heart of the GNVQ.

One emerging problem is that the key skill element is in danger of making the whole GNVQ certification unstable and unattractive. An AS course in key skills - discrete, unapplied, quickly learned and easily forgotten - looks like a much better route to higher education. In all of this debate, the question of sales potential and income development accompanies the talk about education. A General Studies AS Level with credit transfer from A Level courses and a simple one paper examination is commercially a more attractive option than a complicated GNVQ system.

The other problem with key skills is that the performance criteria approach lives on here. Instead of identifying these criteria as the central problem with the assessment of key skills, they have become the starting point for the addition of extra rigour to the system. So, they are to be more detailed, more complex and even more decontextualised than before without addressing the issues of transferability or competency. Even Chris Woodhead agrees that the idea of teaching discrete skills 'in a knowledge vacuum' is patently absurd.

This is a crucial issue because unless the key skills element can be made a success the whole notion of strategic pathways as proposed by Sir Ron Dearing may fall down. The Dearing National Certificate was to require two A Level passes (or equivalent) plus a key skills element at AS Level or equivalent while the National Diploma, the route to university, would require two A Levels plus two AS (one of which would be key skills) and coverage of aspects of science, the arts, a modern language and study of how the community works. Of course, that vision is now a pipe-dream but the idea of a broader base to post-16 study as a prelude to specialisation in higher education should not be.

NVQ

1998 saw the award of the two millionth NVQ certificate. New criteria were published by QCA which - so it was claimed - would create a more flexible and less jargon-ridden certification while increasing the rigour of the assessment and adding more quality assurance and quality control. The numbers involved in NVQ certification continue to grow. It is probable that over two million certificates were issued in 1998 with the biggest increases at level 3. The most popular areas continue to be business, goods and services and engineering.

One area where NVQ started to come unstuck in 1998 was a government attempt to export the qualification. It may be a folk myth but students in Oman were said to have struggled with an NVQ course in heating engineering that included work on radiators!

Current Issues

Business Links

Over 90% of secondary schools and 60% of primaries now have active links with business, and almost 100% of year 11 pupils undertake some kind of work experience. New Labour has been keen to set itself out as the natural partner for dynamic businesses and, before the election, promised to nourish the links between education and commerce. The policy had three aims; to introduce young people to the world of work, to rekindle enthusiasm in a group who were disaffected by schooling and to make more substantive connections between courses in schools, colleges and workplaces.

WHAT SCHOOLS CAN GAIN FROM BUSINESS

• Work experience	• Mentoring programmes
• Teacher placements	• Project information and help
• Money for specialist school status	• Mock interviews and personnel issues
• Visits as part of career education	• New, supportive governors
• Personal development programmes	

Since the election, three areas have emerged as particularly important. The first is work experience and £10 million is available this year to support it. The government may have ideas of linking work experience to key skill training. The second is mentoring and the provision of workplace role-models for young people. Mentoring of this kind has - anecdotally - a good track record in current schemes but quite what that means may yet have to be unravelled. If it is simply a system that allows companies to select and reject, or to 'cherry-pick', then it may have unwanted consequences that are not yet apparent. The third is study support, and some very new initiatives where literacy and numeracy top-up courses are provided away from schools at centres identified - typically - with football clubs and businesses.

Teachers and schools can benefit from business links with management and IT support. Again, this is fine as far as it goes and the relationships can be valuable in themselves. However, there is a growing feeling that industry has taught education enough in the last ten years for schools to be able now to stand on their own feet. In fact, some educationalists think that schools - many of which are highly successful in business terms - could now teach businesses about how to run some of their operations more efficiently.

Education Business Partnerships

Today's Education Business Partnerships (EBPs) show how far work experience has progressed in twenty years but they are still viewed with suspicion by many teachers. The principle behind an EBP is that both schools and industry can gain from the arrangement.

A positive view suggests that for schools, there can be an added momentum for new initiatives within the school and an opportunity to enhance curricular provision with workplace experiences and skills. Workplace links can also help to tackle under-achievement within specific groups while teachers can improve their management skills and come to a better understanding of the skills that their school-leavers will require when in employment.

The employers and companies involved stand to gain from an increased awareness of their work, and from new insights into the composition of the local workforce. Also, the 'wealthy high streets need wealthy back streets' argument is often put. In summary, it means that if the underclass (measured by spending power and its degree of social deprivation) remains stubbornly at around 30% of the population it will always act as a drag on industry's ambitions. Turning even 5% of potential underclass members into cheap, efficient labour would be a very significant gain.

The current schemes fall into three categories. The first is the relationship of schools to a large local employer, the second is the project-based support offered by a major national company, and the third is the support for schools that comes from intermediary organisations which are largely, or exclusively, funded by industry. General Motors in Bedford, Cadbury in Birmingham and Tate and Lyle in Newham operate schemes that come under the first heading. A wide range of companies including retailers (Marks and Spencer), banks (Midland Bank), insurance companies (Royal Sun Alliance), accountancy firms (KPMG) and soap powder manufacturers (Unilever) feature under the second heading and offer a variety of schemes and opportunities to schools and teachers ranging from materials to visits and training courses. Finally, under the third heading is the work of organisations like Headteachers Into Industry, Understanding British Industry, The Prince's Trust and the National Mentoring Network.

The days of trading the cream of your school-leavers for a couple of redundant computers are long gone and, for all schools, there are clear advantages in links with business and industry whether these be local or national. The recent moves towards the development of action zones suggest that industry may have an increasing role to play and those companies that are already in EBPs are the ones most likely to increase their influence over local education.

Careers Education

The status of Careers Education and the Careers Service for schools was weak for so long that its shortcomings were institutionalised and accepted. Although the last government claimed to be set on improving careers advice for young people and introduced a new requirement in the 1997 Education

Act, a report, carried out by Susan Bender on behalf of The Children's Society in the same year, described most advice in schools as 'astronomically bad'. Surveys have also revealed that many careers officers felt that they operated in a vacuum without support from either industry or schools and wanted to see careers education and guidance (CEG) as part of the statutory curriculum. It is also worth noting that under 35% of school leavers go into higher education, fourteen OECD members have more 17-year-olds in full-time education, and around 20% of 19-year-olds can be described as functionally illiterate.

However, things are starting to change as jobs are given a higher priority by government. The Employment Service re-launched itself in 1997 with a new framework of values to enable the delivery of the New Deal programmes, centred on results, service, innovation, partnership and quality. There are currently just over one thousand job centres nationally with a total budget of £1000 million. There are also sixty-six careers services in England - privatised since 1993 - with a budget of £209 million and 8,500 staff. They operate in partnership with TECs as well as schools.

As a sign of its intention to deliver changes, the DfEE announced £5.5 million extra for the Careers Service in June 1997 to support a new focus on students without qualifications or expectations. This was followed up with a publication defining good practice in designing CEG programmes, working with partners and evaluating and improving the service to users. At the same time, the DfEE announced plans for OFSTED to inspect the careers service more widely.

1998 saw the publication of two key documents. In May, the DfEE published a slim circular (*Careers Education in Schools: Provision for Years 9-11*, DfEE 5/98) which followed up the Education Act requirements for a careers education programme in all maintained schools. It called for schools to develop, or review, their careers education and guidance policies, to link these to school aims and the development plan, to name key personnel and their responsibilities, and to state how careers education was either to be timetabled or integrated into the curriculum.

This circular provided the framework for OFSTED's survey which was published in October (*National Survey of Careers Education and Guidance*, OFSTED, 1998). The study involved a collaboration between OFSTED inspectors, DfEE inspectors and regional government offices and covered almost one hundred and fifty secondary schools plus a range of other institutions. OFSTED found that there was a national shortage of recognised qualifications and that only 30% of schools employed a careers co-ordinator. This

was not altogether surprising but the finding that 25% of schools failed to offer a recognisable programme of careers education or satisfactory careers information and that 10% had no proper library of materials was disappointing.

However, in other areas, OFSTED was pleasantly surprised. More co-ordinators than anticipated had achieved some form of qualification in the past three years (30%) and teaching, once a blackspot, was considered to be satisfactory in 80% of observed lessons. The advice from careers advisers was almost always helpful. Teaching allocations for careers varied considerably with a 'circus' in some schools and scheduled lessons in others. The schools which were weakest on the provision of careers advice in years 9-11 were those where there was an expectation that students would remain at school for sixth form education. It is clearly OFSTED's view that some of these schools are concerned that the dissemination of alternative routes will encourage pupils to go elsewhere post-16. Generally speaking, careers service providers were rated more highly than the schools that used their services.

As priorities, OFSTED noted the need to get careers advice into all schools, to develop an additional qualification for teachers and to provide a careers input in initial training. Headteachers were advised to build closer links with careers service companies and to focus the work done by their in-school co-ordinators so that this could be run in parallel without needless duplication.

Provision for careers education in secondary schools comes typically in four forms; separately timetabled lessons, careers lessons within a PSHE programme, integrated activities within national curriculum subjects and extended activities (work experience, withdrawal for interviews and extracurricular activity). Reading between the lines, OFSTED is least enthusiastic about the popular option of including careers with PSHE where it found the least time devoted to careers and a danger that careers education had to fit the programme rather than be offered at an appropriate time as, for example, when option choices are made. Schools that are revisiting their policies will find the old SCAA publication, Looking Forward (*Looking Forward: Careers Education and Guidance in the Curriculum*, SCAA, 1995) as helpful as much more recent material.

Another new initiative in this area in 1998 was the introduction of the plastic Learning Card for all students in year 11. These currently offer telephone numbers but are, perhaps, significant as the forerunners of a personal education and employment record carried on a smartcard.

Schools

Those cynics who stand on the side-line and carp need to understand that this is a revolution which has begun.

Stephen Byers on Education Action Zones.

If we carry on doing the same, we'll get the same outcomes.

John Botham, Sheffield EAZ.

The Shape of the System

As schools started to redefine themselves as required by the 1998 School Standards and Framework Act, there was plenty of controversy over status, selection and admissions policy. Within the school system, the new categories of foundation, community and voluntary-aided schools now hide a multiplicity of organisations. So, there are grammar schools that cream off varying percentages of the local population, schools that have some degree of selection courtesy of the last government, specialist schools for technology, the arts and music, and city technology colleges. Soon there will be beacon schools and specialist schools in the inner cities that receive additional funding for dispensing their expertise. There will be privately run schools and, perhaps, some that are owned by their communities. Most of these schools can, for additional variety, be mixed or single-sex. The outlook will continue to be fluid because, in the longer term, all maintained schools will have the option of becoming foundation schools.

If the government now has a principle about school organisation it is probably that there is not a national policy. Instead, local communities and the people in them can decide what kind of education they want for their children. This is fine where that amorphous thing - community - can easily be defined and better still when the community is prosperous, middle-class and has a view about education. However, it ignores huge tracts of Britain where any sense of community is a joke and where the comprehensive schools have never been mixed by ability because of the areas in which they are located. The real challenge for new Labour is to do something for these organisations within the social inclusion policy which is why the schools in the education action zones and the most recent inner cities initiative will provide the acid test of how the system is shaping up for the next century.

The choice of school status under the new legislation is interesting. Most of the previously grant-maintained schools were inclined to become foundation schools, thereby keeping their current governing bodies more or less intact. This caused a spat when the catholic

bishops realised that numbers of their schools were in the process of cutting themselves off from voluntary-aided status and their diocesan links. Once a school was in the foundation category, the diocese would only have 25% of the governing body under its control and there would be no requirement for additional religious education in the catholic faith. The argument had blown over by the end of the year with all of the schools bar two coming into line with the bishops' request.

However, there was a growing realisation that many grant-maintained schools were not going to slide easily back into the local authority herd. The government has made the point forcefully that there must be give and take on all sides but, in many areas, the opting out process was a very bitter one and some of the people involved are bound to still feel recriminatory. Many grant-maintained schools now operate partial selection and while the new admission code of practice is likely, as soon as there is an appeal, to rule against this, the schools will still be able to select 10% of their intakes by aptitude - in the arts, music, languages, IT, design & technology - courtesy of a deliberate government loophole.

The question of whether the government wants to abolish grammar schools is an interesting one. There is no doubt that it does not want to be seen as the party that got rid of the sector and also does not want to be involved in damaging rows over their future. Therefore, some critics claim, it has made the procedures for voting them out of existence so complicated that no-one will bother to enact them. One odd consequence is that those areas where there are several grammar schools such as Kent, Bucks and Lincolnshire, have a better chance of saving them.

The ballot system has gone through several versions. What is clear, however, is that a petition signed by 20% of the parents at relevant schools is required to trigger a ballot. Then, in ten selected local authorities which have a full grammar school system there will be a ballot in which all parents can vote. The franchise is extended to those with children in neighbouring authority schools, those with pre-school children and those with children in private education. Essentially, this will amount to a local referendum on the issue. In other areas, all the parents of children in feeder schools which have sent five or more children to the grammar school in the previous three years will have a vote unless they also have a child at the grammar school under discussion. Where there are neighbouring boys' and girls' schools their futures must be discussed together. Opposition to these proposals came from, among others, small schools whose parents would be effectively disenfranchised by the process. As to how this arrangement will work out in practice is hard to say but there are some indications that many 'local' schools will not be franchised. As one example, in Barnet which has three grammar schools only a third of the primary schools will be eligible to vote but twenty-four schools outside the authority and fourteen independent schools will be. July 1999 is the deadline for drawing together the first petitions so, realistically, there are unlikely to be any challenges to the grammar system until 2000 at the earliest.

There is a growing movement against selection - Say No To Selection - being brought together by the Campaign for State Education (CASE) with the help of Roy Hattersley, several other Labour members of Parliament and, for the most part, the Liberal Democrats. Roy Hattersley is a powerful spokesman for the campaign because his credentials in the area are impeccable as a lifelong opponent of selection. The aim is to support local campaigns as they arise rather than to make some kind of national challenge and to foster grass-roots opposition to the grammar schools. The first targets are the grammar schools (166 of them) which select entirely by ability.

It is worth mentioning here the potentially interesting role for primary school headteachers in raising awareness about the balloting process. Those headteachers who have been courted by the local grammar schools may keep quiet but those that have been sidelined since 1992 or treated with contempt may well have some scores to settle. It is also worth noting that two grammar schools in Bristol, Cotham and Fairfield, have been given permission to change their status. They will have their first comprehensive intakes in September 2000.

The government's relations with independent schools are also going through a strange period. The abolition of the assisted places scheme and the amendments to the School Standards and Framework Act to make sure that local authorities could not support similar schemes was said to have been the work of Stephen Byers and perhaps he felt vaguely apologetic afterwards. In May 1998, plans were announced for forty-eight linked schemes - where the maintained and independent sectors work together - using £350,000 from the government and £250,000 from the Sutton Trust (the philanthropic arm of the millionaire Peter Lampl). There were over three hundred applicants for the funding after the idea was proposed in November 1997. How the schemes will work out in practice still

has to be revealed but it will be interesting to see whether long-standing animosities can be broken down. This is only the start of things. The government is willing to commit another £1 million but that may depend on persuading Lampl not to set up his own assisted places scheme which was believed to have been under discussion in the autumn of 1998. Estelle Morris became the first Labour education spokesperson to address the Headmasters' and Headmistresses' Conference in 1998. A subsequent DfEE publication, *Building Bridges*, suggested that teachers in independent schools should be involved in local discussions over admissions, and that they should be allowed to benefit from local education authority administered training initiatives in addition to being able to complete their induction years in the independent sector.

TEN THINGS YOU MIGHT NOT HAVE KNOWN ABOUT SECONDARY SCHOOLS ...

1. Nine out of ten secondary schools are non-selective comprehensives

2. Only 5% of schools are grammar schools

3. Only 5% of schools are solely for boys

4. The average secondary school contains 838 pupils

5. There are fifteen schools with more than 1800 pupils

6. The average time spent in lessons each week in 1996 was 24.6 hours

7. In 1996, there were 795 female headteachers and 2799 male

8. The proportion of pupils gaining five or more A*-C GCSE grades rose by 7.5% between 1992 and 1997

9. Grant-maintained schools do not have higher standards of achievement than maintained schools

10. The gap between the top 10% of schools and the bottom 10% in terms of GCSE point scores of schools widened between 1992 and 1996

Source OFSTED, 1998.

The decision to let the business sector run schools has always seemed to be predicated on a desire to challenge the inalienable rights of local authorities to a monopoly over state education. Such a wish may not be the best starting point for a new policy which may yet see communities running their own schools but has, so far, seen a successful CTC, Kingshurst in Solihull, take over the management of a failing school, Kings Manor in Guildford, from a local authority. The latter school has four hundred pupils on a site designed for nine hundred and has a poor academic performance in relation to its neighbours but is now to get an unexpected make-over. Other bids came in from Nord Anglia, CfBT and the American education company, Edison. On the basis of the winning outfit's reputation, the likelihood is that the change to Kings Manor will be technology led but will also include new paint, staff changes, new uniforms, a tough disciplinary and attendance code and a longer school day. It is safe to say that the school will thrive under its new owners which raises the question of why the local education authority cannot deliver the same goods in that situation.

In this sense, the take-over is very bad news for the local authorities as a whole because it suggests that they not only cannot keep their own houses in order but that they are also not the best people to improve them. Another failing school, Ram Episcopal Primary in Hackney, has a headteacher who is contracted from CfBT. Other private sector organisations with their eyes on schools include Timeplan Education which makes money from the provision of supply teachers and Capita which is a systems provider to schools. It is also clear that government is willing to see all of Hackney's schools put in the hands of business.

One source of bitter argument has been over selection and interviews for potential applicants. The grant-maintained sector was persistently criticised by Labour in opposition for making use of these. The argument was that social factors and cultural attitudes were set above the rights of those who applied first. The London Oratory School, which the Blair children attend, held interviews to gauge the enthusiasm of parents for the ethos of the school whatever that entailed and was roundly criticised for it. So, it was no surprise that the draft regulations on admissions made clear that there was no need for interviews as part of the admission process. The only oddity was an additional note that church schools might wish to interview parents to assess their religious and denominational commitment to the school. The Bishops were quick to say that they had not asked for this so clearly there had been some quiet lobbying from some influential school governing bodies.

After a long period of debate, the government has decided to give grant-maintained status to a Seventh Day Adventist school, John Loughborough in Haringey. This puts the church with its UK congregation of 25,000 on a par with the two Muslim schools which have been given new status since the 1997 election. From September 1999, there will also be a voluntary-aided Sikh school, Guru Nanak College in Middlesex. The school has over two hundred students and the percentage of pupils gaining five or more A*-C GCSE grades is 73%.

OFSTED published some interesting data about the composition of schools. More OECD data showed that the average English child spends two years more in school than did his counterpart in the 1980s. The increase comes both from greater numbers staying on after the statutory leaving age and schools making room for early entrants. For the average child, 17.3 years of schooling is now the norm which compares reasonably with other OECD countries (the OECD average is 16.5). Annual spending per pupil runs below average on OECD figures ($4246 in secondary schools against an average of around $5000). Of the OECD group, Australians and Belgians spend the most time at school and Mexican children the least.

For posterity, it should be noted that David Willetts, as Conservative education spokesperson, announced in 1998 that the party would not reintroduce the assisted places scheme even if it was returned to power. In an interview, Willetts acknowledged that the scheme's connections with selection had made it and the party unpopular with the majority of parents.

The End of the GM Revolution

By December 1998, all of the six hundred or so grant-maintained schools had to indicate their preferred new status, thereby bringing to its inevitable end a major educational experiment that endeavoured to use parental choice to break the power of the local authorities. At the Council of Local Education Authorities (CLEA) annual conference, Anthony Tippett, the Funding Agency for Schools (FAS) chair, urged the local authorities to work with the schools that came back under their control and make the most of their knowledge of self-management.

The FAS closes down officially in April 1999 but a transitional team will be left at the York base until October to oversee the final transfer of the schools to their new status. Many of the staff were made redundant in September 1998 but some were offered new DfEE jobs in Darlington and the few who have agreed to remain to the bitter end will be rewarded with generous bonus payments.

In its last years, the FAS has been kind to its servants. Michael Collier, the chief executive, was paid a package worth £110,000, the part-time chairman Sir Christopher Benson was paid £18,000 for a two-day week and there was a 42% increase in fees and expenses paid to members but the FAS has still managed to end with an operating surplus.

It has only recently occurred to the local authorities that there are significant costs to be incurred in taking schools back into their systems. Bromley, Essex and Kent will be particularly affected but several others have reported that they will need to take on new staff.

EDUCATION ACTION ZONES 1998-99		
Blackburn with Darwen	Barnsley	Salford and Trafford
Weston-Super-Mare	Newham	Herefordshire
Croydon	Leicester	Lambeth
Grimsby	Middlesbrough	Newcastle
EDUCATION ACTION ZONES 1999-2000		
South Tyneside	Halifax (Calderdale)	Wigan
Sheffield	Birmingham 1	Birmingham 2
Nottingham	East Basildon	Southwark
Plymouth	Brighton	Hull
Thetford		

Education Action Zones

Education Action Zones (EAZ) are test beds for innovation, a solution to educational failure and the indicators of a new partnership between schools and communities depending on who was talking in 1998. Condemned at one point for being unsexy, at another for being too ambitious, the pioneer dozen took their stuttering first steps in September 1998.

Sixty education action applications were received in early 1998. Spread nationally, the greatest number of bids came from the north-west, the majority came from urban areas, there was an emphasis on areas of relative social deprivation and the bid least likely to succeed came from Solihull! There was argument that the local authorities, often already in partnership with TECs and local business had an unfair advantage. It was also said that, of the sixty applications, forty-seven were rejected immediately and that civil servants had trouble making up the numbers. The criteria were unpublished but guaranteed private sector investment was a key element. Twenty-five schemes were approved, of which twelve started work in September 1998, with thirteen scheduled to follow in January 1999.

Each zone involves two or three secondary schools and their feeder primaries (perhaps, twenty) so the relatively low numbers conceal the fact that this is a major initiative. Around two hundred schools are involved in the first phase and this number will double in 1999. As the zones have emerged, they have undergone some subtle changes. Firstly, the funding has changed. The zones are now required to raise only £250,000 for themselves with the government finding the remaining £750,000 of the annual grant (it was to

be a 50-50 split). Even this figure may be an overstatement since it is said that 'most' of the approved schemes have failed to raise the required £250,000 in private sponsorship and that the money is offered in kind - through support services and advice - rather than in hard cash.

Secondly, the emphasis on innovation and the use of technology has overtaken the notion of partnership and the original intention of taking power away from the local authorities. And, finally, the autonomy of schools and the status of teachers within them has not yet been radically challenged. Few of the bids mentioned performance related pay, for example, and there has been little action in this area since. The need to keep teachers involved and enthusiastic outweighs any possible gains.

Every zone has literacy and numeracy hurdles to climb and a number of other targets that include increased GCSE pass rates, attendance and stay-on rates, more use of information technology and reductions in the number of exclusions. Each zone has a specific set of innovations to explore and develop. These broadly fall under four headings. The first group are concerned with meeting the targets for greater use of IT. One zone will have a laptop computer loan scheme, another has internet addresses for all, another an intranet and one has its own television channel. The second group of innovations link to the school day and include changes in holiday patterns, a longer day, breakfast provision and after school clubs. The third group of innovations concern staffing and covers specialist teachers with advanced skills, a new emphasis on leadership and management, co-operation with outside agencies and less use of supply cover. The final set of innovations are hazier and revolve around curriculum planning where there is specialist teaching of literacy and numeracy, study support and elements of work-related learning and workplace lessons. Most of the zones have gone for change at two levels - quick, high impact alterations to the school day and established routines and longer-term developments like curriculum reform.

It would be churlish to assume that such investment and an evident degree of enthusiasm will not lead to some success. As just one example, Lilian Bayliss school in Lambeth now finds itself at the heart of a zone of twenty seven schools promoting family literacy, breakfast clubs, the Duke of Edinburgh award scheme and residential courses for all of its pupils. This is the same school that was savaged by OFSTED in 1994 for the overtly racist and sexist language used by its pupils and the high levels of bullying experienced by younger children. In 1997, it was named and shamed by David Blunkett but now it is linked to IBM, the Royal Festival Hall and the National Theatre, steered by a forum headed by the director of Corporate Affairs at Royal Dutch Shell and its local business partner is the Marriott Hotel.

Lambeth is one of the zones that is looking for help from one of the expanding education companies. It has close links with the Centre for British Teachers (CfBT) which may go on to have some kind of management role. Nord Anglia, now larger than several local authorities, is involved in Weston-Super-Mare and Arthur Andersen Consulting is in Newham. Unusual partners include Blackburn Rovers (Blackburn with Darwen), Tesco (Herefordshire) and McDonalds (Weston-Super-Mare). The role that business will play has yet to develop but should involve help with management, ICT, work placement and mentoring as a minimum. Two of the zones, Croydon and East Basildon are school-led initiatives and the nearest thing to community zones.

For most of the zones these are very early days. Key staff are only just in post and while it is relatively easy to introduce innovation when the funding is available it is far harder to make it stick and produce results across a range of schools. Also, the targets set by many of the consortia are very demanding given their starting points. Probably, leadership and management will be the most important elements in their ultimate success or failure. Any that become glorified mini-councils and talking shops are doomed because the experience of the specialist schools shows that there has to be a clear executive structure in which partners take, and have responsibility for, action.

One odd event in 1998 showed the government's determination for the zones to succeed when the DfEE parachuted Sir Anthony Tippett, the part time chairman of the FAS which is currently winding up its work, into the Halifax EAZ. The bulk of the money here comes from the eponymous building society and, probably, the DfEE wanted to keep Calderdale local authority in the background after OFSTED had exposed its weaknesses.

Where teachers are concerned, Arthur Andersen Consulting (Newham) was grousing about the lack of cash from business in the schemes, implying the kind of management services that it wanted to offer could not be financed by the government's handouts alone. However, Newham was the first EAZ to contemplate the unthinkable and to discuss competency payments to teachers. In early 1999, the zone announced plans to introduce a competency framework based on headteachers observing lessons, interviewing teachers and inspecting records. A new pay framework will match the competencies demonstrated to a teacher's salary. To achieve this, some aspects of national pay agreements will have to be suspended. There is also a plan to appoint four ASTs in every secondary school and to retain a central pool of fifteen who will be 'on call'. While the government is keen to see prototypical performance-related appraisal schemes, Newham needs to think hard about the dangers of fragmenting teaching skills and about whether headteachers have more important jobs to do than checklisting skills in artificial periods of observation. One unanticipated problem for Newham and for others who move in the same direction, is that the EAZ only has a five year life and, if it pays good teachers more, this could leave the borough with an impossible wage bill once it takes over control of the schools.

Lambeth also has literacy and numeracy advisers on fixed-term contracts with performance bonuses if targets are met. Four of the current schemes have indicated that they are likely to appoint advanced skills teachers. Of major interest is how the role of the EAZ Chief Executive / Project Director develops. To foster change, high quality leadership will be required in this post but the question is whether these individuals can deliver change without annoying those headteachers and governors who value their schools' autonomy more.

The role of business is slowly emerging apart from the general reluctance of any of the companies involved to hand over hard cash for the EAZs to spend. Basically, all the companies from McDonalds and financial organisations to football clubs offer facilities and staff time in lieu of payment. Their involvement is good local public relations that sometimes edges into dubious marketing using branded materials and there are obvious benefits for the companies in being involved.

The future of zone development is not entirely guaranteed but looks increasingly secure. At one time in 1998, the government was talking of seventy-five zones before the next election although its original target was one-third of that number. The most recent plans are for a further fifteen to open in January and September 2000. There has been considerable discussion of encouraging zones which are under community control and this may be in response to a growing awareness that action zones seem likely to tackle educational weakness more effectively than social deprivation. There were hints that the DfEE and Downing Street were in conflict over this but the disagreement may have been resolved by the announcement in March 1999 of £24 million to extend the programme to support forty additional smaller zones around particular estates as part of the new Excellence In Cities initiative.

That may also explain why the latest action zone bidding documentation is community oriented. What is more, around fifty shortlisted applicants can receive help from specialist advisers and grants of up to £20,000 to help them prepare their bids. Sir Cyril Taylor has been appointed as the DfEE's action zone specialist to lead the former aspect. Sir Cyril was the prime mover behind the establishment of the city technology colleges and there is a feeling that his role is to push innovation forward. There was speculation that the government intended a cut in the subsidy from £750,000 to £500,000 but that is not exactly the case. Now, the first £500,000 is guaranteed and beyond that sum the government will match contributions from business. The government has been taking a hard line on this, wanting to see genuine funding agreed in advance. This may be because - as noted previously - some of the first round zones have still not delivered their sponsors' cash. After the second round bidding had opened, it was claimed that around sixty bids were received, of which forty were led by local authorities and the remainder by other groups including headteachers, communities and the burgeoning education business sector.

For schools - especially those in areas of relative social deprivation - the cash is inviting. There are also many national organisations which are not yet involved in the zones so there is the potential for increased outside support. The downside is the distraction that an application might be from the day-to-day business of meeting targets and the realisation that an action zone is a short-term strategy. However, for headteachers who are seeking purposeful change the zones have much to recommend them as a kick-starting mechanism.

New Directions for Schools

Specialist Schools

The specialist schools, once despised for cherry-picking by Labour in opposition, are now the apple of the government's eye. There are over three hundred of these schools and, by 2002, there should be five hundred more selecting 10% of their intakes by aptitude in technology, languages, sports and the arts - not, heaven forbid, by ability. The current rules are that if a school can raise £100,000 locally, it can gain the same from central government as well as the top

up grant of £100 per pupil a year and an extra £20,000 for developing links with neighbouring schools. However, it looks as if part of this funding requirement will be waived for inner city schools. While this is not quite the level of action zone funding it is still a very handy amount. The survival of these schools has been impressive and, as a sector, their covert selection is likely to guarantee continued improvement and government support while not being sufficient to attract the attention of the abolitionists.

The long term aim is for a quarter of secondary schools to come into this category, a figure that presumably includes all schools within action zones. While the 1998 School Standards and Framework Act included clauses that covered their status legally the extension of selection that the expansion of the sector involves is a surprising route for the Labour party to take. Another 1998 innovation has seen the proposed introduction of 'master-classes' as one way of delivering the links between the schools and their neighbours. These will offer extra tuition in the specialism offered by the school to talented 8 to 14-year-old pupils from local feeder schools. ICT development will be prominent with adult computer learning clinics in some of the schools. There will also be more money (£17 million) for the mentoring of disadvantaged pupils. Inner city summer schools for older pupils and new tests of performance will push up standards. Where this kind of activity is already undertaken by schools it has a pronounced impact on transfer choices and that factor may add to the arguments about the selection procedures adopted by some specialist schools.

Beacon Schools

Beacon schools are a new idea. With £1.8 million of funding, seventy-five of the schools deemed most successful by OFSTED are expected to pass on the secrets of their success to neighbouring schools over a three year period. Grants of between £20,000 and £50,000 - usually £30,000 - will allow schools to offer ICT demonstrations or develop new learning strategies, often in conjunction with teachers from local feeder schools. The cash can be used for supply cover in other schools. There was a whiff of the school prize about the activity at the start because only OFSTED's top one hundred and sixty schools were invited to bid. Of these, nine declined. There should be another 125 schools pulled into the scheme from September 1999 and local education authorities are being asked to make specific use of the schools in their education development plans.

In 2000, the Excellence In Cities initiative, announced in March 1999, proposes a major increase in the number and status of beacon schools. The new aim is to have one thousand in the six largest city areas in England by 2002. The areas targeted are Inner London, North London, Manchester and Salford, Liverpool and Knowsley, Birmingham, Leeds and

Bradford, and Sheffield and Rotherham. The schools may provide learning centres - perhaps with ICT facilities - as well as offering other forms of support to the community.

Edison Schools

Whenever the role of the new education companies is mentioned up pops the name of Edison, or more precisely, the Edison Project - a company that runs twenty-five American schools and is keen to be involved in England. It has bid to run action zones and applied - unsuccessfully - to run the Kings Manor School in Guildford. Edison's American philosophy is that it takes over a failing school and pumps in money. It gives teachers and pupils computer access, extends the school day and works on a team basis so that pupils are with the same group and teachers for three years. The American schools have done well but have not made exceptional gains.

The long-term aim is that as the school succeeds and grows it meets pre-set performance targets and makes a profit for the company. In the last year, and in spite of considerable publicity, the company has made few inroads into education perhaps because it has used the wrong faces to front its ambitions. For example, Andrew Turner, failed Conservative MP and the man blamed for politicising the grant-maintained schools organisation, was never likely to be popular with the DfEE people who would have to explain his involvement in any successful bid to the media and James Tooley, the scourge of educational researchers was equally unpopular with teachers.

Links to Local Authorities

The way to stop arguments between the local education authorities (LEA) which have declining powers to regulate schools and the schools themselves is the new voluntary code of practice. The code faces the task of giving local authorities the power to intervene when things go wrong but it is also meant to protect schools from unnecessary intrusions and even interference in their day-to-day work. As if this relationship has not been sufficiently testing in the past, the return of the grant-maintained sector to the fold, OFSTED inspections, the negotiation of targets for improvement, arguments over admissions and the writing of development plans could all make for a lively relationship in the future.

LEAs have to work with three guiding principles that are elaborated in the code. The first is that they are responsible for guaranteeing improvement in the system and therefore need to know what is happening in their schools. Secondly, it is their duty to ensure that schools get adequate support, if not from them then from other agencies and, thirdly, they should not interfere unless a school has serious problems. The tensions in all this when things begin to go wrong are obvious.

The headteacher is the main link to the local education authority. Where there is intervention it can be either formal or informal. The latter could involve sending in an adviser or issuing 'early warnings' but the latter is a draconian strategy where the local education authority can withdraw a school's delegated budget or question the suitability of a headteacher. It is worrying that the code is at its slimmest in just these areas where the relationships could break down. If that

THE NEW UNITARY AUTHORITIES

Bath	Blackburn	Blackpool	Bournemouth	Brighton & Hove
Bristol	Darlington	Derby	East Riding	Halton
Hartlepool	Herefordshire	Kingston-upon-Hull	Luton	Middlesbrough
Milton Keynes	North Lincs	North Somerset	Northeast Lincs	Newbury
Nottingham	Peterborough	Plymouth	Poole	Portsmouth
Reading	Redcar & Cleveland	Rochester & Gillingham	Rutland	South Gloucestershire
Slough	Southampton	Southend	Stockton-on-Tees	Stoke-on-Trent
Thamesdown	The Wrekin	Thurrock	Torbay	Warrington
Windsor & Maidenhead	Wokingham & Bracknell	York		

happens, the secretary of state, is likely to have to adjudicate sooner rather than later.

Unitary Authorities

1998 saw the completion of the local government reorganisation which has taken place over the past four years. Five English counties have been replaced entirely by unitary authorities of which there are now forty-six and no longer can teachers work for Cleveland, Humberside or Berkshire! It is important to underline that there is no guiding logic behind the changes which arose out of political gerrymandering so that in some areas there is single tier local government but in adjacent areas the two tier system persists.

For education the shakedown is not quite complete. OFSTED and the Audit Commission are both likely to make some sharp comments once they start to look at central and advisory services, budget devolution and staffing in the smaller unitary authorities with fewer than twenty secondary schools. However, for most of them, the honeymoon period continues with the changes leading to a new enthusiasm for educational innovations.

Government Priorities

Action on Class Sizes

One of the Labour government's most trumpeted priorities was to adjust class sizes downwards in infant schools. The pledge was that, by 2001, there would be no infants in classes of more than thirty. By September 1998, the government could point to significant progress with 140,000 fewer children in classes of 31 or more pupils after an investment in approximately fifteen hundred new teachers and the spending of around £62 million on salaries and buildings. However that still left 21% of the cohort in large classes. These figures are based on a new school census, the Class Size Count, which - from 1999 onwards will be completed in January and September.

There is evidence that the government hopes that this policy can be delivered a year early. The relevant population is declining, courtesy of a demographic trough and extra money has been offered to denominational schools to help them keep up. Church schools normally have to find 15% of funding for new classrooms but this regulation has been waived for schemes designed to meet the target on class numbers. The rest of the money, £620 million by 2002, is in place and local education authorities have been told that they can use temporary classrooms if that helps to deliver the policy on time.

For primary schools that include the infant phase, the pledge has created some headaches. Staffing ratios, while improved, are not ideal and fluctuations in numbers from one year to another has reportedly meant that the improvement in the infant phase has been at the expense of the remainder of the primary sector in some local authorities. There was an early worry that mixed-age teaching would be the simple response for many schools and, after a Coopers & Lybrand audit was published estimated that much of the overcrowding problem was caused by parents demanding places in popular schools, the local authorities were instructed that they could not use the policy to coerce parents into less popular schools.

The bureaucratic planning process for class size reduction has been interesting as a way of seeing how local authorities will be expected to operate in the future. First, the government set the target but then it was left to local education authorities to forecast the numbers of pupils in the classes by 2001, estimate how many teachers would be needed to meet the required teacher-pupil ratio, propose any changes to school places, set out the capital cost implications including new classrooms, describe the measures that would be taken to avoid prejudicing key stage 2 classes and say how the proposals would extend parental preference for all. This had to be completed within a few months and be set out as a bid for funding but the same period also had to include a consultation phase for schools to give their views. Clearly, this directed and fast-paced role represents the future for the local authorities, delivering precisely stated government ambitions through their schools and being funded for specific projects rather than through global budgets.

New Admission Procedures

The government's new guidelines on school admissions have had some effect in the current year but will really come into their own from September 1999 when local admission forums come into operation and appeals panels are made more independent of schools and local authorities. And, where there is disagreement or an unresolved appeal there will be regional adjudicators to sort the matter out. The practical outcome is to take the local authorities and the secretary of state out of the appeals procedure.

The small print suggests that the working out of the detail for the forums will be harder than the overall scheme suggests. There will be requirements to reduce class sizes, to protect failing schools that are trying to improve and a loophole to allow adjudicators to have the power to abolish partial selection in secondary schools which is unrelated to a school specialism (grant-maintained schools were given the right to introduce 10% selection by the last government). There will be a code of practice to govern the work of appeals committees where volunteers will find themselves doing a dirty and unpopular job without the local authority to shelter behind.

A new problem for parents emerged in 1998 when there were allegations that parents were being told by schools that unless they took up a nursery or reception class place, they could not be guaranteed a school place later. The existing admissions guidelines are vague on this and suggest that schools should follow parental choices but there were signs in 1998 that this was not happening. The reasons are obvious - the schools need full nursery and reception classes to balance their books.

Study Support

If the government is to meet its targets for literacy and numeracy, the provision of study support will be crucial. This is the global term for what used to be called extracurricular activities undertaken outside school time but it now includes homework clubs, sporting activity, voluntary work and a whole lot more and its nature has been fundamentally changed in two ways.

The first is that money - a lot of it - is available to support these activities and the second is that teachers can be paid for helping to run them. The pot of gold that has enabled this is the National Opportunities Fund (NOF) which is the mechanism to divert lottery money into education and the 'after-school' element is a means of saying that this is something new in education rather than a topping up of something that schools should be doing anyway.

There is agreement that schools in action zones and those in areas of social disadvantage will have priority but there is so much money available (around £200 million in 1999) that all schools need to think hard about the possibilities on offer. Bids are to be invited in the first half of 1999 for schemes that will commence from September 1999. A good bid will raise standards or tackle social exclusion and involve people or organisations outside the school. The fund may turn out to prefer bids from schools rather than find itself feeding the money to local authorities.

The things that schools can do include varieties of homework and after-school study clubs. Examination revision classes and the use of laboratories and ICT suites for bright pupils would be unusual examples in this category. Sport and outdoor activities may also prosper. Starting a new school team with business support and links to adults involved in the sport locally is the kind of bid that will attract interest. Linking with business or the local independent schools for outdoor pursuits and character building exercises will also go down well. A drama or film club could work on the same kind of basis with local theatre links, the introduction of outside experts and the wider use of local resources. Activities that get parents into school in learning situations alongside children are also likely to prove popular with the fundholders. As with any

bid funding, the organised early birds should find some worms and schools should already be exploring the options. The DfEE booklet, *Extending Opportunity*, is an important source for pre-planning and the Basic Skills Agency has also published some case histories on how literacy can be developed through study support.

Where after-school clubs are concerned, provision was made in the last pay settlement for teachers to be paid around £9.72 per hour to run them. However, a 1998 report on the pilot schemes discovered that, while there was some skills benefit for pupils, the clubs operated on the enthusiasm of young teachers and required a continuous input to maintain support from pupils and families. Plans to engage home literacy as an issue often foundered because the parents who were targeted were not the ones who volunteered. More bids were called for in early 1999 but this is an area where schools need to have a very clear understanding of what they hope to achieve before engaging their resources. There has been some recent confusion over the status of the hourly rate and it my be worth submitting bids where payments to staff relate in some way (with £9.72 as a minimum) to the hourly rates attached to their posts in school.

School Transfer

The discovery that progress in literacy and numeracy appears to go into reverse between years 6 and 7 caused a small panic in 1998 and has led to a greater emphasis on cross-phase links and on transfer. New admission policies, parental ballots over selection and education action zones have also stressed the need for feeder primary and secondary schools to talk more while common year 6 reports may make the transfer of information easier.

A QCA publication in 1998, *Building Bridges*, suggested a common transfer form, a timetable and a recommended protocol for linking schools more closely. Standards fund money can be used for this purpose. It will be interesting to see whether schools start to make more visits to primary schools now that the formal interviewing of potential entrants is so severely frowned on by the DfEE.

It will also be interesting to track whether the QCA proposals have an effect. The problem with cross-phase links at the moment is that information comes into the secondary school and may well be used to facilitate the creation of teaching groups but that is where it stops. It is rare, for example, for subject specialists in year 7 to receive useful diagnostic information on new pupils - something that OFSTED often complains about - and if that extra link can be incorporated into the system it could be useful. Of course, many successful schools are far ahead of QCA. Their sporting teams, orchestras and ICT suites are used to lure potential applicants in years 4 and 5 and the early booking of school places from the right kind of parents is welcomed. This is a policy that can turn round a school more quickly than any other and with longer-term results.

Home school agreements have a part to play at this time. New guidelines on these were published in August 1998. The main message of the advice was that schools should be careful about making unreasonable demands on parents and children since it would have no legal standing.

Changes to the School Day

There was more discussion in 1998 of the possibility of making changes to the organisation of the school year and the school day. The arguments that premises and the resources that they contain are poorly used when they are closed for twelve weeks a year and only available for half of each day, that pupil performance declines over the long summer break and that teachers have holidays that are too long continue to ferment. However, the increasing investment by schools in expensive ICT equipment does argue for its greater use. An RSA discussion paper suggested in 1998 that schools should move to a shift basis for daily operation and that pupils should be able to make use of distance learning. It argued that the current school day was linked to the requirements of nineteenth century agricultural workers and had to be changed. Technology colleges and action zone schools have both moved in the direction of sessional days and longer terms but, thus far, the three-term mould has not been broken.

Homework

It was back in 1995 when OFSTED first suggested a virtuous circle between homework and school achievement. It followed this up in a research study in 1997 that showed a strong correlation between homework and positive OFSTED judgements. What this study found were striking differences in the amount of homework done by pupils in broadly similar schools and a positive association between the overall performance of a school and the amount of homework pupils do.

The timing of this research was such that new Labour was able to pick up on a Conservative initiative but go one better. Basically, the government had figures to prove that those schools which set more homework in a systematic way achieved better test and examination results and were given more favourable reports from OFSTED. It was also concerned about the quantity of television watched - especially by boys - and the way that children in many areas are unsupervised, or out late, on the streets. Setting more homework looked like a good way to raise standards and tackle social exclusion simultaneously. So the White Paper, Excellence in Schools, promised more action and

passed the work to Michael Barber's Standards and Effectiveness Unit.

HOMEWORK RECOMMENDATIONS	
Years 1 and 2	20 minutes reading plus 10 minutes tasks
Years 3 and 4	20 minutes reading plus 20 minutes tasks
Years 5 and 6	25 minutes reading plus 30 minutes tasks
Years 7 - 8	45 - 90 minutes per day
Year 9	1 - 2 hours a day
Years 10 - 11	1.5 - 2.5 hours a day
Years 12 - 13	Guidance should be included in schools' policies

In April 1998, this group published draft versions of homework guidelines for primary and secondary schools. These were confirmed in November and suggested that children in the top years of primary schooling should be reading for twenty-five minutes a night and spending thirty minutes on homework tasks. In secondary schools, this would rise to over two hours per night as GCSE examinations approached. In January 1999, OFSTED published some of the background work to the formulation of the guidelines in a guide that highlighted some of the best practice uncovered and rehearsed the arguments once again for more, better focused, homework.

OFSTED also published advice in November 1998 on how to involve parents in homework schemes. The agency suggested numeracy and literacy workshops, link books such as diaries and records, shared materials such as games and instructions on topics and shared activities such as family surveys as all having a part to play in establishing good habits in primary schools.

Where homework policies are concerned, OFSTED pointed out the key features of successful policies. These included top management involvement, a sense of partnership with parents, consistent practice across the school with purposive tasks to support learning, high expectations and regular monitoring and evaluation.

Teachers and Pupils

This is not an alternative to next year's pay award ... assuming there is one.
> David Blunkett at the launch of the Lloyds TSB Annual Teacher Awards Scheme.

I have slapped a lot of little legs and I can see a lot of little legs that need slapping tonight.
> Angela Browning, Conservative Education spokesperson, on the vote to end caning in private schools.

I was told by the headteacher that corporal punishment was used to keep order. He then put on a cricket glove and asked me to cane him on the hand ... then asked me to put on the glove so that he could show me how it was done.
> Phil Willis, Liberal Democrat MP on becoming a teacher.

Will superteachers be required to wear their underpants outside of their trousers?
> Inveterate letter writer, Keith Flett, in the *Times Educational Supplement.*

You can kiss goodbye to the old ethic among teachers that sees them sharing their work and the stress in support of colleagues.
> Letter in the *Times Educational Supplement* from Harvey Linehan.

Many male teachers hit the novelty socks stage in their late 40s. They are either eccentric or deeply sad. Girls have more role models in teaching that they would want to emulate.
> Researcher at the BERA Conference explaining the drop in primary recruitment among men.

Teachers

The New Deal

It has become clear since Labour's election victory in 1997 that the master plan is for teachers to be herded with appropriate carrots and sticks to some new pasture which involves separating the racehorses from the donkeys and shooting the old mules. The December 1998 Green Paper started to develop the necessary machinery for the donkeys and horses while Chris Woodhead will deal with the mules!

The carrots proposed included a new spinal pay scale with £35,000 for the top classroom teachers, a fast-track scheme for effective young teachers, a new enhanced scale for senior teachers and Advanced Skills Teachers (AST), bonuses for high performing schools, more classroom assistants, and a competition to redesign the staffroom of the future. The sticks were threshold appraisal at just over £22,000 to extend the salary ceiling (from first to second level or the leadership spine), subsequent annual performance appraisals linked to pay (PRP), targets for teaching and a contractual duty to keep up-to-date, hopefully by the compulsory reading of *Curriculum Confidential.*

For headteachers, there were more carrots and sticks in terms of short-term contracts, explicit performance-related pay and additional training in leadership. And, for trainee teachers, there was more inspection for course providers and formal numeracy and literacy assessments. A new post, the external consultant, will advise schools on performance-related payments and evaluate the headteacher's performance. School Improvement Grants (SIG) will help to boost under-achieving schools with resources and the School Performance Award (SPA) will reward the teachers in those that do well. The fast-track option for new entrants will include industry placements and a longer year but will offer genuine rewards as well. The 1256 hours currently specified in teachers' contracts will not apply for anyone on the leadership spine or in more senior posts.

To summarise what is on offer, it is more money - perhaps 10% per year overall over the course of a teaching career in return for a link between classroom performance, formal appraisal and salary. A new professional structure will differentiate four divisions - senior managers, teachers with 'leadership qualities', advanced skills teachers and fast-track candidates - from the simple - first level - classroom teachers. The teachers in these enhanced posts will work longer hours and carry more responsibilities than at present and their continued pay will be linked to their results.

If the proposals are agreed the new system will come into effect from September 2000.

The argument for change of some kind is inescapable. Recruitment has to be increased and better graduates have to be persuaded into teaching. It is simply not acceptable that the average points score for entry to B.Ed degree courses should be five points lower than for other degree courses (13.3 points at present) and the long-term effects of this trend could be devastating. Also, while teachers are clearly under-rewarded they also have poor job status and a public perception that, as a group, they are old fashioned, resistant to change and unwilling to be accountable.

What could be good about this for teachers and schools? If you are ambitious, capable and hard working there is every prospect of making more money at the job. You are probably already working longer hours than some of your colleagues and have the feeling that you are adding more value to the institution than some who are paid the same or perhaps more than you are. You welcome appraisal as a form of useful professional review and a chance to refocus your aims. For you, this deal could be motivating and that feeling could lead to more successful outcomes for the school. What could be bad? You could be the backbone of the school, a reliable classroom teacher who is willing to take on dirty jobs with rough classes and who gets the best out of low achievers. At the same time, you have a life and would rather not run the after-school homework club. You are likely to experience a drop in status and your salary will not continue to rise unless you commit yourself to additional responsibilities.

The appraisal model will be crucial. There is an argument that the main reason why previous teacher appraisal systems have been less than successful is simply because they have no bite. The have neither offered rewards nor been focused on specific goals. However, there is widespread support for some kind of diagnostic and formative appraisal often seen as essential to counter the one-off judgements made by OFSTED. The Green Paper has cleverly put teachers in a position where they have to request appraisal in order to secure a pay rise but the ministers may be missing the point that most teachers are not concerned about appraisal *per se*, but are very concerned about who does it and by what criteria. The feeling that headteachers are too busy or idiosyncratic to do it properly and that line managers may be inconsistent in their judgements is a common one and it will be interesting, therefore, to see how the role of the external consultant develops. Finally, there is also a sense that if the appraisal works then everything else in the Green Paper will fall into place because that is the experience that teachers will measure the rest of the package by.

Clearly, the government is going to tough this one out. Later clarifications in a technical paper from the DfEE after the Green Paper publication suggested that

appraisal would be undertaken by senior staff - possibly the headteacher or the school assessor - against at least three performance targets with at least one appraisal objective linked to pupils' statistical performance. Progression to the leadership spine would be dependent on successful appraisal and all senior staff would be selected from this group. As part of the appraisal process, teachers will maintain a professional portfolio - personal analysis of results, details of training, ICT experience. Headteachers' contracts will be modified to include their work on appraisal and performance management. There will be a list - implying registration - of independent assessors and they will be trained. All this leaves some questions unanswered. For example, the balance between pupil performance and other objectives would need to be explicit.

Further union responses will be interesting. Worries about appraisal are understandable, particularly if the link is explicit between measurable outcomes and salary, but there was also criticism of the fast-track approach as undermining the status of current members. One NASUWT poll showed 57% of teachers supporting appraisal but only 17% willing to see a link with pupil performance. 54% of the teachers surveyed were opposed to the fast-track route. Annual appraisal is seen as too frequent, bonuses are cosmetic and there are worries that the package will not address recruitment problems. As to how far the opposition will succeed - perhaps by industrial action - in watering down the proposals remains to be seen. But, it may also be the case that if the profession is to be subject to appraisal and performance targets, then clear and specific requirements will serve teachers better than woolly statements and peer group waffle.

However, it is worth noting that PRP has been less than successful either in teaching or in other public sector employment. The bonus increments for excellent teachers have not been a long-term success because governors and headteachers have never liked to use them. And, at least one piece of research has found that both civil servants and nurses believe that PRP de-motivates good staff, that line managers have favourites among staff and that the link to salary reduces the formative benefits of appraisal because people lie about their achievements. An interesting MORI survey in 1998 found that only 9% of employees in the public sector feel valued by their employers and only 15% have confidence in their line managers.

Finally, it is also worth looking at how business is moving. The Barclays Bank partnership deal with its employees may be a better model for the future, introduced at the same time as teachers are yoked to the managerial model of the 1990s. The latest theories in industrial relations talk about businesses as organic organisations within which the intellectual capital brought to them by the workforce is as important as the product. Nurturing people, developing their skills and making them feel engaged with the company's activity is much more important than setting them targets or offering performance-related pay. Of course, this is what charismatic headteachers always used to do, it is just that now we are beginning to understand why they did it!

There have been some interesting diversions from the main agenda. The first was over the provision of teacher assistants. The suggestion in 1998 was that there would be 20,000 by 2001 but Tony Blair's idea that they would be made up from the young unemployed panicked those who are doing the work at the moment as well as the teacher unions. There is no indication yet as to how this new army will be recruited or introduced into schools where, as all teachers know, good assistants are a boon and poor ones can be disastrous! Another announcement concerned the offer of £5000 welcome packages for graduates in mathematics and science who enter teaching. These should be available this year at around the same time as there is a relaxation of the employment regulations to allow retired teachers to work for up to six months of each year. The government and the TTA are also looking to develop more 'on the job' training opportunities for late entrants to the profession from other employments.

Pay and Conditions

The 1999 recommendations from the School Teachers Review Body (STRB) were the first for some time not to be staged. Perhaps that is because people have become wise to this strategy which allows a government to accept the pay review body's recommendations but then to limit the overall percentage increase quite dramatically. An NASUWT official who went through the complicated calculations discovered that he was almost £500 out of pocket on the 1997-8 salary deal over a two year period assuming a salary of £27,500.

There is a 3.5% rise for all teachers from April 1999. This is complemented with bonuses amounting to around 3% for primary headteachers (6% for those working in the smallest schools with fewer than 100 pupils), and about an extra 1.5% for secondary headteachers (3% for those working in the smallest schools with fewer than 400 pupils). Failing schools can award three extra points for recruitment and retention of key staff.

Working conditions will come into line with the European Union Working Time Directive (48-hour week), headteachers and ASTs will have responsibility for overseeing NQT induction years, and teachers can earn additional points for time worked in education action zones - a move that will ease the return of the zones to local authorities at the end of their five year life.

There were some earlier worries about the government's plans for the teaching profession with a rumour that the employers favoured lengthening the teachers' working year. Currently, there are 190 days for pupils and five for training but it was suggested that this latter figure could rise by a further ten days for classroom teachers and by fifteen days for those on higher scales. One leak suggested cutting teachers' holidays from thirteen to eight weeks and, later, it was suggested that a five term year with no extended summer break was a good idea as well. It is worth noting that if the Green Paper proposals are enacted and the 1256 hours rule no longer applies to teachers on the leadership scale then all of the above could be feasible.

The timing of the package is interesting. From September 1999, the leadership scale is to be introduced for headteachers, deputies, ASTs and some other senior staff. For new headteachers, fixed term contracts may also prove popular now that the gates have been opened to allow them. For other teachers, point 9 on the scale is the point at which they can move to the leadership spine with an immediate 10% increase in salary. This is a clever move that should undercut the opposition to the introduction of the new appraisal model.

The School Performance Award Scheme will benefit up to 30% of schools. The awards will be based on improvement, using QCA's benchmark data over a three year period. There will be unique targets for special schools, referral units and very small schools. The payments will not be massive and it is not yet certain how the cash will be shared out. However, they will provide a small incentive. On a per capita basis, a typical secondary school might reckon on about £150 for each member of staff.

Awards for Teachers

Not content with proposing redesigns for school staff rooms, David (Lord) Puttnam, the ex-film director, has been at the heart of the plans for what are generally thought of as teacher 'Oscars'. There are ten award categories, ranging from teacher of the year to the year's greatest contribution to school leadership, each with subdivisions for primary and secondary so that around twenty trophies will be handed out each year. Nominations opened in September 1998 and the process is to culminate with an award ceremony which the BBC has agreed to cover. Lloyds TSB has stumped up £3 million to fund the party. It will be interesting to see how the awards pan out and how schools and local education authorities will take up the opportunity to nominate people. Weary cynics may laugh but it is possible that the process might get teachers more recognition.

The 1998 Queen's Birthday Honours list included more awards for education. The lollipop ladies still got the press coverage but about one hundred headteachers and people with educational credentials received CBEs, OBEs or MBEs. The New Year

Honours List in 1999 included a knighthood for two headteachers. As the new honours system develops, there is a sense that the local authorities are getting wise to the nomination process and are operating more formal processes in their decisions about who to recommend.

The General Teaching Council

The General Teaching Council (GTC) gets underway in September 1999 under the auspices of a chief executive on £80,000 a year and with teacher elections to follow in April 2000. Membership is compulsory for all 470,000 teachers and will cost around £20 a year.

The GTC will have sixty four members; twenty-five elected teachers, nine union appointed teachers, seventeen members from representative bodies (higher education, churches, equality and antiracist organisations among others) and thirteen secretary of state appointments (including two representing parental interests and coverage of special needs education). It is likely to be based in Darlington but will almost certainly have to relocate to London if it is to have a sensible media voice.

How its role develops will be fascinating. Presumably, the unions will try to dominate the teacher elections and will slog their way through those next April but that is unlikely to leave the GTC in any one trade union's pocket. What it will benefit from is a positive agenda to promote what teachers do and to raise their status in society so that it does not find itself simply reacting to events.

One interesting role for the GTC may lie in its power to strike off teachers where there is reasonable doubt rather than legal proof of their criminal behaviour. In Scotland, the existing GTC can do this and it stops local education authorities from maintaining secretive lists of people who the officers believe may be a danger to pupils - as opposed to those who have criminal records to prove that they are.

Headteachers

It is hard to gauge nationally how dire the shortage of headteachers actually is. An NAHT survey in 1998 showed that two-thirds of primary schools received fewer than ten applications for advertised headteacher posts and, in the smallest schools, only a handful of jobs attracted more than ten applicants. London is said to have the greatest problems with almost half of all primary headships being re-advertised but the figures for Southeast England as a whole are not much better.

A bigger problem is that the headship vacancies in the primary sector are overwhelmingly in schools with problems. A matching of headship vacancies with key stage 2 assessments in 1998, carried out by John

Howson, showed that over 70% of the inner London vacancies were in schools with below average test performances.

The union view is that pay and conditions are at the heart of the problem but, perhaps, the problem is more complex than that. It may also be the case that people generally are less willing to uproot their families these days, that the greater differences between schools mean that there are increasing disparities in the numbers of applications for posts and that the process of appointment is hopelessly outdated.

Employment consultants are regularly disparaging about the way that schools work in making senior appointments. The details that schools send to applicants tend to be scrappy or even misleading, many schools still expect handwritten forms to be completed, the reference process is hit and miss, selection committees are randomly chosen and untrained and the 'interview' format still dominates. In some ways, it is no surprise that selection committees end up disappointed or deadlocked.

One solution is the short-term contract, favoured by government as a means of attracting good headteachers into poor schools and highlighted in the Green Paper. Local authorities have wrestled with these in the past because of concerns about long-term job security but if they are going to end up paying over the odds to a recruitment agency many may feel that the time is ripe to bite this particular bullet. Where they have been introduced there have been complaints from other headteachers about 'bonus' payments and dowries - the practice of giving the parachuted headteacher extra cash for resources. In larger authorities, OFSTED has found that the 'pool' system can work well. It might yet also be possible, with some judicious regulation, to use the contract as a mechanism for tapping into the reservoir of people who took early retirement and who are finding regular OFSTED work both hard to find and poorly paid.

Headteacher Training

The jury remains out on the Teacher Training Agency's flagship qualification, the National Professional Qualification for Headship (NPQH). This is the prelude to a compulsory headship qualification from 2002 onwards but, thus far, the number of applicants has been under target and the courses have come in for more criticism than praise. The TTA has needed to advertise constantly and, as an additional perk, the local education authority contribution has been cut but workload, underfunding and the quality of needs assessment and teaching remain the key issues in dissuading teachers from making applications. In the first year from September 1997, only 4150 potential headteachers signed up against a projected figure of five thousand and it is alleged that even fewer were recruited from September 1998. Primary numbers are most below target. The first awards were made at a gauche public ceremony where Anthea Millett handed out the plaudits.

It may be the case that teachers, realising that the qualification is a necessary evil to be endured, will start to apply in greater numbers over the next few months, and there is some evidence that this may be happening, but there is also an argument that the NPQH model is terminally flawed. The weaknesses include the fact that it starts with its own notion of the successful headteacher who is defined in terms of a rag-bag of performance criteria. However, it is also overly directive in that it attempts to reshape its students in that grey managerial mould. And, finally, in an attempt to be practical, the courses have become anti-theoretical. The idea that theory can be derived from practice is sound enough but not if the notion of good practice is as restricted as it currently is. The assessment process has been widely criticised for involving long written exercises that are time consuming and refer back to previous practice (what the teacher has done) rather than forward to headship, while the much vaunted accelerated route still places the same assessment burden on teachers. On the plus side, there is some preliminary evidence that women in primary schools are being helped to make a move into headship by the training but this picture is not reflected in the secondary sector.

Headlamp training which gives £2500 in training money to newly appointed headteachers has trained another five thousand teachers. The success of this scheme is equally hard to measure. Headteachers are the last people to turn down grants but whether the money really goes into buying well-structured training or simply finds its way into the local authority coffers for a 'headship' course is not apparent.

1998 saw the addition of another strategy. The Leadership Programme for Serving Headteachers offers those who missed out on the NPQH and Headlamp a chance to recharge their mental batteries and to challenge their own thinking. The courses start with a needs assessment - looking at the headteacher's and the school's performance - then the crux of the work takes place in a four-day residential conference and is followed up with some sort of business partnership. As with any such enterprise, it is the quality of the training that makes the difference between, on the one hand, changing how people work forever and, on the other, giving them a pleasant few days for reflection out of the school environment.

The problem for the TTA is that the clients' perception is what matters as far as these courses are concerned. Perhaps there was a feeling a few years ago that the fear of OFSTED's judgements would make headteachers run like frightened rabbits into whatever trap was set for them by a self-confident government agency, but there has been a subtle change recently and headteachers are now more valued both by the DfEE and the local authorities and are more confident as a result. So, currently, it is the

TTA that is on the rack and, in early 1999, there were increasing signs that the DfEE ministerial team was feeling increasingly frustrated at the inability of the agency to deliver the goods and was wondering whether it could be trusted to develop the criteria for performance threshold appraisal. If the TTA does not get that job and if the timing coincides with the start up of the GTC, it may even spell the end of an organisation which has promised and published much without having a noticeable impact on what teachers do. If that happens, its epitaph will have to note how, despite having some good ideas, the TTA never conveyed its enthusiasm to the profession.

The National Standards

The National Standards set out the professional knowledge, understanding and skills required to carry out the key roles for headteachers, subject leaders, special educational needs co-ordinators (SENCOs) and those seeking qualified teacher status (QTS). In one sense they are crucial documents for all teachers and central to their status and purpose while, in another, they are an irrelevance. For the last government, the master plan was that national standards would set down what teachers should do and be able to do and then OFSTED would check that they did these things. Those that could not meet the standard would be rooted out with the unticked checklist as the clear evidence for their lack of competence.

Advanced Skills Teachers

Unlike teachers with merit awards, advanced skills teachers (ASTs) are already having an impact on the system - the first one was appointed in 1998. Most are to be found in action zones where the peripatetic teacher consultant has a genuine role to play. In larger comprehensive schools, although there have been appointments, the posts are simply a reward for faculty heads but this will change and ASTs could have a major part to play once teacher appraisal and performance-related pay is introduced. An AST with a clearly defined role would be likely to do a better job in this area than a headteacher or a deputy with an existing portfolio of responsibilities.

Red Tape and Workload

The DfEE must have been driven to despair by its attempts to combat red tape and make teachers jobs a little easier. After the election in 1997, a working party was established to report to Estelle Morris. It included representatives from the teacher unions, business and local government. Its establishment was meant as a signal to teachers that the new government cared about their working conditions.

In January 1998, the group reported and recommended the establishment of a permanent working group within the DfEE, a sampling procedure for government consultations over plans, a pilot scheme to show schools how to operate waste-free administration systems, a review of the demands made by government agencies and a simplified bidding process for additional funding.

So far so good, but immediately afterwards the NASUWT was said to have taken exception to what it saw as a suggestion that headteachers should not be criticised as a primary source of red tape to save the face of the NAHT. Then, the union began to develop the view that the red-tape discussion was simply a smoke-screen to avoid discussion of the real issue - workload. By the end of March 1998, red tape was going to be the first test of strength between the new government and teachers. The NUT and the NASUWT held ballots, using large quantities of precious paper for the forms which 50% of their memberships failed to complete, and discovered that only 5% of teachers were either in favour of more bureaucracy or confused over which box to mark.

By the conference season, the NASUWT had produced a list of bureaucracy-cutting measures for its members to impose. These included limiting all written documents to fewer than four hundred words, only writing one report for each pupil in a year and only attending one after-school meeting a week and then leaving after an hour. There were other clauses about the preparation of documents for OFSTED, schemes of work and the monitoring of pupils under the SEN Code of Practice.

Fans of Harry Enfield will have recognised how this was all a bit like inviting Frank Doberman for tea. The initial bickering was childish and it made the final recommendations of the working party more anodyne than they need have been, while the petulant approach to the serious issue of workload that followed showed the teacher unions in a poor light. The lack of enthusiasm shown in the ballots was an indication that the rank and file was taking a more professional view than its leaders.

The government had promised to respond and did so in June with a circular which broadly proposed that meetings should be necessary, documents pithy, reports crisp and schemes of work concise. It was basically a statement of good intentions and failed, it might be argued, to address either the issues of bureaucracy or of workload at anything more than a superficial level.

Teachers and Sex

The number of male teachers in primary schools is in serious decline. Recent statistics, analysed by John Howson, show that there are fewer than one thousand men under the age of twenty-five teaching in primary schools or, in other words, there is one for every twenty schools. The reasons why young men prefer not to go into teaching are usually thought to be related to salary, promotion prospects and the appeal of other employment areas, but the truth is more likely to be found in the cultural shift towards the view that men around children - especially young children - are a cause for suspicion. There is absolutely no incentive to take on a role which will lead you to be branded as a pervert by most of your contemporaries and to be viewed with suspicion if you comfort an unhappy child or are left alone with a happy one. This is a sad state of affairs which may also have a bearing on the poor performances of boys in primary schools. However, it is hard to see how things can change, given the current media preoccupations and the anxieties of parents. There are also considerably more women than men being appointed to primary headships and deputy headships and the total numbers of men in both categories are dropping fast.

It will be interesting to see whether the trend continues as remorselessly in secondary schools where the proportion of female teachers increases year by year. In the 40-plus age range, there are slightly more men than women at the moment but, if the current trends continue, men will make up less than one-fifth of the typical secondary school staff in twenty years. In the circumstances, it is surprising that there is still a stubborn glass ceiling in place which allows only around 30% of headships to go to women.

The female head of PE in a private girls' school who discovered that her equivalent in the boys' school was earning £7000 more than she was, took her case to an industrial tribunal on the basis of sex discrimination and won. If there is not a successful appeal, several private foundations which run parallel schools for girls and boys are likely to face similar cases.

Finally, when both sexes are taken together, there was a drop in 1998 in the number of graduate applications for teaching - the first time in five years that this has happened.

List 99

Concerns about child abuse have led to some confusion over the status of this infamous DfEE list. The truth is that anyone convicted of a sexual offence involving a child under the age of sixteen is barred from working in a range of areas of which teaching is one. The police hold this information and can vet job candidates before a formal offer is made.

List 99 contains the names of people against whom such allegations have been made, including those people facing cases which have yet to come to court as well as those who resigned or were dismissed before disciplinary action was instigated. Schools and local authorities have a duty to keep List 99 up-to-date but there have been instances in the past where this was not done with damaging consequences. At the moment, List 99 is updated twice yearly and local authorities, independent school associations, teacher unions and supply teacher agencies are all entitled to copies. However, not all of them take up the offer. Schools which intend to take over responsibility for staffing under the new arrangements for devolved funding need to know where they can have easy access to the most recent information.

Additionally, it is also possible that local authorities will introduce positive vetting for teachers once the new Criminal Records Agency gets underway in 2001. This privatises the service previously operated by police, opens it to a wider range of clients and makes a charge for its services. Teachers could have to pay up to £25 for a certificate stating that they have a clean criminal record. It is an interesting situation to monitor because there are probably many teachers in post with criminal records of a minor sort that they do not admit to on application forms.

Reasonable Force

The 1997 Education Act was a hotchpotch, largely abandoned by the last government because of time pressure in the run up to the general election. However, in the salvaged part of the act was a clause which allowed teachers to use reasonable force, in the common law sense of the term, to intervene in violent or potentially violent situations. Those with longer memories will remember that this came in to the bill after a rebellion by the back-bench education committee which wanted a return to corporal punishment in defiance of European legislation.

While a return to corporal punishment attracted very little support from the profession, the situation that schools had gradually come to find themselves in required action. In the early 1990s, a handful of assault charges brought by parents and the concerns of local authorities and governors that they might be liable for damages in such cases had left teachers in what, with hindsight, was a completely untenable situation. Teachers risked their careers if they stopped playground fights or removed pupils physically from their classrooms and had, ultimately, no response to physical aggression or defiance.

The legislation was followed by advice from the DfEE (DfEE Circular 10/98). This states that teachers can use force to come between angry pupils or to block a pupil's path. They can hold, push, pull and lead recalcitrant pupils in the process of 'shepherding' them, a useful term, out of the classroom. In self-defence or in extreme cases they can do more but neck-holds, slaps and kicks are banned as is any touch that might be considered indecent. The guidance also outlines the situations where intervention is reasonable, including where pupils refuse to leave classrooms, are causing malicious damage or seriously disrupting lessons. However, teachers should not show aggression or lose their tempers.

Obviously the circular needs to be mediated through a school policy which is widely discussed and understood within the community. It is also worth making the point that this new law has yet to be tested in the courts. One piece of solid advice the circular includes is the need to keep careful records of any incident, including who else was present as well as what happened, and to log events centrally within the school. The other advice, of course, is to defuse tensions in advance and to use disciplinary procedures which are less confrontational. The Suzy Lamplugh Trust (0181 392 1839) offers advice and training in the area. Finally, as part of the School Standards and Framework Act, caning was banned in private schools in 1998.

Proof of Qualifications

It was the Billie-Jo Jenkins murder case which opened this can of worms, when it was revealed that Sion Jenkins, the foster father and teacher found guilty of the murder of the 13-year-old, had lied about his qualifications to obtain a deputy headship at a school in East Sussex. He also lied in a subsequent application for a headship in Hastings. As a result, the local education authority instigated checks on the qualifications of seven thousand employees. Since that time other local authorities and schools have followed suit, with teachers raiding lofts and cupboards for old examination and degree certificates. Those who had gently massaged their A Level passes and notched up their degrees over the years have been forced into embarrassing climb-downs. The responsibility for checking qualifications is the local authority's or, in the case of the grant-maintained sector, the school's.

One headteacher reported that he had asked fifteen short-listed NQTs over the course of the year to produce written evidence of the qualifications listed on their application forms. Two out of the fifteen were unable to do so and withdrew from the interview process which suggests that, nationally, deception could be rife.

It is also worth noting that, since 1994, both new employers and the subjects of references are entitled to take legal action for compensation against referees if they believe that they are guilty of making negligently inaccurate comments. This has led to an increase in anodyne commentary, particularly where NQTs are concerned and places an even greater burden on what candidates have to say about themselves. However, other legal experts claim that if a case came to court a referee could still claim 'qualified privilege' for making a negative statement which later turned out to be false.

Whistle Blowing

A 1998 amendment to the Employment Rights Act protects those who make disclosures in the public interest about the wrong-doings of their colleagues. It will be possible for an employee to argue at an industrial tribunal that an employer dismissed or disciplined him or her for blowing the whistle over lawbreaking or a health and safety issue and to win compensation - quite possibly very considerable - as a result.

In one sense this legitimises the public disclosure of confidential, or internally confidential, information from public bodies in a new way and carries the implication that whistle-blowers are good for organisations. Of course, some people would disagree and there are critics who feel that this is a wrecker's charter and a new agenda for malcontents in schools. The best advice for schools - as in so many areas - is to develop a public interest disclosure policy in advance. This can define the areas of wrongdoing that are covered, designate responsible staff, set down the procedures which will be followed and outline the safeguards for the organisation and for the whistle-blower. It does not have to be a lengthy document but once it is in place it will be much harder for a malicious whistle-blower to be successful in seeking compensation at a hearing if he or she has ignored the school's procedures for disclosure by going directly to the media or to local politicians.

Pupils

Educating the Most Able

OFSTED published a report in April 1998, *Educating the Very Able*, into the teaching and support available to the most able children in the UK and in other countries. It noted differences in international practice but found no compelling reasons for any form of 'hothouse' education, arguing instead that teaching should be appropriate to the needs of the child. However, there have been suggestions that teachers overlook the clues which would tell them that they have an above average pupil in their class. So, to identify potentially brilliant children, OFSTED suggested that teachers look out for early symbolic activity (reading and writing), an ability to concentrate for long periods, a liking for complexity, the capacity to see through problems and an excellent memory.

It is possible that had the report been published - rather than merely set in motion - under a conservative government, committed to expanding the assisted places scheme and safeguarding the grammar schools that its findings might have been slightly more emphatic!

Exclusion

The whole business of exclusion and the placement of excluded pupils continued to be a headache for headteachers in 1998. In retrospect, it is quite surprising that it was necessary in 1997 to underline that an appeals panel should consider the interests of the school as well as the rights of the individual but that decision - while undoubtedly helpful to schools - did not resolve the problems.

Matters can still easily get out of hand. Litigious parents can use the law and, specifically, a pupil's rights in terms of statutory education and admissions, to force the hand of an appeals panel. And, when this happens, schools and local education authorities tend to capitulate which leads, in turn, to unofficial industrial action by teacher unions. This - apart from its damaging effect on the school and relationships - is also probably unlawful.

However, where cases come to court which they rarely do, the law is less of an ass than some people imagine. In the case of Hebburn School, for example, where the outcome of a successful appeal against exclusion together with subsequent union action meant that a pupil was educated outside the classroom, the judge found against the school but did not enforce the judgement on the grounds that the pupil had a choice of other schools to attend.

Exclusions are rising steadily at the moment but in single figure percentages not in leaps and bounds. In 1996-7, there were 10,500 secondary exclusions and just over sixteen hundred in primary schools. Over 90% of those excluded were boys. Permanent exclusion is more common in London than in the north of England and some schools have much worse problems to face than others. In 1996-7, for example, under 5% of secondary schools were responsible for almost 20% of the exclusions. Special school suspensions are a particular worry, often covering younger children in key stage 3 who become increasingly unmanageable in the remedial education departments of mainstream schools, move to special schools and end up on the streets. Another worry is the low figure for excluded pupils returning from exclusion to education - a statistic that limps along at around 35%.

The level of exclusion among black children is also a cause for national concern. Compared with a white average of 3.6% of pupils who are permanently excluded, there are 3.7% of pupils who are of Indian origin, 7.4% who are black Caribbean and 18.4% who are black Africans. While Asian boys nationally are no more likely to be excluded than white boys, this is not the case in areas where there are high concentrations of Pakistani families. The conclusion that an unacceptable proportion of black children fail in English education is inescapable.

However, it should be remembered that the poor white criminal class is a clearly identifiable group.

Levels of recidivism are as high as ever and the majority of those in young offender institutions turn out to have siblings, parents or other family members who have been before the courts. Surveys show that almost all of those serving time in young offender institutions have been either excluded from schools for long periods or have truanted persistently. It costs about £75,000 to keep someone in one of these institutions.

In their families, there are patterns of instability, violence, of grinding poverty on long-term benefits and of interventions by social services. Increasingly, there is associated drug use but not dependency. However, while this underlines the near impossibility of the task facing schools in compensating for society, it will be unfortunate if a poor black criminal class is allowed to develop as well.

Apart from the problem of placing excluded pupils elsewhere, another weakness in the system is the absence of proper conciliation and reintegration procedures for excluded pupils. A new problem identified in 1998, concerns the effect of the admission of excluded pupils on other pupils in a school. A Birmingham University researcher uncovered high levels of hostility towards the school management when pupils excluded from other schools were admitted. The study also confirmed the well-known fact that children are far less tolerant of misbehaviour than their teachers.

The government's social inclusion programme is tackling the problem by setting local authority targets designed to reduce the number of exclusions and the days lost to truancy each year. One discussed device is the additional inspection of schools where the exclusion rate is considered to be too high and local authorities are also likely to be monitored against given performance targets in this area.

Truancy

It will be interesting to see over the next few years what the Social Exclusion Unit makes of schools and how it assesses their contribution to social inclusion. There are those, for example, who see the national curriculum as an exclusive strategy and there is an argument that there is something in the nature of schooling that creates the problem of truancy. At the same time, teachers should recognise the benefits of a multi-agency approach to the problems posed by exclusion and truancy and the advantages of involving parents - who may well otherwise be unconcerned or acquiesce in a child's absence - are clear. As a barometer of this, when student attitudes are sampled roughly half of all truants think their parents know what they are up to, and the same proportion of non-truants give worries about their parents finding out as the main reason for not truanting!

Secondary school truants take an average of ten days off school each year and primary truants around half

this time. The Crime and Disorder Act (1998) gives the police powers to take truants back to school and courts can impose orders which require their parents to deliver them to school each day. This has stirred up controversy among both teachers and social workers. The latter are worried about the increase in police powers, suggesting that they will simply lead to more confrontation and alienation for the disturbed young people who end up excluded or as semi-permanent truants. Meanwhile, the teacher unions are concerned about limits being placed on the school's right to exclude as a way of meeting someone else's targets. They also know that once the police have delivered some pupils back to school, they will be off again at the first opportunity. It may even be the case that steering clear of the police will give truancy - generally a rather cold and dull activity - an additional *frisson* for some pupils. A surveillance exercise, carried out in Kent in 1998, to see how the new powers might work found seventy truants, mostly under the age of 12 and out of school with some degree of parental connivance.

An OU researcher, Janet Collins, published some interesting work in 1998 about pupils - mostly girls - who simply withdraw from work in schools by avoiding teacher contact, working on the periphery of groups or by quietly getting on with something quite different. She argues that this mental truancy is as significant as any other.

Meanwhile, a school in Hillingdon, Mellow Lane, has appointed a truancy adviser to tackle high levels of condoned absenteeism with the support of local partnerships. Absent children will be followed up from day one of the absence and patterns of absence will be studied to find curriculum links that can be addressed.

Pupils in Care

The anxieties over the education of what are sometimes now called 'looked-after children' have emerged with the increasing analysis of performance data from schools over the past five years. However, there is no reason to think that things were ever any better. The category includes children in children's homes as well as those in foster placements - these are not necessarily long-term arrangements and the population is transient. The statistics are shocking. 26% of the 14 to 16-year-old children in the group were not in full-time education in 1994, around 75% leave school without a qualification and less than 20% stay on post-16. The government's target is to get 75% of them to achieve one GCSE grade by 2003.

The Utting Report, *People Like Us*, outlined the issues in 1997 but it was the House of Commons Health Committee that raised the temperature, slamming schools, local authorities and social services in July 1998 for creating a service devoid of respect, kindness or support. It said there was poor communication

KEY INDICATORS OF DEPRIVATION AND SOCIAL EXCLUSION IN THE UK IN 1998

Falling ...

■ Living in a household where no-one works (2.5 million)

■ Living in a family with children and less than half of average income (3.3 million)

■ Suffering an accidental death to a child (600 a year)

■ Achieving no GCSE passes (220,000 a year)

Rising ...

■ Having low birth-weight babies (7.1%)

■ Having a child on permanent exclusion from school (12,000 a year)

■ A family birth where mother conceived at under-16 (4250 per year)

■ Children in young offender institutions (11,000 per year)

■ Drug treatment 'starts' (23,000 per year)

Steady ...

■ Children whose parents divorce (166,000 per year)

■ Low - minimum - rates of pay (1.2 million)

■ Suicides - but increasing in 20-24 year olds in lowest social group

between those involved and an absence of clear policies. Even, at the start of 1999, many local authorities were unable to report on the academic performances of their looked-after children and there was little public evidence that schools had responded to the concerns.

Schools usually blame social workers for problems with this group of children but, as long ago as 1994, a Department of Health circular made clear that schools were responsible for tackling the educational problems that social workers missed. And, like it or not, schools are front-line services where the children are under 16 years of age.

What is needed is a fundamental shift in attitudes in education with some priority being given to these pupils. It is, of course, likely to be hard and unrewarding work given that this group is substantially over-represented among the prison population, the unemployed, the non-literate and the unskilled but it is something that the caring school has to do.

What They Think!

Every few years, MORI goes out to ask children what they think about education and learning. In 1998, four thousand were polled and, in general, they revealed themselves as solid and middle of the road in their attitudes to school work. Most children think they learn most at school but, otherwise, television is well ahead of libraries and computers are ahead of museums. Most prefer to learn in groups or through practical work. For teachers, there were some interesting findings that went beyond the attitudinal. For example, 20% find learning boring - rising to 25%

of boys in secondary schools - and 80% of year 11 pupils believe that some of their teaching is below standard.

Part Time Work

The notion that school pupils are lazy and shiftless is taking a battering as more and more take on part-time jobs to fund their designer life-styles. The most recent Labour Force Survey reckons that up to 50% of sixth form and college students are doing substantial work outside school. A West Midlands College linked hours worked to A Level performances and tracked an eight points drop in those who worked for more than fifteen hours a week. This was an interesting finding given that supermarkets prefer their sixth form and college students to work for around eighteen hours a week and will be keen to recruit more of them as the national minimum wage, with its lower levels for part-time young people makes them extra attractive while 24-hour opening creates more jobs.

Nutritional Standards

The government's introduction of nutritional standards for school meals is not some old Labour policy being rewritten but is, instead, an essential safeguard once responsibility for school meals passes from local authorities to schools as part of the devolved funding initiative. One interesting possibility is that local authorities, rather than trying to manage a contracting service with a fluctuating client base, may contract out their meals services and then leave the contractors to negotiate with schools. The London

Borough of Lewisham has done a deal with a catering firm, Chartwells, to provide its school meals service. The firm's parent group has the franchised right to use the Kentucky Fried Chicken, Taco Bell and Upper Crust names in the kind of grouped counters seen in shopping arcades, railway stations and higher education institutions.

Gay Bullying

The National Union of Teachers stirred up controversy with a finding that 80% of schools admitted to some level of toleration of homophobic name-calling and bullying. The union also claimed that it had received legal advice that it was permissible for teachers to discuss their own sexual orientation with pupils in lessons. There was further pressure to repeal Section 28 of the Local Government Act, the pernicious clause that gags local authority employees from talking about homosexuality. The survey confirmed previous findings (Stonewall, 1996) where almost 50% of gay people under the age of 18 said they had suffered bullying and abuse at school. Lord Tope, a Liberal Democrat peer, used the gay press to try to uncover first-hand accounts to measure the extent of the problem. One boy replied, to tell how the deputy head at his school, seeing him standing near the school Christmas tree, asked him why he wasn't on top of it!

Sunburn

Primary schools are being asked to think about the medical consequences of packing children outside every lunchtime in hot weather when the sun is directly overhead. In Australian schools it would be unthinkable not to supply adequate shade and this view is spreading to Europe particularly as, outside school, parents are more vigilant than ever before. Half of an individual's lifetime exposure to sun comes in the first twenty years and there are forty thousand new cases of skin cancer each year as the ozone layer evaporates. The best advice for schools is to suggest suitable clothing to parents and to be accommodating about parents who send their children to school with sunscreen lotions.

Hearing Impaired Pupils

OFSTED reported in 1998 on the teaching of reading for hearing impaired children. The covert aim of the report (*The Teaching of Reading to Pupils with Hearing Impairment in Mainstream Schools*, OFSTED, 1998) was to show that pupils with hearing impairment could benefit from the kind of teaching associated with the Literacy Hour and this was achieved with the overall finding that provision and teaching was generally sound. However, training issues were raised and the inspectors criticised the use of assessment information and ICT support.

The Gender Debate

Now it is clear that girls do better than boys at baseline tests on entry to primary schools, the educational system has no-one left to blame for the disparities between the performances of boys and girls: it must be society's and the parents' fault. More evidence for this thesis comes from a 1998 OFSTED analysis of the performances of boys' schools which shows, unsurprisingly, a lamentable picture as part of which almost 10% of boys' comprehensives are considered to require 'substantial improvement'.

In such schools, the low achievers are white, aggressively heterosexual, working-class boys immersed, allegedly, in the 3F culture (fighting and football are two of them). They view themselves as hard, and schoolwork, teachers and diligent pupils as soft.

OFSTED suggests that there are three areas where the gender gap can be identified and confronted. The first is in primary literacy and, later, English where boys lag consistently behind girls. The second is GCSE examinations where a gap that was identified in the late 1980s remains today, and the third is mathematics, science and technology where girls drop out of courses after GCSE. As remedies, OFSTED suggests regular monitoring by gender, and a deliberate attempt to make literacy and 'girly' subjects more macho.

The increasing body of evidence on differential performance at all ages has encouraged researchers to come up with more explanations and different advice. One of the front-runners in 1998 is the idea that boys are starting school too early and are simply not ready, in terms of the brain development of fine motor skills, for the learning and concentration that school requires from rising five-year-olds. Other research suggests that their emotional development is also lacking because underfathering is now the norm in the western world and, where fathers do not play or interact sufficiently or adequately with their children, aggression and a lack of control is a common result. It is unfortunate that this advice coincides with the government's determination to offer school places to 3-year-olds but it may be another reason why there has been increasing disquiet about the overly academic Desirable Learning Outcomes for the pre-school curriculum and why there have been proposals to change them.

Another interesting piece of 1998 research looked at how boys do better on 'male' computer games - featuring fighting, danger and weapons - but girls quickly catch up when the subjects are made more anodyne. In one game, a hunt for pirates' treasure was replaced by helping bears to find some honey without any alteration in the problem solving requirements and, when this was done, girls quickly caught up. It is worth noting that the reading materials given to primary children mostly come under the 'honeyed' heading!

What do the statistics reveal? An analysis of key stage 2 results showed that 62% of girls reached level 4 in writing but only 44% of boys did so. In reading, the gap was nine percentage points. In contrast to these figures were the findings from a small study of fifteen hundred students in year 6 in Manchester. On key stage 2 tests, the girls streaked ahead in line with the national statistics but on standardised tests of mathematical ability, reading and self-esteem, the boys did better at mathematics, showed greater self-esteem and were less behind in reading than the key stage 2 scores indicated. Overall, the scores for boys covered a greater range than those for girls. This raises the question of whether national assessment has become girl-friendly in unsuspected ways.

From another quarter there is OFSTED evidence that girls in single sex schools do better than those in the remainder of the system. Of the 226 maintained secondary girls' schools, sixty are grammar schools, eight are partly selective, nine are secondary moderns and the remaining 149 are comprehensive. There are also just under 350 independent schools for girls. An unpublished OFSTED analysis in 1998 showed that while girls' schools, taken as a whole, are less disadvantaged than boys' schools they have, even when this factor is taken into account, better gradings for attitudes to learning, progress, attendance and behaviour.

One area where boys continue to outstrip girls - albeit by a tiny margin - is in science, or more precisely in physics. When the separate sciences and double and single award GCSE results are aggregated, boys are around one percentage point ahead. However, if the physics element is identified separately, boys are seen to be over 10% ahead in this area. This probably explains why only three in every thousand girls but twelve in every thousand boys obtains a grade A at A Level Physics. This is in itself interesting since that subject is considered - even by most scientists - to be dull, theoretical and requiring of considerable hard work and application and these are often considered to be the 'female' attributes in education.

So what are schools to make of all this confusing data and advice? Firstly, there is a case for suggesting that OFSTED, and many schools, paint too extreme a picture of the 3F group and run the risk of pathologising it. They behave as if these pupils are an external problem for the education system rather than an outcome that it has taken ten years to refine to this point of unpleasantness! Also, such accounts leave out the weaknesses in the performances of Afro-Caribbean boys which it is politically incorrect to mention.

Secondly, there is increasing evidence that the national curriculum offers a model of knowledge and learning that girls find easier to handle. That there has been a shift in the epistemology of education is obvious in subjects like technology, the humanities and English where, since the early 1980s, the emphasis has moved from facts to processes and to a form of assessment that asks for exposition rather than quick answers. However, it is less clear, and was certainly not understood at the time when the changes were adopted, why these changes should benefit girls or disadvantage boys and there may have been other cultural and social changes which have also had a part to play. There has certainly been a change in the economic status of women in society and a change in the relationships within families to reflect this. Male unemployment may also be a significant factor since it has risen rapidly over the same period.

It is also beginning to look as if national assessment and, to a lesser extent, the GCSE examinations that are predicated from the curriculum are favouring girls. At one time, coursework was blamed but the coursework limits introduced in 1994 have not had an effect on differential performances in the subjects. It is also sometimes argued that girls like to write down what they know and that boys like to use their knowledge so that exposition benefits girls and that girls also like to write empathetically and imaginatively while boys would rather not.

A simpler argument is that it still all comes down to fine motor skills. The examinations that girls do better in are those where there is a hefty writing component and girls handwriting is neater than boys for the same reason that they are, allegedly, better at knitting. Because writing comes easier, girls write more and for this reason and because it is more legible, their writing is, firstly, praised more by their primary school teachers and, secondly, corrected more closely. That leads to reinforcement and an improving performance while boys, in contrast, move in the other direction.

Thirdly, there is not a lot of evidence that compensatory education programmes are working effectively. Perhaps this is because so many of them are essentially remedial reading classes and the educational gains have to be balanced against losses in self-esteem. It may also be the case that secondary school managers cannot bring themselves to run 'boy only' lessons or to divert resources to one gender rather than another after years of discrimination which has worked against girls. It is interesting to see that many of the action zones are tackling the issues, usually with more ITC, work-related learning and links with boys' interests like local football clubs, and this work may come up with something more than provisional answers.

However, it is still the case that the experts and the practitioners are riding the same old hobby-horses, looking for solutions in the same areas of compensation and support. The things that they do not think about include the possibility that boys in the 1990s spend a good deal of their time being extremely frightened and do not feel personally 'safe' in their schools or on their way there. They also would rather not think about the fact that too many of their teachers are women who place expectations of silence, stillness and decorum on young boys with motor skills that are not up to what is asked of them and are disproportionately 'strict' with them when they offend. And, it is quite beyond the scope of education to contemplate the possibility that learning under the national curriculum has somehow got confused once again with the old monastic notions of discipline so

that passivity, regurgitation and neat handwriting have taken the place of fascinating facts, enquiry and interaction. And, as for literacy, perhaps someone might ask why the decline in boys' reading coincided with the invention of children's literature in the 1970s so that, just as underfathering was becoming an issue, reading stopped offering boys a means of accessing the world of adults.

Finally, someone might also like to ask, when the fuss about disadvantaged boys has died down, why working class girls - a large section of the population - only make up 1.6% of all students in higher education.

Computers in Schools

Michael Barber says that the Net is the future of communications. One hopes ... that he will now practise what he preaches and confine his further thoughts solely to the World-wide Web where we can log on to them or not as we please.

Letter from Keith Flett in the *Times Educational Supplement.*

The Millennium Bug

If the doomsday scenario is correct, schools can expect to find their records, timetables, telephone switchboards, heating, security and fire arrangements in tatters after the next Christmas holiday. A British Educational Suppliers Association (BESA) survey in 1998 showed that most schools knew about the problems but fewer than 3% of primary schools and 5% of secondary schools had allocated specific funds to investigating the issue. Most expected any funding to come from the ICT budget. The principle behind the millennium bug is that even the smallest computers have internal clocks, often embedded in the software that controls the hardware, which will not recognise that the year 00 follows 99 and will, therefore, shut themselves down terminally. There is also a worry about September 9th because a sequence of 9s (9/9/99) is said to trigger an error message in some older computers. The Local Government Association reckons that it would cost around £150 million to correct a problem which may or may not exist. Meanwhile, various operators are selling their services to schools offering to run bug checks. The option is not available to schools, but one aircraft manufacturer did this by flying a plane across the international date line with the clocks set to December 31st. Out of the thousands of systems on board, a few functions went wrong but none were considered to be critical.

The best advice is that any management or accounting system installed in the past three years is probably okay but anything older should be backed up before December 31st 1999.

Education and the Web

The National Grid for Learning

At the start of 1998, around six thousand schools (out of approximately 31,000) were connected to the internet. By 2002, if the government reaches its target, all schools will be connected through superhighway-fast ISDN connections, as will every library. They will be making use of the National Grid for Learning (NGfL) - a massive complex of resources, advice and information for schools, teachers and lifelong learners.

The architecture of the NGfL is designed to pull together school learning, lifelong education (through the University for Industry and the Public Library Network) and business. The NGfL map separates three areas - government, public service and business and commercial interests - in an ambitious scheme that opens amazing possibilities. The vision is of thousands of schools permanently wired to the grid with teachers calling down lesson material as required, talking to colleagues and pupils engaged in similar projects in other schools and receiving advice and information electronically. One aspect, the funding, is assured. The government has assigned £700 million up to 2002 to get schools connected and to build the infrastructure, £230 million to train teachers (see overleaf), £9 million for library links and £50 million for library learners. These are enormous sums in any language.

It also has to be said that the grid - in the planning stage at least - is making considerable efforts not to repeat the mistakes of the past. There are repeated assertions that the grid will be a market not a monopoly, that access will be cheap, that content is crucial and that continued support is necessary.

At the moment, the grid is developing wildly in various directions some of which, in the fullness of time, will probably prosper; there is the 'GridClub' for the young independent learner that sounds like a Ben Elton skit on teenage broadcasting; the virtual staff room for teachers who want to spend their evenings in a virtual school; and, there will soon be community grids linking local schools, councils, businesses and libraries. The ICT industry is being drawn in with the notion of managed services where approved suppliers will - probably - lease and maintain access equipment and services to schools so that the budget 'hit' can be spread over a number of years. There are also suggestions that there will be 'home-learning centres' for children which could be a good way for a manufacturer to off-load its redundant PCs! And, finally, educational broadcasting will be part of the mix, providing high quality information and programmes by request not according to broadcaster's timetable.

It is very easy to be cynical about the grid. The enduring problems are over access and content. For teachers to use the grid in the way that its architects describe its possibilities will involve both a massive investment in hardware and connection charges that are manageable. However, it will also require a change in the way that classrooms are conceived of, a shift in teacher pedagogy and a more flexible learner-oriented curriculum. With OFSTED, national targets and appraisal linked to salary to consider, that may be much harder to deliver.

The problem with content is equally deep. Even if the grid sets out to kid itself that it is not, education knowledge remains a commodity that has value and is traded. Publishers, including local authorities and some agencies, cannot give material away for nothing and if they are simply advertising their wares then the grid becomes a catalogue not a resource. If the government grasps this particular bull by the horns and starts to commission and promote its own learning materials (as it is planning to do anyway) then the curriculum and the resources to deliver it will both be under its control in what might be considered to be an unhealthy way.

The current advice for schools is to monitor developments closely and to stay involved. Partnership will be invaluable, either in getting into the ground floor of community developments or as a means of getting help with ICT innovations. Schools also need to watch out for bid opportunities and funding. Getting in early where national ICT training is concerned may also be advantageous if it opens subsequent doors to useful cash. There is some evidence that reconstituting the school as ICT friendly, or even applying to become a specialist school in the area, is a way of attracting funds over the longer term. Undoubtedly the biggest mistake will be to buy into the technology too early and all spending in the area should be scrutinised. Much better to change the curriculum, the timetable or whatever and then to buy the hardware to implement the change.

It is also worth noting that the NGfL is one aspect of a government revolution which is targeted to see 25% of all business conducted electronically by 2002 and to offer a largely paperless administration. The GSI (government secure intranet) will have the potential to massively extend the influence of government over people's lives. As examples of where things are going, the DTI server received two million hits in February 1998 - a figure that should double this year - and it is not a joke that government minister have virtual red boxes - they do. Schools will undoubtedly start to conduct more of their business using internet connections. Some devolved services such as payroll and other aspects of finance lend themselves to this.

Another growing trend is internet policing where almost all governments have revealed a natural tendency to control the information flow, using spurious excuses like the growth in pornography, to cover their tracks. Our own 'nanny-state' with its long tradition of concealment can be guaranteed to be at the front of the pack in this area.

And, lastly, it is worth underlining that schools can never keep up with technology. DVD technology (digital versatile or video disc) looks much more education-friendly than the cumbersome whirring of the CD-ROM and will take over the videotape market but downloading digital materials from satellites on a pay-per-view basis may turn out to be a better way of distributing commercial broadcast materials than along the telephone line. And, somewhere along the line, there will be electronic teachers to assess written work and offer personal diagnostic feedback more competently than many teachers.

Elsewhere on the internet, there are the DfEE pages and the Standards Site which was launched in 1998 and now carries a wealth of useful statistical information and links to other sites. Elsewhere on the government pages there is lots more about education but it is sometimes hard to track down specific information. OFSTED's site has a vast collection of inspection reports but carries some useful publications as well. QCA's web pages have the sense of being aimed at the general public rather than at those who work in education. There is also a plethora of 'education sites' which claim to do all sorts of things but really sell advertising space to agencies, publishers, consultants and look like it.

More rumoured than real are cheat sites. The theory is that these sites will provide dishonest students with the chance to download coursework and modular assignments but, thus far, there is little evidence that they exist let alone that they are a threat to examination rigour and standards. In the end it is probably much easier to borrow your older sibling's document disk than to root around on the internet for something similar!

Developments for Teachers

Teacher Training

Courtesy of the New Opportunities Fund a massive reskilling exercise is in hand in ICT. This will cost £250 million by 2002 and offer every teacher a needs assessment and a distance learning package or regional training. Currently, Approved Training Providers (ATP) are being validated. Some are approved to work nationally and others within particular areas. The typical ATP is a consortium including local education authorities, not-for profit educational companies, hardware and software manufacturers and distance learning practitioners. As an example, the Open University, Research Machines™ and several local authorities form one ATP - Microsoft™ and an education company make up another. The training - valued at £500 per teacher - should be available from April 1999 but the bulk of the programme will get into gear from September.

The enterprise - orchestrated by the Teacher Training Agency - is currently in a state of some chaos. The needs assessment materials have not been made to work effectively and the training is facing two major obstacles. The first is that the cash cannot be used to buy time so the training has to take place in the teacher's own time, and the second is that the money cannot be used for hardware. Teachers, asked to define their problems with ICT, put time and equipment in the first two places so it is likely that they will be less than enthusiastic about waiting after school to watch a CD-ROM (pictures of children playing with up-to-the-minute computers) chugging along on their old machines. It is possible that astute schools will head for the consortium in which Microsoft™ is involved since they are more likely to get free copies of software to play with at home. Those with RM machines may stay loyal to their provider. Local authorities will undoubtedly try to take the role of the middle-man and to offer special deals to their schools but the bidding is at school level and it will be, in theory, possible for different departments to spend their entitlement for each member of staff with their own choice of provider.

While there is more than a whiff of a hotchpotch about these plans, the skills that serving teachers are expected to acquire are those outlined in the new ICT initial teacher training curriculum. This document is mostly mumbo-jumbo because it was written to be future-proof (no mention of existing technologies or examples) but it is very detailed in the requirements that it imposes on higher education institutions whose courses are inspected regularly by OFSTED. It is less use to schools because, while it covers considerable ground, it fails - perhaps just as well - to identify levels of competency or standards.

Laptops in Schools

After a successful £5 million pilot project, the government's plans to give teachers laptop computers received a boost in April 1998 with the decision to extend the scheme and to give it another £23 million of funding. The 1999 Budget provided funds to extend the scheme further but not, as some had forecast, to give all teachers a machine. However, there is also talk of cheap loans and grants under the 1999 inner-cities regeneration initiative as well. One way or another, most teachers should, within the next few years, be able to get some assistance with the purchase of a machine to help them do their work.

In the pilot phase, two teachers in almost six hundred schools were given multimedia portables with internet connections. The computers came with limited training and a support network. The evaluation of the pilot found that the machines were well-used. Over 90% of the teachers experimented with CD-ROM's, 76% tried out the internet and 62% tried e-mail. Almost all of the teachers felt that the availability of the machines had benefited their work and noted exclusive use, portability and support as the key features in the success of the scheme. The latest funding should allow around a further thirty thousand teachers to be allocated machines with an emphasis on primary schools (there are 470,000 teachers in the UK). One of the successes of this scheme has been in establishing that teachers need their own computers - as opposed to them being institutionally managed - if they are to make much use of them. Also, when they have sole use of machines, they are lost much less frequently.

There has been some discussion of whether teachers who are given laptops are receiving 'benefits in kind' and should pay tax on 20% of the computer's initial value. This would probably be the case if a teacher had a school computer permanently at home but for one which is taken back and forth, most experts agree that there should be no tax liability. However, where the school 'owns' the machine it is a good idea to clarify the insurance position. Some insurers may insist, for example, on a 'booking-out' procedure.

A few local education authorities have been threatening draconian penalties for teachers who use their machines for anything but educational purposes. Potential misdemeanours include visiting websites that are classed as pornographic and sending the pictures to the headteacher by e-mail or selling them to the woodwork teacher for profit. Teachers may also find themselves in deep trouble for visiting non-educational chat rooms, playing silly games, passing on SPAM e-mails or downloading anything that is in breach of copyright. And, as Gary Glitter allegedly knows only too well, it is not that easy to delete what you have been up to over the weekend before you go back to school on Monday. It is probably advisable to cross out any such nutty constraints when signing agreements over laptop use.

OFSTED & Inspection

You break out a vicious circle of failure into a virtuous circle of success.

Dame Helen Metcalf, headteacher, Chiswick Community School.

If we are saying inspection judgements are only accurate when there is reliable test data to base them on, why do we spend millions sending OFSTED inspectors round schools?

Don Foster, Liberal Democrat Education spokesperson.

Inspectors must be alert to schools which are coasting - where standards are not high enough given the abilities of the pupils.

OFSTED briefing on changed inspection requirements, 1998.

A post that is out of control.

Professor Eric Bolton on the role of HMCI, *Oxford Review of Education*, 1998.

By the end of Wednesday, I knew I had a predator on the premises and there was nothing I could do about it.

John Harries, ex-headteacher on the work of the struck-off RgI, Geoffrey Owen.

The worst thing Mr Blunkett could have done for teacher morale.

Doug McAvoy on Chris Woodhead's new contract.

Does School Inspection Work?

1998 figures showed that, since 1993, 573 schools have been subjected to special measures and another seventy are waiting in the pipeline after adverse reports. Over the same period, 110 schools did enough to leave special measures and thirty-one were closed. In 1997-98, there were just over 7500 school inspections and 213 complaints about them. There are now 223 approved contractors but twenty of them do the bulk of the work.

However, with the completion and reporting of a full cycle of school inspections, the question of whether inspection works is one that has to be posed, and answered. It has been asked recently by the House of Commons Education and Employment committee which has just completed an investigation of OFSTED across four headings: public accountability; reliability of judgements; effectiveness in raising standards; and value for money. In the discussions, other questions have emerged. For example, has the legislated system of inspection - introduced at enormous cost - had the effect of improving the education system? Would any other alternatives have done the job better? What are the side-effects of a national system of inspection? What priorities have been overlooked by schools? Has

naming and shaming some schools damaged them beyond repair? What effect would the six hundred plus headteachers who left their primary schools to become inspectors have had on the system if they had stayed in post?

The House of Commons inquiry followed on from Margaret Hodge's grilling of Chris Woodhead, Her Majesty's Chief Inspector of Schools (HMCI), in February 1998, when he was called before the previous committee over the OFSTED inspection of the Birmingham local education authority. However, the new committee proceedings were initially chaired by Charlotte Atkins after the promotion of Margaret Hodge to the ministerial ranks. In the opening rounds, Peter Mortimore told MPs about the team of 'Kafka-esque' inspectors (he may have meant Gogol-like) who vetted his ITT courses, claiming that their visits were politically motivated and undertaken without clear criteria. John Macbeath argued that, in attacking education research, HMCI was undermining school improvement initiatives and Harvey Goldstein claimed that OFSTED's gradings obscured sound judgements. Tim Brighouse appeared to talk about contentious and unreliable findings in Birmingham, Nigel de Gruchy commented on the inspection overload for teachers and John Bangs discussed stress. Surrey's CEO told the committee that his authority believed that one in six inspection reports was inaccurate.

Later, a quartet of headteachers supported OFSTED's work, on behalf of an alleged 'silent majority' who think that the agency does a good job. They were Gary Yates (Crosshall Junior, Cambridge), Jim Hudson (Two Mile Ash Middle, Milton Keynes), Brenda Bigland (Lent Rise Primary, Slough) and Geoff Hampton (Northicote School, Wolverhampton). In contrast, a survey of registered inspectors showed disgruntlement over the inspection process - they wanted to give more advice and help - and over the financial returns now available to them.

Meanwhile, Greg Wilkinson, who was previously responsible for the Audit Commission's policing of local education authorities and is very close to the DfEE, raised the temperature by suggesting that OFSTED needed a management board and a chief executive. He pointed out that it was now the only non-ministerial government inspectorate and that its accountability to the prime minister and to Parliament was largely theoretical. He backed up his view with some critical comments on local authority inspections, the area where OFSTED is probably most at risk from the members of parliament who have close links with their local councils. In February 1999, Chris Woodhead appeared. The current chair of the committee, Malcolm Wicks, talked about the schizophrenic nature of OFSTED and its impact on teacher morale. HMCI said that this was a result of how the agency is reported and resisted the idea that it should have a management board

The final report of the committee will make interesting reading. It is quite possible that it will take forward the reining in of Chris Woodhead's power which started with David Blunkett's target-setting exercise. Advice on the need for accountability to the DfEE or on the establishment of a management board is a strong possibility. If there is criticism of OFSTED's work it will most likely be in the area of local authority inspection where the agency's apparent dependence on limited evidence and its failure to publish its criteria could both be slated. Could it have been a coincidence that OFSTED published its most positive reports on local education authorities just as the committee deliberations were coming to a close?

Elsewhere, a piece of 1998 research, shared between the University of Reading and the Institute of Education produced a mixed set of findings about inspection. There were some benefits. The headteachers of good schools enjoyed the free management advice, for example, and most headteachers found the delineation of key issues useful, but these gains were usually outweighed by problems. These included poor practice by individual inspectors, lengthy periods of notice, over-preparation and an increasing dependency on the framework. The authors suggested more retraining for inspectors on an inservice basis.

Other research, this time by the University of Huddersfield, confirmed a disquieting trend that has

been alleged before. This is that inspection can damage a school's GCSE results. In the study of over four hundred schools, there was a 12% difference in the percentages achieving five or more A*-C grades at GCSE (40% as opposed to 52%) between schools that had been inspected in the run up to examinations (March to June) and those that had not been. May and June inspections appeared to be even more damaging and autumn term inspections less so. The findings mirror those produced by Philip Hunter in January 1998 but OFSTED claims to have worked the data for all schools and to have identified no 'clear trend'.

The OFSTED grading system is seen by both its friends and enemies as flawed. The seven-point scale with its draconian descriptions of failure and its unrealistic vision of success has become in practice a three point scale - above average, satisfactory and below - with fewer than 5% of judgements (according to the latest primary data) outside this area. What this suggests is that inspectors - for the most part decent people - feel insecure about making judgements outside this sphere of generalisation and this, in turn, suggests that the criteria are not as absolute as OFSTED sometimes likes to suggest. It is interesting how little actual data on gradings surfaces in the annual report from HMCI.

In some areas, OFSTED has been willing to take on its critics. The agency points to the substantial majority of schools which agree that the findings of their inspection are fair (although that may be because inspection tells them what they already knew and their views are not always trawled anonymously) and it points out that the research into the validity of inspectors' judgements - while contentious in its approach - does suggest that serious unreliability is rare.

However, if the evidence in these areas is variable, there is not the faintest doubt that OFSTED inspection, and the criteria in particular, have had a massive impact on education. In the 1980s and before, HMI celebrated diversity and even a degree of eccentricity as long as schools delivered a positive ethos and adequate results but, since 1992, the OFSTED criteria have provided either a straitjacket for schools or a sensible organisational model depending upon one's standpoint. Because of OFSTED, schools have become much more alike in terms of staffing, structures and policies. While that may have developed the cohort as a whole, it is arguable that within the 90% of schools which are defined as mixed comprehensives, there is an enormous range of institutions of which some have proved too small, too socially disadvantaged, too mixed culturally, or too specialised to adapt to the OFSTED model. Most teachers can think back to a time when they knew of highly successful schools with charismatic leaders that operated with few rules or stated policies other than some version of 'do as you would be done by'. Such schools pioneered change and innovation and saw development in technology, curriculum or pedagogy as central to their role. Their local education authorities recognised this and let them grow organically as a breeding ground for new ideas and inspirational teachers.

Of course, there are still many excellent schools and many charismatic leaders but, for many teachers, the imposition of an OFSTED way of doing things has taken much of the challenge and excitement out of their day-to-day work, and it a well-known fact about organisations that exploring innovative ways of moving forward - not simply meeting someone's criteria - is essential to thriving in the present.

One source of evidence should be the performance of the schools after inspection. There is an argument that a school which has re-assessed its teaching and learning methodologies in advance of an inspection, faced a rigorous inspection process and then responded to the key findings of the inspection through an action plan should see some clear measures of improvement in performance emerging within one or two years depending on the date of the inspection.

Another source is OFSTED's own inquiries. The post inspection questionnaires sent to schools show that only 10% of schools disagree with the findings of the inspectors but, as Carol FitzGibbon has pointed out, that figure is quite high since the questionnaire is not anonymous. OFSTED also conducted a reliability survey using paired inspectors which proved that the judgements of inspectors were broadly similar but was undercut by the fact that the inspectors who took part in the survey had previously worked together on teams and were highly self-selected - only 17% of those asked to participate agreed to do so!

Failure and Poverty

The links between school failure and poverty are a key area in considering OFSTED's success. Carol FitzGibbon's colleagues at Durham University were commissioned as part of the *Dispatches* programme on OFSTED in 1998 to look at the link. They found that fifty-nine out of eighty-three failing schools had more than 35% of their pupils eligible for free school meals (FSM) while a further twenty one schools had FSM figures of above 22% - the national average is 18%. OFSTED figures reveal the same trend with 71% of failing schools with FSM figures above 22% in a cohort that includes only 35% of schools.

Later in the year, the *Times Educational Supplement* compared failing primary schools with their performances according to QCA benchmark statistics. The enquiry found that seventeen out of one hundred recently failing primary schools were performing at or above average when the QCA benchmarks were applied to their performances. This more or less confirmed FitzGibbon's belief that around one quarter of failing schools are actually performing at or above their average level. This suggests, on the one hand, that OFSTED has underestimated the levels of

poverty and deprivation in these schools in formulating its judgements and, on the other, that if poverty is such an important factor in school performance, the search for a solution to a non-existent problem concerned with teaching methods is chimerical. Clearly rattled by this evidence, OFSTED decided that from September 1998, inspectors should follow the benchmark data in commenting on standards and would have to explain in writing where they varied from its conclusions.

However, OFSTED continues to emphasise that there are disadvantaged schools that do well and give the lie to any deterministic belief that poverty inevitably leads to poor performance. Chris Woodhead's argument is that teachers can make a difference even where the social odds are stacked against them. While that may well be true, of course, that does not make it a good reason to inspect all schools.

The London Borough of Ealing is engaged in an interesting longitudinal study which may eventually come up with some findings. At reception, it found that 30% of pupils scoring between nought and three out of twelve on a baseline assessment scheme were on free school meals and, at key stage 2, 54% of those scoring level 3 or below for English were in the same group. However, by tracing the children involved back through postcode information and census data, the study has also showed that children from the 'best' backgrounds migrate steadily to the most successful schools and that increasing wealth or a new job is the trigger.

OFSTED's Year

It is impossible not to admire the Machiavelian way that Chris Woodhead has reoriented OFSTED in 1998 to meet a change in government and new political priorities, as well as to gain a four year extension to his contract and a 34% increase in pay.

The secondary school review of inspection evidence (*Secondary Education 1993-97*, OFSTED, 1998) is an impressive piece of work but few would believe that its tone in relation to, for example, grant-maintained schools would have been the same were the Conservative Party still in power. And, as for 'naming and shaming', the impression left for history is that this was the impetuous action of a new government and nothing to do with Chris Woodhead. And, there is the way that OFSTED has stopped being so - intentionally - nasty to teachers and has become much more positive in its findings in a whole range of areas. Of course, the brilliant sleight of hand at the end of the trick is to point out that the evident change in attitude is solely brought about by improvements set in motion by OFSTED inspection in the first cycle. It was no coincidence that 1999 started with the chief inspector publishing a MORI survey showing how much schools felt that they had benefited from inspection and appearing in the media to celebrate this new sense of partnership.

In agreeing to Chris Woodhead's new contract, David Blunkett requested five specific emphases in the next four years. These were the introduction of a light touch inspection for successful schools by January 2000, more reports on local education authorities and on initial teacher training (ITT) courses, a development of the beacon school policy and a continued improvement in the quality and consistency of OFSTED's work. The suggestion that 'coasting' schools should also be brought to book was mentioned, as was the need to work closely with the Standards and Effectiveness Unit (SEU) on literacy, numeracy and standards. Some people have read this list as a statement of where HMCI can tread and as an attempt to limit Chris Woodhead's influence but others point out that there is plenty of leeway for independent action.

However, although Chris Woodhead survived 1998 unscathed, OFSTED was attacked from many quarters. Channel 4's *Dispatches* programme pulled together a full house of the agency's most strident critics to slate the organisation. Those contributing included Tim Brighouse, Chris Woodhead's co-leader of the Standards Task Force, Carol FitzGibbon from Durham University and Colin Richards, former HMI. They were supported by the findings from a specially commissioned survey which showed, among other findings, that fewer than fifty out of three hundred headteachers felt that inspection had improved their schools significantly and that 95% of them felt that the inspection model was flawed.

Eric Bolton, an ex-chief inspector from the 1980s and an HMI of the 'old school', launched a savage attack on his successor in 1998. Writing for the *Oxford Education Review*, he argued that OFSTED needed to be brought back under DfEE control, that its role as both the accumulator and the processor of data on schools made its judgements hard to challenge and that its criterial framework was too rigid to recognise either strengths or weaknesses in the system. He also claimed that HMCI's polemical statements were damaging the organisation.

OFSTED also found itself in trouble for interfering in other areas of the education system. The first occasion was when the agency analysed GCSE results to show that the top 10% of schools (on OFSTED ratings) were pulling away from the bottom 10%, demonstrating that OFSTED was a good judge of performance and that poor schools deserved to be blamed. However, the figures were distorted by the claims. In fact, the average GCSE points score in 1992 for the bottom 10% of schools was 15.7 but, by 1996, it had risen to 19.8. This 26% increase was arguably a greater achievement than the 10% increase shown by the top 10% of schools.

Later, at the Keele Annual Education Conference and at the Council of Local Education Authorities (CLEA) Conference in June, Chris Woodhead was advising QCA that the national curriculum at key stage 4 needed to be cut back further. He called for less prescription, more emphasis on key skills and fewer initiatives. Afterwards, he went on to savage key stage tests in a lecture at the London School of Economics. He claimed that the tests were vague and unreliable and were used 'creatively' by schools.

In other areas, OFSTED published a document about 'parachuting' successful headteachers into failing schools. Based on case studies from a number of authorities, *Making Headway* (OFSTED, 1998) set out to show how tenacious and charismatic headteachers - the word 'streetfighters' was used - can make an impression in a failing school. However, it also cautioned against the assumption that such people can leave existing posts on secondment and then drop back in a few terms later as if nothing had happened in the meanwhile.

The agency also conducted a revealing analysis of what parents think about their children's schools based on its questionnaire responses. Unhappily for OFSTED, there was no tangible link between parental views and academic achievement or with quality of learning. Basically, the analysis showed, as many surveys have done previously, that parents are most concerned about homework, national assessments, behaviour (in secondary schools) and the safety of their children.

OFSTED was forced to say sorry once in 1998 when it admitted that its reports on primary religious education were variable in standard and coverage after a complaint by the SACRE (Standing Advisory Council on Religious Education) for Hampshire that some inspections were not aligned to the approved syllabus or were simply misleading in their findings where they confused RE with collective worship.

Next, OFSTED is planning a foray into in-service training which presumably fits somewhere above its work in inspecting the local authorities. This is an odd venture because inset is almost entirely a commercial enterprise, and where local authorities undertake courses these are usually self-funding. If inset provision is really a marketplace, it is hardly the government's role to go around assessing the quality of the bananas on the various stalls; quality control comes from the buying power of the clients.

Finally, at the start of 1999, the agency dived into antiracism with a critical commentary on the way that schools and local authorities monitor the progress of ethnic minority pupils. It urged closer monitoring among other steps to take but did not stop to consider whether this was an aspect of schooling that could have featured more positively in its own inspection framework since 1993.

Elsewhere, over half of the staff at a secondary school in Dorset burned their teaching grades in a lunchtime ceremony. The grades which had been, at the staff's request, given to them in sealed envelopes by the inspection team were burned - allegedly, at least - without being looked at. OFSTED also completed a 30-page report on Holy Island School in 1998 at a cost of around £1500. The school had one pupil at the time, who attended when the causeway to the shore was closed by high tides.

Secondary Education 1993-97

Depending on one's point of view, this flagship publication (*Secondary Education 1993-97*, TSO, 1998) either drew together the findings from the first cycle of inspections or rewrote history to ensure that OFSTED will be seen in a good light. It tracked how the educational budget diminished in this period and how teacher workload increased. Pupil-teacher ratios rose from 15.8 to 16.8, average class sizes rose by 0.5 of a pupil, spending per pupil went down by over 5% and teacher contact time increased by 3%. At the same time, standards were raised. A Level pass rates went up from 81% to 87% and the percentage achieving five GCSE A*-C grades rose from 35% to 43%. Where they were poor (around 40% failing to reach the required standards in English and mathematics at key stages 2 and 3) it was the QCA's fault! Information technology was the weakest subject but standards of classroom teaching overall and of leadership and management were all improving. One in ten schools was shown to have serious weaknesses and one in fourteen was failing.

Where the document was silent was on the links between failure and poverty and between inspection and subsequent improvement. It also did not review the links between OFSTED failure and school performance - the cycle of decline. Its style was largely anecdotal and the report's use of data was considered surprisingly thin by some commentators. Its exhortations to teachers to expect more, to pitch work higher and to assess progress more accurately were more closely aligned to the DfEE's new position than to OFSTED's previous injunctions to root out the rotten core of the profession.

The launch of the document was what gave OFSTED the chance to pull extra data to show that the gap between the highest performing 10% of schools and the bottom 10% was widening. A gap of 30 points in 1992 had grown to 32 points by 1997. As noted previously, it subsequently materialised that in fact the bottom schools were improving more quickly than those at the top.

The Annual Report 1999

The Chief Inspector's Annual Report represented OFSTED's new policy of 'tough love' in action. Much more positive in tone than in previous years and presented to the media as such, the report tracked

substantial improvements in teaching quality. The 8% of unsatisfactory lessons in primary schools contrasted with figures of around 25%, four years ago. The equivalent figures for secondary schools showed that between 7% and 10% of lessons were unsatisfactory - again a fall of around 50% in five years. In primary schools, 50% of lessons were good and 74% of lessons in secondary schools were satisfactory or better.

That left six thousand weak teachers in primary schools and nine thousand in secondary schools (those given ratings of 5, 6 or 7 by inspectors) but the figure was not given its usual weight in the report. The secondary figure is even recognised as possibly an over-estimate since OFSTED no longer inspects a completely balanced sample because of its focus on failing schools. Poor leadership came in for criticism in over 10% of schools but this judgement was linked to schools in disadvantaged areas where either the job is impossible or the right people cannot be found for the job. ICT was considered to be the worst taught subject.

There are some trends over time emerging from these reports. One is that teaching is improving and that teachers are matching up to OFSTED's yardstick, assuming that the application of criteria by inspectors has been consistent. Another is that the percentage of failing schools is settling at a figure of 3% of all schools which suggests that the system is doing better as a whole than its critics have sometimes implied. It is also noticeable that weakness - at school level through failure or in unsatisfactory judgements about headteachers - is very closely linked to social disadvantage. The final trend to note is the way that HMCI has the uncanny ability to spot weaknesses in areas close to the government's heart. A few years ago it was literacy and numeracy and now it is information technology, perhaps as a consequence of OFSTED's accountability to Downing Street rather than the public.

In 1998, OFSTED published, as a follow up to the Chief Inspector's report for the year, a series of leaflets for primary schools summarising the standards observed across individual subjects. These are likely to appear again in 1999.

Naming, Shaming and Failing

In June 1998, the government decided on a new, firm approach to failing schools to commence from September 1998. This was on the basis of some approximate information which suggested that 3% of primary and 4% of secondary were falling into the category between 1997-1998, compared with 2% in both sectors over the majority of the first cycle. In other sectors, the percentages were higher. 6% of Pupil Referral Units (PRUs) were failing and 5% of special schools. The policy - not exactly new apart from the deadline - requires a failing school to be turned round within two years. If, at the end of this time, it is still in special measures, it must either be closed or given a 'fresh start'.

So, once a school has been put on special measures, the governors and the local authority have six months to show OFSTED that an action plan has been developed and implemented. After this visit by OFSTED, the agency will decide on the timing of future visits. After eighteen months, if the school continues under special measures, the local authority and OFSTED must decide what to do, but it is clear that closure is the preferred option where there is a surplus of places. Seventy-four of the schools on special measures had been in that category for more than two years when the change was signalled.

This new policy - sometimes described as 'tough love' - replaced the previous naming and shaming initiative which was formally abandoned at the Labour Party Conference. The decision to get rid of this, reviled, policy came too late for one grant-maintained school in Kent. After being 'named' in 1997, Southfields School started the autumn term in 1998 with fewer than 200 pupils in a building designed for 1200 and the Funding Agency for Schools (FAS) announced that it would close in August 1999. The FAS blamed the government for undermining parental confidence in the school. After OFSTED put the school under special measures in 1995, there was widespread agreement that the school had improved but parental confidence was fatally damaged. Three other schools, Dulwich High, Handsworth Wood Boys' (Birmingham) and Mostyn Gardens Primary (Lambeth) are scheduled for closure.

Two 'fresh-start' schools opened in September 1998. Blakelaw School in Sheffield and Earl Marshal in Newcastle re-opened in their new guises - Fairvale School and Firfield School. Fairvale has a Sheffield College unit on site and courses for parents while Firfield, aided by almost £2.5 million of government cash is now a community school with an almost completely changed staff.

Of the other named schools, six are out of special measures and four others are expected to follow shortly; one is still being monitored by the DfEE. The bare figures conceal some harsh experiences for the schools involved. Upbury Park GM lost a large number of staff after being named and Selhurst High was involved in competency arguments with fifteen of its teachers. The successes are impressive as well. Abbey Farm Middle School in Thetford, Norfolk saw a 29% increase in level 4 English gradings while the Lilian Baylis School in Lambeth is now at the heart of an education action zone.

Two merged Orthodox Jewish schools in North London, Pardes House in Barnet and Beis Yaakov in Brent, were also failed by inspectors. Since half the lessons were devoted to Jewish studies there was never likely to be sufficient time to deliver the curriculum even if the teaching was up to it. However, these were probably the first schools to be failed for delivering

too much religious education! They are reported to be planning to demerge and extend the school day to fit the curriculum in.

Although OFSTED has registered an increase in the percentages of failing schools this may be an anomaly related to the fact that OFSTED is deliberately selecting some less successful schools for scrutiny. However, failing schools will face more problems from September 1999 because a clause in the Teaching and Higher Education Act which comes into force then will prevent them from employing NQTs who are starting their induction years or from co-operating in school-based training courses. In London, this will be welcome news for the large numbers of itinerant Australians who now cover around 10% of teaching hours in the capital and a much larger proportion in failing schools.

Inspections are still seen as stressful, even the second time around. An NAHT survey of 1200 headteachers noted increasing teacher absence and a slump in morale after the inspection. More surprising perhaps were the headteachers' complaints about errors in reports, particularly discrepancies in the grades given to individual teachers and those recorded on the teaching profile.

OFSTED did one group of pupils a favour. A private school in Herefordshire that catered for dyslexic children was found to be providing poor teaching in dangerous buildings. The school, Grange House, had twenty-one pupils between the ages of 8 and 14 but was found to have unheated classrooms and faulty plumbing. The dangers noted by inspectors included discarded rat traps, unfenced ponds and old agricultural machinery.

Attacking Educational Research

There were times in 1998 when the allegations about OFSTED being out of control seemed to be developing some substance. One was with OFSTED's support for, and financing of, James Tooley's highly critical survey of educational research (*Education Research: An OFSTED Critique*, OFSTED, 1998).

The rationale for the work was that education research had failed to provide hard information about teaching and learning in schools and was, according to Chris Woodhead's introduction, concerned with 'irrelevance and distraction'. And, the choice of James Tooley - a right-wing thinker whose views on higher education were always likely to colour his findings - suggested that OFSTED was pursuing its own agenda.

During the arguments, Carol FitzGibbon took the opportunity to point out how OFSTED's methodology was that much more questionable than that employed in the research that Tooley sought to slate. It has also been alleged that, at the time of publication, Tooley was working for Edison, the private educational company which would love to pick up the odd contract in this area. More fundamentally, the research was considered to be limited in its coverage. Based on limited evidence from few sources, it overlooked the broader role of higher education in questioning assumptions and raising new issues and it implied that research should be an arm of educational policy rather than a safeguard against its excesses.

Complaints Against OFSTED

The Geoffrey Owen saga was an odd event even for OFSTED. After a stream of complaints and rumours about a maverick inspector out of control in the south of England, OFSTED capitulated to demands for an enquiry at the end of which the inspector involved, Geoffrey Owen, lost his registration for the conduct and the reporting of an inspection at an infant school in Bristol. Some of the circumstantial evidence was straightforward in that Owen had failed ten out of the sixty-five schools where he led the team when national statistics would have suggested that two or three would be the more likely figure. In his defence, Owen argued that the selection of schools must have been accidentally skewed and that his approach was simply rigorous and challenging.

However, fuel was added to the flames after his deregistration by the publication of a personal letter from Chris Woodhead, admiring his work and offering to 'oil the wheels' in helping him to find other work. This was in sharp contrast to a meeting at the Liberal Democrat Annual Conference where, for a different audience, Chris Woodhead promised to deal ruthlessly with inspectors who took ideological baggage with them or who failed to engage with a school's vision. There are two thousand inspectors currently registered as RgIs, twenty-five have been deregistered since 1993, including fourteen in the past year.

The decision to appoint Elaine Rassaby as the OFSTED Complaints Adjudicator (OCA) was seen by many as a victory; the fuss over the dismissal of Geoffrey Owen and the chief inspector's subsequent comments certainly underlined the need for the role. OFSTED received over two hundred complaints about inspections in 1998 - that is about three for every hundred inspections. Elaine Rassaby's background is in mental health adjudication and tribunal work. Her experience in defending the mentally ill against intransigent organisations may make her especially suited for this job! However, her actual role may be less important than some OFSTED critics imagine. The OCA is an ombudsman and as such is concerned with processes rather than findings. In simple terms, if a school makes a complaint of unfair treatment against OFSTED, the agency's procedures will have to be completed before the OCA comes in and she can then only comment on the handling of the complaint, not on OFSTED's conclusions about its validity. She will be able to offer some form of conciliation and hold meetings but not to overturn the findings. It is thought that there are around forty cases which could eventually land on her desk, many of which concern the work of individual registered inspectors. When asked by the Education Select Committee how she would describe the way OFSTED deals with complaints, she said that the agency was 'assiduous'.

Changes to the Inspection Protocol

Changes to the inspection protocol were introduced in September 1998 and major proposals for new short inspections were unveiled in November. As a result of the primary curriculum changes, OFSTED advised inspectors that from September they should no longer assess standards in the non-core subjects and PE in primary schools. That left English, mathematics and science - where there would also be test evidence - information technology and RE. Inspectors were told that, for the core subjects, they would need to be able to explain if their observations differed from the test results.

There were two reasons for this change apart from the obvious need to adapt to curriculum change. Firstly, OFSTED wished to place an additional emphasis on literacy and numeracy but could not be seen to be adding to inspection requirements and, secondly, a 1998 review of standards judgements alongside test results, showed only 'a broad match' between the two scores, so this was one way of writing correlation into the system!

OFSTED also introduced changes to the summary reports - partly based on a survey of parents' who were asked what they liked and disliked about reports from nine schools. Luckily, they all agreed with Chris Woodhead that reports should be short, jargon-free, clear and unambiguous and should focus on standards, teaching and ethos. Summary reports are now limited to four pages and are expected to use tables to highlight strengths and weaknesses as well as giving information on gradings and a space for views expressed by parents. The headings are written in straightforward language - what the school does well, where the school has weaknesses and how the school has improved. OFSTED has claimed that it plans to give inspectors additional training or support in handling and interpreting data for inclusion in the summaries.

In other areas, OFSTED indicated its concern for 'coasting' schools, stressed the importance of looking at value-added data and unravelled its focus on school improvement which includes looking at the school's capacity to improve as well as the evidence that it has or has not.

The September changes tidied up the regulations about how inspectors should report on teaching. The profile of the quality of teaching drawn up by the RgI and showing, for each teacher, the number of grades in the categories of excellent/very good, good/satisfactory, and less than satisfactory is a document whose confidentiality rests with the headteacher. He or she can make use of it to fulfil official requirements, implying that it should not be bandied about or used to discredit individuals. However, teachers must also have been told their own grades in feedback sessions. It is hard to believe that the handing over of the teaching profile will not be accompanied by some discussion but its status as a management document (as opposed to a series of verdicts) is emphasised, as is the message that it only provides a partial picture of an individual's competence.

In November 1998 in response to government requests, OFSTED unveiled proposals for shorter inspections for effective schools; about 30% of schools fall into this category. The plan was to consult for three months, pilot the new regime in the rest of 1999 and then introduce it more widely in January 2000. An effective school is one with good national assessments and GCSE results when compared with similar schools. Its trend data shows sustained high standards or above average improvement and the findings from previous experiences of OFSTED must have been favourable.

This new 'short' inspection has some interesting features. Firstly, it will provide a health check for the school, using approximately half the lesson observation time of a 'full' inspection. This varies with size so that a large secondary school could expect thirteen days of inspection compared with over fifty on the full version. Lay inspectors would be reduced to a single day of inspection which would mean the virtual end of this controversial aspect of inspections. Primary school inspections would take perhaps five days in total. To put this in perspective, OFSTED figures show that on a current 'full' inspection, a primary teacher will be observed seven times and a secondary teacher three times.

Secondly, the reporting arrangements will change. The short report will be briefer but the summary section will be identical so that comparisons between schools are made easier. Thirdly, should they so wish, governors will have the right to request a full inspection and, finally, a new framework will be written in which the full inspection criteria will build from those for the short version.

If a school is found to have serious weaknesses as a result of a short inspection, it will receive a full inspection within six months. There will also be a new inspection category of a 'coasting' school - one that does all right on its own terms but could, when

national comparisons are taken into account, do even better. Also, the proposals suggested that the notice period for all inspections should be reduced from two terms to between four and eight weeks. This is an interesting clause since, earlier in the year, Chris Woodhead floated the idea of spot-checks where a group of inspectors would visit a school and 'decide' on the basis of the visit whether a full inspection was necessary. This idea sent the NAHT into a panic!

The consultation phase led to agreement on a six to ten week warning period - basically half a term and the decision to implement the new protocol, so are short inspections a good thing? One problem is that the judgement on standards will predominate over judgements on teaching and will be statistically led. The information on improvement will also be statistical so there is likely to be less overall focus on quality. For headteachers and senior managers, the quality of leadership will be most important. Also, where there are adverse findings it may be hard to dispute them because the evidence base - other than the figures - will be very slim. Another worry concerns the framework changes which might allow OFSTED to sneak in additional emphases on literacy and numeracy and more reliance on statistics. The reduction in the notice period, which will apply to all inspections is a double-edged sword. If inspection teams play fair then it will make the process less threatening but if some demand the full documentary evidence associated with some first cycle inspections, then the burden on teachers will simply be telescoped into a shorter period.

One other 1998 initiative concerned the grading of governing bodies by inspectors on the basis of their strategic effectiveness. It is likely that OFSTED was contemplating the inclusion of this into the framework and was exploring some of the criteria that might be used. However, the idea was anathema to those organisations that represent governors and might politically have become a hot potato. The idea did not resurface in the proposals to change the framework.

OFSTED has a range of government performance targets to meet. These include inspecting 20% of schools in 1999-2000 and inspecting 8,000 nurseries, twenty-six local authorities and 240 initial training courses in the same period. The target cost of the inspections is £54 million, a lowered figure that reflects the move to shorter inspections.

One problem that the agency faces is disgruntled inspectors. The competitive bidding system combined with the proposed move to short inspections has left more contractors and more inspectors than are needed to do the work and fees have dropped through the floor. As OFSTED squeezes contractors, they squeeze the inspectors. The cuts are significant, so that a secondary registered inspector leading an inspection team who could have earned £5000 in 1997 is now likely to be offered £3000 or less. The inspectors argue - rather emptily if the monitoring is competent - that quality is as risk and there has been critical comment of car-park teams - inspection teams which meet for the first time outside the school.

The truth is that this has always been a competitive market and that sometimes this has been to the benefit of the inspectors. It has always also been inviting for inspectors to skate over the framework and to avoid making unnecessarily critical judgements which create extra work, and this has been to the benefit of schools. There is also an argument that school inspection - especially second time around - is not that difficult in terms of the overall judgement about whether a school is making progress.

Local Education Authority Inspections

The whole business of local education authority inspection seems to have come down to 'boots' and 'other feet' with the government deciding, early in 1999, that the entire cohort will have faced OFSTED teams by the end of the parliament. It is interesting to note how this process mirrors the previous government's plan for schools and rests on its legislation. So, by the end of 1998, nine local authorities had been inspected prior to the changes in the law, twelve were inspected during the year under the 1997 Education Act legislation and seventeen were scheduled for 1999 under the 1998 Teaching and Higher Education Act. The Northumberland inspection will be interesting because it will cover education and social services together as an investigation into whether such inspections can help to tackle social exclusion.

The basic OFSTED inspection strategy is straightforward. It covers priorities, the management and organisation of services, support for school improvement and an analysis of the context within which the authority operates. After preliminary meetings and a documents trawl (the initial review), the inspection team comes in and gives the organisation the once over, then it retreats and works out what the key issues are, and then it tests these out by visits to schools. The report goes to the Chief Education Officer (CEO) in draft from for a factual accuracy check and then has to be published by the local education authority within thirty days of receipt. Any lack of agreement between what the authority officers say they are doing and how schools perceive what is actually happening gives OFSTED a bone to chew on. Meanwhile the Audit Commission, at the request of HMCI, rummages through the finances. The process can add up to almost two hundred days of OFSTED time and another fifty days for the Audit Commission's work. The current cost is around £60,000 per authority.

In one sense, this is a fair process. The authority has a chance to define its own key areas of interest and the simplest test of these is to ask teachers and schools whether the central messages arrive intact or at all. However, it is also a mechanism for stitching people up in the way that OFSTED can manipulate the evidence base - outside of the local education authority's direct control - to suit its premises. The further problem for the authorities is that none would claim to be ideally structured organisations. The impact of the first round of devolved spending, the break up of advisory teams, the slow growth of the grant-maintained sector, the need to operate as businesses, internal profit targets, financial squeezes and an uncertain future role has made it very hard for any local authority to sustain either steady growth or internal consistency in the last five to ten years. And,

LOCAL AUTHORITY INSPECTIONS

Carried out as pilot or voluntary reviews	Carried out in 1998	Planned for 1999		
Barking & Dagenham	Brent	Barnet	Islington	Plymouth
Bedfordshire	Bury	Barnsley	Kingston-upon-	Rotherham
Birmingham Cornwall	Kent	Bristol	Hull	Rutland
Kirklees	Kingston-upon-	Bromley	Knowsley	Salford
North Somerset	Thames	Bucks	Lambeth	Sheffield
Staffordshire	Leicestershire	City of Leicester	Lancashire	Solihull
	Manchester	Derbyshire	Leeds	Solihull
Carried out at	Nottingham	Doncaster	Lewisham	Stoke on Trent
request of	Sandwell	Durham	Middlesbrough	Walsall
government	Southwark	Greenwich	Newcastle-upon-	Warwickshire
Calderdale	Sunderland	Halton	Tyne	Worcestershire
Hackney	Surrey	Haringey	Northumberland	
	Tower Hamlets	Hertfordshire	Oxfordshire	
			Plymouth	

even as the round of inspections continues, the organisations are being bound to fair funding and the devolution of services which that entails, compulsory target-setting and a code of practice to regulate their dealings with schools. When all this is set alongside the common feeling among officers that OFSTED and its inspectors have only a very limited understanding of what they do then, all in all, it is no surprise that there have been some critical findings and some vicious arguments.

The Hackney saga limped on in 1999 with the government's 1998 improvement team, led by Richard Painter, giving its final report. It was complimentary about the work done by Liz Reid and other new key managers but criticised proposals to re-open Hackney Downs School, the borough's financial controls and support for ICT. It suggested that there should be a fresh OFSTED inspection before Easter 1999 with the possibility of reorganising the borough into two action zones if there were still problems in the management and delivery of the education service. David Blunkett has made it clear that he is willing to see the private sector take over education in Hackney.

Manchester was the first inspection carried out 'involuntarily'. The event was a major blood-bath which showed that OFSTED had learned no lessons from the skirmish with Birmingham in 1997. The report was, allegedly, bounced by OFSTED into the public arena in June 1998, some ten days early, and was given to the media before the CEO had received a response to his commentary on the first draft. The press release and summary were also attacked for headline grabbing. Unsurprisingly, the report identified failings in the schools - and hence the local authority - including below par examination and national test performances, high levels of truancy and exclusion rates. It highlighted inadequate provision for one hundred and forty excluded pupils and a slow process for dealing with pupils with special needs.

The city expected criticism but hoped to be credited for its attempts to innovate through partnerships and its efforts to free itself from a crippling deficit in the budget. Also, while the city admitted to problems, levels of performance were close to national averages and levels of improvement were above. The arguments over the publication simmered as the city was given partial approval for its action plan in September.

Calderdale, first inspected after the problems with The Ridings School in Halifax, was given six weeks in August 1998 to publish another action plan. The alternative would be a government hit-squad - another agency - to run the education authority. This was as a result of an OFSTED re-inspection which found that there had been no progress against five key recommendations from the original report. These included calls for a strategy for behaviour management, moves towards school reorganisation, new links between the education committee and the

officers and the effective analysis and use of educational data. The local authority recognised that it still had problems but took the view that it was addressing them at a reasonable pace. However, faced with OFSTED's demands and, in particular, its criticism of senior management, it decided to call in outside experts in August 1998 rather than face any loss of control. Simon Jenkins, an ex-CEO from Devon, helped to draft a new action plan which was approved in outline in September. At that point, Calderdale was given another year to achieve substantive improvements.

Leicestershire (now excluding Leicester and Rutland which are independent authorities) was in the spotlight for not challenging schools to do better. The education authority was unlucky that the inspection coincided with the new OFSTED determination to pinpoint schools that coast along on better than average results without really challenging their pupils. The other criticism was that it had allowed too many small primary schools to continue without reorganisation but, given the previous government's ambivalence in this area, that was a political point. Other local authorities reported on in 1998 included Southwark (high spending but variable progress and poor national test results) and Surrey (good results but needs to work on its partnership with schools). However, there has been a change in 1999. By March, four authorities - Brent, Nottingham, Newham and Bury - all received very positive reports suggesting that OFSTED has realised the need to back-pedal or that the agency is starting to appreciate the difficulties that many local education authorities face. One authority, East Sussex, commissioned its own inspection using a team led by Margaret Maden from Keele University. The team employed agreed criteria - unlike OFSTED - and covered a wider range of services.

Liverpool could yet be the sacrificial cow of 1999. The authority has more than its fair share of failing schools (thirteen including three secondary) and another twelve schools with serious weaknesses. Around one third of 16-year-olds achieve five A*-C grades at GCSE in contrast to the national average of 45%. The decision to prioritise the inspection for early 1999 was ominous. Other low performing authorities where reports are due in 1999 are Kingston-upon-Hull and Islington.

Experience suggests that to survive an inspection, a local authority needs to be well-prepared and its schools well-briefed. Surrey nominated a senior officer to co-ordinate with the inspection team, it gave visited schools supply cover to help them prepare and invited staff to meetings to remind them of what the local education authority was up to. All of the information submitted for initial review came in the same format and house style, and the 'interim findings' made by the team at this stage which would direct their further enquiries were challenged or complemented with the more detailed information.

Inspection of Initial Training Courses

There is little doubt that Chris Woodhead has a low opinion of initial teacher training (ITT) courses and those who operate them. His statements about the 'heart of darkness' in education were aimed in this direction and OFSTED has relished the chance to shake up the higher education institutions (HEI) that deliver the courses. The TTA has been quick to support the moves so that there are now two-yearly inspections. However, the exact protocol for these remains unclear and some HEIs have been closing courses under the pressure.

The process started with the introduction of teacher standards in ITT (*Teaching: High Status, High Standards*, DfEE Circular 4/98) designed to exert a common model on the training system. These standards cover nine overlapping areas for HEIs to work with, including the overall QTS standard and overall course requirements, the ICT curriculum for all teachers, and separate primary and secondary English, mathematics and science curricula. There is a high level of prescription in all these documents covering pedagogy, effective teaching and knowledge and understanding. The year also saw the introduction of performance tables for the providers showing how many of their students went into QTS employment and teaching.

Meeting the standards and performance requirements has not been easy. OFSTED appears to operate rather as it does with a local authority inspection by identifying issues and then following them through the system rather than taking an overview. Failing a course can mean that accreditation is partially withdrawn from the institution in the sense that it will be lost with another failed inspection.

There is an argument that the policy went out of control in 1998. The HEIs were not given enough time either to respond to the criteria - which were over-detailed and prescriptive - or to put their own houses in order for the simple reason that OFSTED wanted to hammer them as part of its blame culture. However, this same policy is now in danger of backfiring. Closed courses, questions over the future of HEI provision and endless criticism engenders low morale among staff and students which will lead to fewer applicants and completions and no resolution of the recruitment shortage which bedevils the government.

School-centred teacher training (SCITT) schemes, in particular, came in for constant criticism in 1998 with seven schemes judged inadequate or failing by the end of February. Those that have been approved are generally considered to be adequate rather than good. As a result, the Open University (OU) which has to operate with schools at a geographical distance withdrew its primary distance learning course (three hundred candidates were affected) rather than face the problem of compromising it and is quite likely to withdraw completely from certificating teachers. The OU complained that the TTA/OFSTED quality assurance requirements and criteria had not existed when the courses were devised and that OFSTED deliberately focused on the weakest students to further its own agenda. Sussex University is also to close down its primary postgraduate course in 1999 claiming that the new layer of regulation makes it uneconomic to continue and Nene College closed all of its secondary courses after a failed inspection of geography.

The providers have been equally critical of the evaluators. Essentially, the model - fragmented and criterial - is a straitjacket on teacher training that may or may not be necessary. There is an argument that turning graduates into teachers involves giving them a chance to experiment with pedagogy and philosophy as well as drilling them in literacy, numeracy and low-level managerial skills. As with many of the current approaches to training in education, the assumption is that the starting point is a defective individual who has to be put right by criterial re-programming - this may not be the best approach for a new millennium.

In 1998, the Teacher Training Agency also published needs assessment materials in literacy and numeracy which schools could use with new teachers to ascertain where there are gaps in their knowledge and to identify inset needs. It is hard to gauge how popular they will be in schools but they will certainly be disliked by NQTs.

With the end of the first phase of what has been a disastrous policy - how can the removal of training places in perfectly adequate institutions be justified when teacher shortages are so acute - there is a supreme irony. Now, it is the TTA which is getting the blame for the resultant mess in recruitment and training while OFSTED has slipped quietly off the hook.

Literacy and Numeracy

Fantastic news for teachers.

Michael Barber, on the publication of the National Literacy Strategy.

Work with the Community Programme in Professional Football to strengthen links with local professional football clubs - encouraging them to include items about players' favourite reading in the club programme.

Idea from the DfEE document on preparation for the National Year of Reading.

OFSTED will indeed judge each school on its merits. You need have no worries on this score.

Part of a letter from Chris Woodhead to David Hart of the NAHT which asked whether the NLS was compulsory.

In two or three years time, we'll have teachers more or less cheating on how they do the literacy hour, teachers doing it regardless, and teachers who think they're doing it when they're not.

Chair of Governors quoted in the *Times Educational Supplement*.

Everyone can learn to read unless they are mentally retarded.

Diane McGuiness, *Why Children Can't Read.*

Literacy

The National Strategy

With suitable fanfares the National Literacy Strategy (NLS) was launched in September 1998. The initiative is costing £60 million with an additional £20 million for new books and all of the funding is coming from central government. Most has already been spent on training for headteachers and literacy co-ordinators (two days in the summer term of 1998) but primary teacher training (three days) is continuing throughout 1999. To help keep teachers 'on message' there is now an additional raft of regional directors working under the national directorate and monitoring the work of three hundred literacy consultants in the local authorities. There is more money in the pipeline to provide compensatory education in years 5 and 6 either in schools, in after-school clubs or in summer schools. There are six monthly evaluations of national progress under the auspices of the SEU at the DfEE.

It has not all been plain sailing. Welsh schools were told in August 1998 that they were no longer obliged to follow the NLS and there was a similar debate about whether schools in England were obliged to. Ruth Mishkin, Chris Woodhead's partner and a devotee of phonics, caused a furore by announcing that her school with a large proportion of ESOL children would be ploughing its own furrow. On the assumption that everything is by design, this may have been an intentional move to flag up that opting out would mean more phonics and more direction, not less. Ms Mishkin's school, Kobi Nazrul, has a large ESOL population and achieves excellent results at key stage 1.

The upshot was that the NLS is a voluntary framework but opting out is only likely to gain approval if the school has, in John Stannard's words, a teaching programme that is 'demonstrably as effective or better'. In practice, the only genuine argument for not adopting the strategy is where a school has an intake for which the strategy is inappropriate. A high ability intake, a large percentage of pupils from multicultural or ESOL backgrounds or considerable social deprivation locally might be reasons why the NLS was unsuited but it is clear that there would also have to be a rigorous well-argued alternative in place. In a letter to the NAHT, Stannard later suggested that local education authorities would have a duty to ask schools why they were opting out and police the process, and that this would not be the government's role.

Reporting on the introduction of the National Literacy Strategy is a bit like checking whether the trains run on time in Cuba. The timetable is followed up with so many documents trumpeting the arrival of trains, celebrating the pulling powers of particular locomotives or discussing their colour schemes that whether the trains even exist almost ceases to matter.

It only becomes a problem when you want to go somewhere and, in the government's case, the destination is 2002 when 80% of the key stage 2 cohort are expected to reach level 4 in English.

One way to reach this particular destination is by passing the buck for improvement to the local authorities. That was probably why the DfEE produced literacy targets for local authorities that, if achieved, would allow the national target to be reached. However, there is a feeling that these targets may be set too high. Local authorities that already appear to do very well are being asked to deliver figures at, or around, the 90% mark while those that have problems are being asked to make even greater progress. Hackney, for example, has to move from 38% to 70%, a rural county like Suffolk from 58% to 83% and a prosperous middle-class area such as Hertfordshire from 66% to 88%.

Another way is to show the big stick. At the start of December 1998, HMI published interim findings on the success of the strategy that had been in place since September. Many things were said to have improved with the new policy. Teaching quality ratings increased, expectations rose, lesson planning was better, headteachers were supportive and pupils enjoyed the lively structure and pace of literacy hour lessons. The downside was that around half of all lessons failed to emphasise word level work sufficiently, support mechanisms sometimes broke down and evidence of monitoring and evaluation was lacking. Chris Woodhead used the opportunity to berate schools and local authorities over the teaching of phonics with the odd result that local authorities have since been told to develop new polices on phonics. The problem with this report was the circularity of the evaluation process. Chris Woodhead's reporting on his inspectors' findings from an enquiry into a project largely of his design was - almost inevitably - going to focus on his continuing convictions that, firstly, phonics are the answer to poor standards in literacy and that, secondly, teachers try to subvert initiatives which ask them to emphasise them.

Where targets are concerned, it is hard to see how the efforts of schools alone can reach this chimerical target of 80% success without some adjustment of the goal posts. There were inklings of improvement in the 1999 performance tables which showed that previously low scoring authorities were beginning to do better but there was less sign of improvement at the top. One serious concern is that the assessment agencies may not even be able to detect improvement as it happens. It is well understood that while norm referencing is not to be associated with national assessment, every agency involved in the work uses year-on-year statistics to confirm its mark boundaries. To achieve an annual shift of around 9% from these baselines will be very difficult. The other area is the teacher assessment and, again, it will be hard for teachers to shift their perceptions of pupils and to

recognise improvement, if it has actually taken place. Teachers have been taught that national assessment is rigorous and severe and have gradually adjusted their own judgements accordingly; many will find it hard to move in another direction.

More Arguments Over Phonics

Apart from Chris Woodhead and Ruth Mishkin sounding off about them, the arguments about phonics reached absurd proportions in 1998. The NLS was accused of imposing its own version of 'eduthink' by Diane McGuiness, whose book, *Success for All*, relies on a slightly different analysis of phonics, when the title was reviewed in the *Times Educational Supplement* in June. There also seems to be an unnecessary divergence between experts and practitioners so that the NLS polemicists, of which there are more than a few, are obsessed by word-level phonic training throughout key stage 2, while the practitioners argue that reading experience is increasingly important as children move through the key stage so that, by the end, there is no call whatsoever for phonic support for children who have reached the stage of independent reading.

WHAT ARE PHONICS?

Phonics is the relationship between the sounds and the written form of a language but it has come to mean a teaching procedure based in the separating, or segmenting, of these sounds and their subsequent linking, or blending, to make words.

The key terms in segmenting are **phonemes** (the forty or so different sounds that distinguish words in English), and **graphemes** and **digraphs** (the letter or letters that represent them). **Blending** (putting the separate elements back together) is helped by an understanding of vowels (the twenty sounds, not the five letters), syllables, consonant sounds and blends. Achievement is measured in terms of **phonological awareness** (the capacity to segment and decode and then, subsequently, to blend).

The truth probably lies somewhere in between. Few mature, competent readers have any recollection of phonics as an influence on their reading but some children - maybe those who did not learn to read on their mother's knees - undoubtedly find a way into reading through phonics. What happens is that there are four stages to reading. The first is where children recognise words by their repetition in picture books and stories, the 'Ladybird' phase. The second is where teachers lead them to analyse these words, and others, into their phonic components. The third is where this knowledge is applied to spelling rules and patterns and the final stage is where children operate orthographically, recognising new words without analysis. Much of the debate is about what happens at stages two and three because there is a suspicion that 'clever' children simply internalise phonic analysis by reading widely and then refine it by focusing on spelling.

The trouble with this analysis is that, when it is carried to any logical conclusion, it appears ultra-patronising, as if phonics is most suitable for those who missed out, either because they are 'stupid' or their parents were not of the right class. It is particularly worrying when phonics is the method of choice for black, Asian and non-English speaking immigrant children but superfluous for the white, educated middle-class which may explain why those who advocate phonics so loudly have to be evangelical and inclusive in their approaches.

Finally, as is familiar in education, the Scots have a better way. Scottish schools have been testing a system called synthetic phonics which introduces phonic learning letter by letter. Within the scheme, six letters are taught at the rate of one a day and are combined to form words. So pupils master S, A, T, I, P and N and the possible phonic links between them before moving on to the other letters of the alphabet. This differs from the analytic phonics in the NLS which starts with whole words and then breaks them down into their phonic components. A pilot study conducted by the University of St Andrews showed significantly greater gains in reading for the synthetic method, while the mix of analytic phonics and word rhymes espoused by the NLS did even worse than a traditional phonic approach. It is also noteworthy that the most recent American research suggests that when phonics is taught in the context of favourite stories and poems, pupils develop better phonic knowledge than when they are taught in isolation.

Other Developments

In 1998, the National Foundation for Educational Research (NFER) published some interim findings based on the data from the national literacy project schools in 1997. These showed substantial gains for all pupils apart from those with special needs, particular gains for bilingual children and an increased enthusiasm for reading among the pupils involved. Even allowing for the halo effect of a new scheme and the enthusiasm of teachers and pupils, these were pleasing results for the government.

Another report, commissioned by the TTA and conducted by David Wray at the University of Exeter, asked what makes an effective primary teacher of literacy. It turned out - amazingly - that these people were mostly reflective English co-ordinators who used support groups and inset opportunities. They had their own models of literacy teaching and taught grammar in the context of developing reading and writing skills. The control group was - rather cruelly - composed of mathematics specialists. The conclusions were that the English co-ordination role might be rotated and that more inset would be helpful for everyone else. As part of the research, the teachers involved were set a quiz. Those judged to be good teachers as well as bad scored about the same on phonic knowledge!

OFSTED inspectors were given guidance in 1998 on what to do in schools where the literacy hour sessions were timed simultaneously. Chris Woodhead also assured the headteacher unions that schools would be judged by the existing criteria and that inspectors would not comment on the implementation of the strategy in individual schools.

OFSTED also quickly published additional guidance on bilingual children in response to allegations that the strategy was based in a deficit model of language for these children. The new materials came in the form of additional guidance to accompany the framework and also responded to criticisms of how to introduce the strategy in small schools and how to work with children with special educational needs.

Two 1998 surveys found problems with the literacy hour. In the first, conducted for the ATL, 80% of teachers said that the hour was not working well for children with special needs and 60% made the same claims about the most-able children. The workload was said to be excessive and the training inadequate. An NUT survey came up with similar findings but also noted that teachers were modifying the strategy to suit their own classrooms.

There have been other indications that schools are finding ways to colonise the new environment. One senior adviser was using images of Salvador Dali's surrealist clocks as part of his literacy hour training and that was typical of a prevalent attitude among teachers who were prepared to sift through what was on offer and take the useful resources and the sound advice while rejecting the fussier requirements within which they were embedded.

As one example, many schools have found the pedagogy of the NLS helpful. The notion that there are times in the lesson when the teacher is not available to pupils because he or she is focusing on a group has proved genuinely helpful. So is the affirmation that in whole class teaching it is sensible to target the top 20% or so in a group on the basis that the spectators benefit from being there! These are radical shifts in practice and only a few years ago a young teacher would have been criticised by trainers and inspectors alike on both of these counts. There was also agreement that the school pack, lunchbox or attaché case as it was variously described, contained a good deal of sound information and advice.

Living With Literacy

It is anyone's bet as to where the NLS is headed but it is clear that it has to be a success and that its outcomes have to be measured qualitatively in raised key stage 2 outcomes. There is a growing theoretical critique of the strategy - effectively silenced in the mainstream education media - which argues variously that it involves a throwback to Victorian models which were as ineffective then as they will be now, that it is predicated on bad research (the easy idea that it works in Australia has been increasingly questioned), that the way that literacy is socially constructed and quantified actually excludes the poor and disadvantaged and that the government, after years of attacking commercial 'one-approach' reading schemes through the work of HMI has now invented one of its own.

So what are teachers to do? The best answers come from the longitudinal studies of population cohorts carried out since the 1950s. These indicate that school organisation and the curriculum do not outweigh the shaping forces of poverty, deprivation and social background but that two factors can make a difference. The first, and the most important, is parental support. Where parents and teachers work together and education is prioritised in the home, children develop beyond their cohort. The second is social mixing. There is overwhelming evidence that some children are dragged to higher levels of achievement by mixing with those who are culturally defined as cleverer. Thus, one can hypothesise that where the NLS really makes inroads into the culture and practices of parents it will succeed and, where the class is truly mixed, there is more chance that the literacy hour will advantage less successful children.

Schools might benefit from measuring their literacy policies against these two yardsticks and from making their main development target for 1999 the involvement of as many parents (especially fathers) as possible.

There is some funding available for this through the family literacy initiative which is operating in over one hundred local authorities with grants that total around £5 million. British Telecom has also funded the BT Reading Challenge which provides grants for small-scale reading initiatives in communities and workplaces that do not fit under other grant headings. A 1999 survey found that primary teachers have on average spent £25 of their own money thus far to obtain materials to support the literacy strategy in their classrooms.

Summer Schools

In March 1998, almost six hundred schemes for summer schools were approved. In June, fifteen special school summer schools were added to the list. The summer school programme is set to expand in 1999 but the jury is still out on whether it makes a measurable difference to pupil performance in secondary schools after the discovery that most children appear to go into reverse gear anyway when confronted by their new school environment.

The National Year of Reading

Launched with considerable media razzmatazz in 1998, the National Year of Reading has proved to be more of a media event than one which changes the lives of those that it touches. The National Literacy Trust's determination to stop local authorities from making off with the funding, and an enthusiasm for local initiatives has made the provision patchy and disparate and caused many people in schools to ask where the party is taking place. However, most schools welcomed the announcement of an additional £1000 for book spending.

The 1998 World Book Day (23rd April) gained media coverage but few schools did anything more than give it a passing mention although it was supported by UNESCO, the BBC, the DfEE and QCA and subsidised by a large number of publishers. QCA claimed that one thousand schools were involved in activities of one kind or another but that added up to less than 3% of the total. The secondary sector was particularly ill-informed and uninvolved. Schools received a pack with a list of ideas they could develop and six sheets to photocopy for their colleagues but the secondary sector seems to have decided that the focus was on primary and carried on preparing for examinations and national tests.

Book vouchers for £1 were given to every pupil in primary and secondary schools but it is not known how many were actually made use of. They could be used to buy *The Children's Book of Books* where celebrities wrote about their favourite books. Tony Blair, David Blunkett and a group of educational luminaries turned up at the Globe Theatre with their favourite books for a celebratory junket.

Why did it all fall a bit flat? The pack was slick in presentation but short on ideas and devoid of funding. There were not enough real writers to go round, the media events were manipulated so that teachers felt left out and so on. It was probably a mistake not to get the local authorities more involved as well. However, they were so busy implementing the literacy strategy that they had little time for additional initiatives.

Some large companies are on board for the whole year - possibly for their own reasons. Sainsburys is funding a national Bookstart project that will give away a million books in the next two years at a cost of around £6 million. Parents attending their child's post-natal health check will get a bag of goodies including a free book. Local libraries are also involved in all sorts of activities and the year may yet involve all pupils in schools rather than just those who find their way to libraries and clubs.

Literacy at Key Stage 3

The twenty-two pilot projects in literacy, funded by £3 million from the DfEE, were launched in September. The projects employ a variety of targets and approaches, so that while some have literacy hours for all pupils others target special needs groups only. Some work through English departments while others are more clearly crosscurricular in approach. The DfEE has gone out of its way to underline that this is not the start of a national literacy strategy for secondary schools but it will be interesting to see what impact the philosophy of the projects has on the rewriting of the national curriculum.

A Reading University survey of headteachers - completed in 1998 - painted a bleak picture of secondary literacy. In over one-third of schools, the headteachers said that even their English departments - let alone their schools - lacked a literacy policy and two-thirds - when asked - admitted that their schools were not examples of good practice in the area.

There is funding for training in literacy for secondary English teachers in 1999. This will operate regionally through local education authorities but be led by the NLS regional co-ordinators. The aims are to spread good practice and to underline the importance of picking up individuals who have not reached level 4 in year 6.

Numeracy

The final report of the Numeracy Task Force was published in July 1998 and, in March 1999, the numeracy framework packages were sent to all schools. These included the massive ring-binder framework, a booklet on mathematical terms and a CD-ROM with everything on flash-cards. As has become customary with such DfEE materials, the range, quality and production of the materials was first-rate.

The model proposed for the introduction of the numeracy strategy mirrors the programme devised for literacy so that there will be a framework for learning, designated key teachers, a cascade system of training and specified numeracy lessons from September 1999 for all children in primary schools. However, after one implementation, the model has been slightly refined to close loopholes and to remedy weaknesses.

The monitoring system will involve OFSTED, regional strategy directors and consultants but their work will be supplemented by skilled teachers in local areas to be known as leading mathematics teachers (LMTs) who will give demonstration lessons in schools. Another change in the training regime will see a three-day training conference for headteachers, mathematics co-ordinators and SENCOs (where

appropriate) in the summer term of 1999 and three in-school inset days in the summer and autumn terms of 1999 and the spring term in 2000. Schools which are deemed by the local authority to need intensive support will get a five-day course for the mathematics co-ordinator and one other teacher and six days of support from the consultant. While these are proposals at present, there seems to be an underlying intention both to target training where it is most needed and to drive it back into schools - perhaps to avoid groups of rebellious teachers meeting together! There is certainly enthusiasm for small clusters of schools rather than large. Another change concerns the funding for materials. Although this may yet change, the task force preferred to spend money on training rather than on materials.

The definition of numeracy is possibly more controversial than that for literacy. The emphasis on knowing numbers by heart, on mental arithmetic and on calculation is seen as presenting a very circumscribed view by many mathematicians. There is perhaps more of a sense here than there is with literacy in English of a discredited mathematics curriculum model being reinstated by statute.

The pedagogy is - perhaps, depressingly - familiar. The numeracy lesson of forty-five to sixty minutes breaks down into rapid whole class work (mental and oral) for five to ten minutes, a main teaching session of thirty to forty minutes (clear objectives, directive or interactive teaching, groups differentiated by ability), and a final plenary of ten minutes giving feedback and summarising key points. This is not to be a mechanistic model - so the report claims - but there should be an emphasis on direct teaching and a high proportion of work should be with the whole class.

The target is slightly less demanding. The government wants to see 75% of all key stage pupils at level 4 by 2002. To meet this there will have to be facilities for compensatory lessons in year 6 and also, for those who fail, in the first year of secondary schooling. The report also recommends a range of secondary school numeracy projects similar to those at key stage 3 for literacy and meetings with regional directors for secondary mathematics teachers in 2000. And finally, along the way, the national curriculum rewrite will reflect the strategy, giving more weight to mental arithmetic and number in the primary phase.

While the proof of the numeracy pudding will be contained in the small print of the framework and how it is delivered in schools, there are several points to note about this massive re-orientation of teacher pedagogy and mathematical knowledge. The first is the sheer competence and style of the operation. The task force, headed by David Reynolds, contained people with real vision and its report, while directive and dogmatic in its recommendations and short on research evidence, always sounds eminently authoritative and reasonable. The second is the extent of the funding and training available. Even the literacy

THE NATIONAL NUMERACY STRATEGY - WHAT HAPPENS WHEN ...	
Summer Term 1999	• The DfEE sends its three-day distance learning programme to all primary schools. • Local education authorities host conferences for schools using the materials, attended by headteacher, mathematics co-ordinator and one other teacher (probably the SENCO) from each school. • The attending teachers hold a one-day inset session in their schools. Schools audit and review their curricula and schemes of work in the light of the framework and the training.
Autumn Term 1999	• The DfEE launches a publicity campaign to raise awareness. • The new Initial Training Curriculum for Mathematics is introduced. • Schools start to teach the hour with consultancy/LMT support and all teachers see demonstration lesson. Schools have a second inset day. • OFSTED inspectors visit schools to monitor implementation. • Additional courses take place for those schools needing intensive support.
Spring Term 2000	• Conferences take place for secondary mathematics teachers and primary liaison co-ordinators focusing on year 7 performance.

strategy's most vociferous opponents were forced to recognise the quality and usefulness of the training materials and the same looks certain to be true for numeracy.

Of course, with three hundred numeracy consultants, employed for three years at a cost of £14 million, fifteen days inset for each school at a cost of £31 million, an extra £5 million for intensive support and £1 million for key stage 3 initiatives, one would expect to see some return and, whatever happens, there will be useful spin-offs for teachers. Thus far, there has been an OFSTED report on the pilot phase and a longer report from the National Numeracy Project. Both registered improvements in the pilot schools but the rate of change was erratic and a few schools did worse than previously. OFSTED reported the biggest increases in performance among 8 to 9-year-olds but the NNP found a stronger effect among slightly older children. Large classes were a negative factor and where there was improvement it was often replicated in English, perhaps because new methods were being adopted there. Overall, the NNP showed a 9% gain in the percentage reaching level 4 in mathematics compared to the 4% gain made nationally.

However, there are some concerns to be voiced as well. It will be hard for the framework not to look like a mathematics scheme, it will be possible for publishers to run off cheap materials very quickly to meet its surface requirements and its introduction may harm good mathematics teaching in primary schools and the kind of mathematics that stretches the most able pupils.

There are also the implications for schools when both the literacy and numeracy initiatives are running in tandem. Aside from the effect on teacher workloads, it could mean that the mornings are given over to directive teaching in English and mathematics but something different happens after lunch. It is likely, to have a knock-on effect on the teaching of science, ICT and the humanities and to significantly damage provision in art and music.

Raising Standards

Part of the LEA's role is to secure that the targets set by individual schools will collectively add up to the targets set for the LEA overall. The government looks to every school to play its part, with other local schools, in helping to meet the target agreed for the LEA.

DfEE Circular 11/98.

A target can be something you aim for rather than something you hit.

Michael Barber, SEU, at a *Times Educational Supplement* Literacy Conference.

Raising Standards

It has been acknowledged that new Labour took a policy decision well before the last election to shift the focus of its policy on education from entitlement to standards. It was a shrewd move and it has allowed the government to avoid the pitfalls involved in confronting the grammar and the grant-maintained schools on egalitarian grounds; a move that would undoubtedly have been reported as 'dumbing down' education. Eighteen months into the life of the parliament, the standards agenda is clear but it has not been fully implemented and has yet to bring tangible outcomes. It is worth underlining that a significant problem for new Labour is that having couched its targets as measurable outcomes it cannot employ qualitative outcomes to justify its achievements, and David Blunkett's job is on the line as a result.

The starting point for all schools is that they can do better. So, the process of raising standards starts with an evaluation of strengths and weaknesses, moves to the identification of areas for improvement, plans how change can be effected in these areas and sets deadlines for the achievement of measurable change. This is now such a familiar mantra that it is sometimes hard to believe how education once muddled through without it. It is institutionalised in post-OFSTED action planning, local authority and school development plans and schemes such as Investors in People (IiP).

The strengths of the approach are well-rehearsed as well. The job to be undertaken is clearly signposted in terms of stated statistical outcomes and the resources required, minds are focused, and deadlines, monitoring, success criteria and evaluation procedures are waiting to confirm whether the result has been achieved. So, is there a downside? There may be,

PROGRESS AGAINST NATIONAL TARGETS					
Primary Schools					
	1994	1995	1996	1997	1998
end of key stage 2 percentage at level 4 in English	-	48%	58%	63%	**65%**
end of key stage 2 percentage at level 4 in mathematics	-	44%	54%	62%	**59%**
Secondary Schools					
end of GCSE percentage with five or more passes at A*-C grades or equivalents	43.3%	43.5%	44.5%	45.1%	**46.1%**
end of GCSE percentage with one pass at A*-G grades or equivalents	92.3%	91.9%	92.2%	92.3%	**93.4%**
Average GCSE points score per pupil	33.9%	35.1%	35.5%	35.9%	**36.9%**

STATUTORY TARGET-SETTING FOR 2000

Primary Schools should identify target percentages of pupils:

- at level 4 in English by the end of key stage 2;

- at level 4 in mathematics by the end of key stage 2.

Secondary Schools should identify target percentages of pupils:

- with five or more passes at A*-C grades or equivalents at the completion of key stage 4;

- with one pass at A*-G grade or equivalent at the completion of key stage 4;

- and also, identify the average GCSE points score per pupil.

according to some commentators. Firstly, there is evidence that living with a failed action plan is a dispiriting experience for a school and, secondly, engagement with the evangelical aspects of action planning invests the process with a personal significance that may be unwelcome in the long term if objectives are not met.

Thirdly, a focus on one area of the school - increasing the percentage of A* -C grades at GCSE, for example - may lead to unanticipated outcomes such as poorer results at grade F, increased disaffection, a decline in attendance rates and so on. And, finally, it is well known that an emphasis on the measurable makes the measurable outcomes more important than the qualitative. Chasing an elusive statistical target may lead a school to throw out the very things - mixed-ability classes, excellent teacher-pupil relationships, inclusive polices - that were previously its true strengths.

In 1998, improvement was pursued across a number of fronts. The Schools Standards and Framework Act provided the legal framework for target-setting against benchlines, and compelled the introduction of school and local authority development plans. OFSTED subtly realigned its procedures to put its emphasis on getting the best out of schools rather than focusing on those with severe weaknesses. For the first time, the agency shared its Performance and Assessment (PANDA) documentation with schools that were not being inspected while Michael Barber's Schools Effectiveness Unit (SEU) at the DfEE expanded its workforce and started to set the agenda for agencies like the QCA and TTA.

However, the much heralded Standards Task Force, co-chaired by Messrs Woodhead and Brighouse, failed to have its anticipated clout, one consequence of which has been an occasional absence of continuity between the different elements of the standards policy as it has unfolded for schools.

Setting Targets

From September 1998 schools or, more accurately, their governing bodies, have been required by law to set targets for improved attainment in English, mathematics and science. Schools should by now have reviewed their 1998 performances (national assessment results and/or GCSE pass rates as appropriate) and set targets for 2000. These will be published by their local education authorities in June 1999 in Education Development Plans (EDP) and, in the autumn, the process will start again when targets will be set for 2001 and agreed and published in 2000. While target-setting will become an annual event, the proof of the pudding will not come until the autumn of 2000 when schools will be expected to make the first review of progress. However, along the way, it will be interesting to see, by the summer of 1999, how far the local authorities have passed on to schools the responsibility for meeting their government-set targets. After some debate at the end of 1998, it transpired that local education authorities could not set targets for schools - these are the responsibility of the governing body. However, the EDP would be able to identify schools which, in the authority's view, were setting targets too low in their education development plans - the plan was to include a letter Y alongside the school target, perhaps for 'Yellow'!

The writing of the local authority EDP is a challenging exercise - particularly with the prospect of OFSTED inspection within the life of this Parliament. A DfEE analysis of draft versions, early in 1999, showed clear weaknesses in meeting targets and in setting out policies for improvement. However, the real problems will come when local education authorities discover how far away the aggregated targets of their schools are from the government's target for the authority.

A change of emphasis under Labour, and one that is in line with the policy of social inclusion, is the new concern over the percentage of students who simply drop out of the GCSE statistics. The stubborn 8% adds up to just under 50,000 pupils and the total includes excluded pupils, permanent truants and the disaffected, as well as some pupils in special education with severe learning difficulties.

Most teachers are now familiar with target-setting terminology and know that targets have to be SMART - Specific, Measurable, Achievable, Realistic and Timed - but there are questions to be asked about how the government's current targets, once they are delegated to local authorities and thence to schools, rack up against the third and fourth of these requirements. The latest anxiety for schools is that, as some have alleged, they may 'run out of arrows'! A new term to conjure with is the *indicative target* - the target that you will go after next, if you hit this one.

NACETT Targets

It is sometimes hard for teachers to unravel just who is setting the targets, what with demands coming from the literacy and numeracy strategies, the government, local authorities and the people who started it, The National Advisory Council for Education and Training Targets (NACETT). NACETT has now been setting targets since 1993 and its 1998 publication, *Fast Forward for Skills*, both updated the national targets and brought the DfEE targets into the framework. Thus far, the nation's record on reaching targets is ambiguous because the astute moving of goal-posts and the postponement of some targets has avoided any embarrassment. As a typical example, one 1994 target was that by 1997, 80% of 19-year-olds should reach NVQ Level 2 which is broadly equivalent to GNVQ Intermediate Level or four A*-C grades at GCSE. It would be hard to find out whether that

target was ever reached but, on balance, it was probably missed since it is known that 72% of 19-year-olds currently hit the magic figure of five A*-C grades equivalent and the difference between the numbers with four and five passes is likely to be less than the required 8% of the cohort. However, another target that 50% of young people should reach NVQ Level 3 (GNVQ Advanced or two A Level passes) by 2000 has already been reached.

The latest NACETT targets are not split up into foundation and lifetime learning and their status has been clarified with their formal adoption by the DfEE which may give them extra credibility where schools are concerned. As can be seen from the table, the literacy and numeracy strategy targets have been bundled with them.

Benchmarks

Benchmarking is intended to help schools set realistic targets and measure how effective they have been in making changes that impinge on the attainment of individual pupils in classrooms. Benchmarks are simply aggregated data showing the typical performance and setting typical expectations for a range of schools.

In January 1998, QCA published national benchmarks for performance based on a categorisation of schools by reference to the percentage of pupils for whom English is an additional language (EAL) and the percentage of pupils who qualify for free school meals (FSM). At secondary level, the FSM figure and school type (grammar or secondary modern) was used.

NACETT TARGETS FOR 2002		
% Target	for 2002	1998 figure
11-year-olds at level 4 (expected standard for literacy) in English.	80%	65%
11-year-olds at level 4 (expected standard for numeracy) in mathematics.	75%	59%
16-year-olds with one GCSE pass.	95%	93%
16-year-olds with five GCSE passes at A*-C grades.	50%	46%
19-year-olds with five GCSE passes at A*-C grades or equivalent.	85%	72%
21-year-olds with GNVQ Intermediate / NVQ Level 3 or two A Levels or equivalent.	60%	50%
Adults with GNVQ Intermediate / NVQ Level 3 or two A Levels or equivalent.	50%	42%
Adults with degrees	28%	25%
Larger firms recognised as Investors in People	45%	18%
Additional Target: Smaller firms recognised as Investors in People	10,000	3,000

The tables look deceptively complex but the process is straightforward. The primary school procedures are outlined on page 32. In secondary schools at key stages 3 and 4, there are eight tables. The first six link to FSM percentages (fewer than 5%, 6-9%, 10-13%, 14-21%, 22-35%, more than 35%) and the last two relate to the type of school - grammar or secondary modern. The key stage 3 measures are the same six national assessment measures as at key stage 2 but these are replaced at key stage 4 by three measures - the percentages of pupils with five or more A*-C GCSE grades, five or more A*-G grades and one or more A*-G grades.

These key stage 4 measures have the weakness that there is no significant difference between the final two measures for the majority of schools and to predicate that a school was over or under-performing on the basis of these would be absurd. Using the more popular five or more A*-C GCSE grades measure, a move from 9% to 10% FSM eligibility would take a school from a median performance in one table to the upper quartile in the next.

It is clear that benchmarks are not the panacea they were meant to be. They are just another fragment of statistical data to be made use of when drawing together a school's targets. It has been argued that because they are based so closely on FSM percentages they are hopelessly flawed. One reason why is that in areas of social deprivation, schools encourage parents to take up their FSM entitlement and the figure is inflated. In contrast, in more prosperous areas there is a stigma attached to FSM applications, they are not seen as the norm and so there is a tendency to underestimation. Another often stated argument is that FSM ratings take education in the unacceptable direction of accepting that social deprivation is a measure of under-achievement - the tables assume the link that Chris Woodhead so ferociously denies.

However, while these are valid criticisms, the tables do have their uses. They are easy to use and, despite their failings, they do provide broad indicators for teachers and governors to look at. Perhaps they should be seen as the starting point in the target-setting process and not - as is sometimes the case - as its destination.

PANDA Data

OFSTED's Performance and Assessment Reports (PANDA) arrived in schools for the first time in 1998. The reports included the QCA benchmark data discussed above and the statistical information usually contained in the OFSTED pre-inspection PICSI report. In addition to this, there was comparative data on similar schools. Local authorities were sent not only the PANDA information for each of their schools but also a statistical analysis of their overall performance in relation to similar and neighbouring areas.

It was noticeable how a change in government realigned the PANDA information so that, instead of a pointed stick, it became a user-friendly guide to school self-evaluation. OFSTED argued that the figures should be read alongside the inspection framework criteria as the best route to self-review. Interesting data included covered the relationship between inspection grades and poverty as measured by pupils on free meals. Basically, schools in prosperous areas with low FSM figures attract massively fewer adverse gradings from inspectors. On the other hand, the poorest sector of schooling is hammered, particularly where standards are concerned. 82% of these schools are categorised as needing improvement in this area but the equivalent figure for the wealthiest schools is 6%. The figures confirm what many experts have previously argued; that prosperous schools in wealthy areas have nothing to fear from OFSTED inspection but those that already labour under a burden of disadvantage are almost certain to face further suffering. As to whether there is a category of schools in between that can yet be persuaded to improve, only time will tell.

Measuring Progress

Performance Tables

Secondary school performance tables were published in November 1998. There was trouble over the government's attempts to write a value-added measure into the statistics. The original plan was to include a School Progress Measure on a scale from A-E based on the progress made by schools from key stage 3 tests in 1996 to performances in English, mathematics and science in 1998. The calculation of the measure was to be made by identifying a cohort of schools - around 120 - with similar patterns of performance at key stage 3 and then comparing the GCSE performances of individual schools (average point scores) with the average performance of the group. This 'median line' analysis is similar to the process used in developing benchmark data. There is an argument that it is unfair to use median line analysis to assess the performances of individual schools. Since the technique categorises groups and averages performances, most schools - treated as individuals - will receive a technical underestimate or an overestimate of their actual performance.

Thus, it soon became clear that this measure would give schools with below average performances that had improved over the two years a higher coding than those that had consistently good results. So, North Halifax Grammar School would end up with a D grade - the same as its close neighbour, The Ridings School. As the headteacher of the grammar school pointed out, even if all of his candidates were to gain

A* grades, the best rating achievable was likely to be a C. Faced with mounting criticism, the government ditched the plan only a few days before publication and, instead, used a tick to denote the schools (around eight hundred of them) which fell into the A or B category.

Another problem emerged when it was discovered that the key stage 3 statistics would be based on those actually taking the tests (ignoring absentees) while the GCSE figures would be based on numbers on school rolls. The outcome would be to inflate the performances of schools at key stage 3 and to limit the degree of achievement at GCSE. Schools in disadvantaged areas that were doing their best were likely to suffer most.

In a separately planned move, a supplement published with the tables explored how a fuller value-added picture might be compiled in the future. This analysis was based on a national pilot of two hundred schools using individual rather than cohort information. However, although advertised as truly measuring added value, this project actually banded the key stage 3 pupils as cohorts rather than tracking individuals from one assessment to the next. This is something which will only be possible when pupil identity numbers work through the system.

It is interesting to speculate on why the progress measure and, to some extent, the pilot failed to deliver. The prime reason was almost certainly the unreliability of the 1996 key stage 3 data, where it is likely that the variations between schools were greater than the differences in subsequently added value. There is also an obvious problem with the school that does very well at key stage 3, lifts the performances of its pupils and subsequently registers little added value between 14 and 16 years of age while, in fact, it has made significant gains between 11 and 16. And while this may all seem to be nit-picking to politicians, if statistics are the major measures of school performance, such issues become central.

Another new measure was the introduction of the average points score (APS). This includes all pupils so it can be considered to be more politically correct than the five A*-C grades hurdle which, so it is said, leads to an unfair emphasis on a relatively small group. The 1998 tables showed that schools with GNVQ courses totted up points more easily than others so that is one way to lift an APS score. Another way - and educationally sound - is to lift the performances of the bottom 20% of pupils, where it is possible to make the significant gains that will show in percentage terms. In a typical comprehensive school, the statistics suggest that it would not be impossible to double the performances of some pupils in this cohort. Harvey Goldstein continued to attack performance tables in 1998 and the 'alarmingly simple' mathematical models that they are built on. Goldstein is an advocate of multi-level analysis which attempts to incorporate all of the factors which may make a difference to a school

- peer group performance, home, previous schooling and so on. As an example of what he is interested in, one of his studies has suggested that primary schools are a greater influence on GCSE results than secondary education. If that were true, the search for improvement in secondary schools independent of this key factor would be almost pointless.

GCSE AND GNVQ POINT SCORE EQUIVALENCE			
GCSE	**Points**		**GNVQ**
A*	8	7. 5	Intermediate Distinction
A	7		
B	6	6	Intermediate Merit
C	5	5	Intermediate Pass
D	4	4	Foundation Distinction
E	3	3	Foundation Merit
F	2	1. 5	Foundation Pass
G	1		

For short course GCSE subjects, the point score is divided by 2 For Part One GNVQ multiply the point score by 2 For Intermediate GNVQ multiply the point score by 4

John Dunford, the new and busy General Secretary of the Secondary Heads Association (SHA), has suggested that rather than include the percentages of pupils with five GCSE A*-C grades, performance tables should include the average points score in the best seven subjects in the school.

Behind all of this debate, there is an underlying worry that comparative measures of the value which is added to education by 'schools' may be chimerical or unattainable. The suspicion is that while schools do make a difference to individuals and while key stage 3 performance is an improving indicator of GCSE outcomes, the differences between tests at key stage 3 and examinations at key stage 4, the lack of reliability in key stage 3 assessment and the lack of absolute comparability of GCSE awards all combine with the data on aberrant individuals to make the derivation of school measures much more unreliable than they need to be as measures of national accountability or educational excellence. If this is the case, it will be a bitter pill for the government to swallow.

Elsewhere in the tables, and to its credit, the government is gradually sorting put the mishmash of entry level certifications and reporting on certificate of achievement awards. And, to tidy up an area of long-standing confusion, approved educational activities carried out off-site, such as work experience, no longer count as authorised absences.

The independent sector was complaining again about performance tables in 1998. After an earlier fuss about candidates who take examinations early was resolved - they are simply counted later - the schools realised that they have a significant minority of candidates who sit their examinations late, usually because their families have been working overseas. Winchester College turned in an APS of 30.3 because its candidates take International GCSE examinations which do not feed into the DfEE's statistics.

Taken as a whole, the tables that show local authority performances are becoming more interesting as the data accumulates. Allowing for boundary changes and aberrant performances, there are significant differences in the improvement figures which must be greater than any population fluctuations. Manchester, for example, with a 6% improvement in the APS from 1995 to 1998 is a large enough authority for the change to be more than a blip on a scale that went from the Isles of Scilly (up by 14.3%) to Merton where there was a drop of 1.7%. Once the grant-maintained schools are included, the veracity of these figures will improve still further.

Primary tables were published in February 1999. One noticeable feature was that, while there were nation-wide improvements, the rate of improvement was nowhere sufficient to guarantee that local authority targets will be met. In other words, there has to be a distinct acceleration to meet government targets. The *Times Educational Supplement* conducted an analysis that related free school meal provision to performance in local authorities and found that Liverpool, Bradford and Sheffield were facing problems in making improvements, that OFSTED's favourite local authority Newham was not doing as well as expected but that Bury - also reported on in 1999 - was doing well. Other analyses showed that some poorly achieving local authorities were falling further behind the average performance in 1998.

Interestingly, there are still two schools that have not given in on testing. Rosslyn Primary in Nottinghamshire has never put its children through national tests and St Laurence RC in Cambridge does not submit results. The former school is being put under increasing pressure to conform but did receive a good OFSTED report in spite of its defiance.

Making Comparisons

In an unguarded moment in 1998, Mike Cresswell, a senior research officer with the AEB, pointed out to an audience of leading academics that the comparison of examination results year-on-year as a measure of school improvement was a sham. The essence of his argument was that examinations in England and Wales had never adopted what he termed 'strong' criterion referencing but, instead, used common criteria to underpin syllabuses and papers, and a loose form of norm referencing to relate one year's award to the last. In contrast to this approach, a mechanism that was designed to measure improvement with strong criterion referencing would use examination papers that barely differed from one year to the next and would not require an awarding meeting to look at the implications of the results.

He pointed out that the government's own study had failed to find any sense of a rise or fall in standards over time because it looked at a limited sample of papers and mark schemes. However, this approach was also flawed because, for example, it overlooked the widespread tendency for examiners to set difficult papers and then to compensate for this severity by adjusting grade boundaries at awarding. The examining system, therefore, relies on a mix of criterion and norm referencing as, increasingly, do national test assessment awards.

It is obvious to teachers who are also examiners that the system of making examination and test comparisons is not ideal. As an example, if the overall - national - pass rates for GCSE or A Level vary from year to year, then the school system as a whole - and the individual 'units' within it - will record a consequent 'improvement' or 'regression' which may be genuine, because the examiners are really seeing better work, or may have something to do with changes in the papers - a change of syllabus or the introduction of modular courses, for example.

This situation is clouded by two other factors which, in practice, sway awarding committees to underwrite improvements. Firstly, the government expects the system to improve as a matter of policy - it expects to see better examination results as a consequence of its policies and investment - and the examining boards do not want to see their market share threatened by what appears to be a 'fall in the pass rate'.

Taking the consequences of this back to the level of the individual school, it is impossible to unravel what a detected improvement really means. Is it genuine or simply the consequence of a national trend which may or may not be itself fully justified? The government's hope is that a mixture of better teaching in schools, better tests and examinations - and a sense of optimism about the future - will work together to cause standards to rise but that is hardly a fair way to measure the achievements of school departments and teachers.

International Comparisons

There has been a constant pressure in the 1990s to show how badly pupils in English schools perform in relation to those in other countries. Reading and number work in mathematics have been two areas, in particular, where teachers have been criticised for not keeping up with other European and Pacific Rim education systems. However, Margaret Brown, Professor of Mathematics at King's College, raised some questions about the politicised nature of some of these comparisons in 1998. For mathematicians, the main measure of comparison is the International Maths and Science Study which has tested children at ages nine and thirteen and in the final year of compulsory education on three occasions. The media treatment of the results has been to show that the UK performs very badly but Margaret Brown has pointed out that, in fact, the results for 13-year-olds are very similar internationally and that sampling disparities are probably greater than the differences from one country to another. She has noted, for example, how English children were compared to their Thai counterparts, overlooking that only 32% of Thai children attend secondary school and she found similar differences in the size of the cohorts from country to country - the UK sample excluded only 1% of pupils as opposed to 20% of low-achievers in other countries.

Evidence to support her belief that the findings have been manipulated for political ends in the past also comes from the fact that an embargo on the publication of results in 1996 was broken only by the UK - just at the same time as mental arithmetic tests and calculator-free test papers were introduced into national testing at key stage 2!

English 1999

We will also ensure proper alignment between relevant parts of the English and mathematics Orders and the national frameworks for literacy and numeracy.

QCA recommendation on curriculum review to David Blunkett.

The study of English is at the heart of the school curriculum, so I am pleased to see rising attainment in this subject at GCSE.

Tessa Blackstone announcing the 1998 GCSE results.

SUMMARY: *The current curriculum came into force at key stages 1-3 in September 1995. A revised version will be introduced in September 2000. GCSE syllabuses were introduced in September 1996 for first examination in 1998. New A and AS Level cores have been published from which syllabuses will be developed by April 2000 for examinations commencing in September 2000.*			
Attainment Targets Key Stages 1-4	*Speaking and Listening (AT1)*	*Reading (AT2)*	*Writing (AT3)*
1999 Teacher Assessment:	*Key stage 1, 2 and 3: Assessment of AT1-AT3 based on levels of attainment averaged and rounded to the nearest whole number. GCSE 1998: 40% coursework - 20% En1 (Speaking and Listening), 20% En2-En5 (Reading and Writing).*		
1999 Test Assessment:	*Key stage 1: Reading task for levels 1-2 plus comprehension test at level 2 (for all those achieving the level on reading task) and level 3. Level 2 is graded A-C. Writing task covering levels 1-3 (with sub-grades A-C at level 2) and spelling test for level 1 (optional) and levels 2-3 linked to writing task.* *Key stage 2: Teacher Assessment at levels 1-2 for Reading, Spelling and Handwriting. 60-minute Reading (12th May) and Writing (13th May) tests at levels 3-5, 15-minute Spelling and Handwriting test at levels 3-5 (12th May). 60-minute extension test at level 6 (13th May).* *Key stage 3: Teacher Assessment for levels 1-3. Paper 1 (4th May) is a 90-minute (+15 minutes reading time) test of Reading and Writing covering levels 4-7. Paper 2 (4th May) is a 75-minute test of Shakespeare scenes covering levels 4-7. A 90-minute extension paper (5th May) covers Reading and Writing at level 8 and SEP level. 'Twelfth Night' replaces 'A Midsummer Night's Dream' as set Shakespeare text.*		
MAJOR CHANGES:			
1999:	*Training in remedial literacy for secondary school teachers. Curriculum review consultation period.*		
2000:	*New curriculum and A Level syllabuses to be introduced.*		

Subject Update

■ Unpublished research carried out on behalf of QCA suggested that English pupils are better at writing English than their counterparts in France. They are more adventurous, spell better and employ more tenses. The fact that the research was not widely disseminated may have something to do with the fact that the French teach reading and writing in a structured, grammar-based way that emphasises syntax and is constantly drilled into pupils. The French were, however, better at using commas!

■ An NFER survey of over 300 primary schools found that, even before the literacy hour was introduced, nine out of ten primary teachers were already spending more than five hours a week on English. This adds up to 190 hours a year which is ten more than recommended by Sir Ron Dearing.

In almost one-third of the schools surveyed the English co-ordinator had no non-contact time to support his or her colleagues.

- The Secondary Heads Association (SHA) published a supportive document on drama teaching in 1998. Drama Sets You Free (Gulbenkian Foudation, 1998) claimed that the subject was the ideal vehicle for transmitting an awareness of citizenship and social responsibility. The National Association for the Teaching of English (NATE) also published a position paper on the subject.

- After sterile debates over the past few years about the teaching of grammar and a slow realisation that English teachers have to engage with the issue, a new avenue to explore is about to open with the publication of the QCA Technical Accuracy Project findings. This has, for the first time, analysed the genuine strengths and weaknesses of writers and is likely to have a major effect on the teaching of the subject.

- OFSTED produced a useful summary leaflet on primary English that could be equally applicable to key stage 3 teachers. It identified improvements in teaching and learning but was critical of children's sustained writing, their handwriting skills and their understanding of spelling patterns. It suggested that management and the use of resources, and the performance of boys were key areas for teachers to address.

National Assessment

Key Stage 1

The 1998 assessment results in English revealed another consistent pattern with the test and teacher assessments (TAs) for Speaking & Listening, Reading and Writing all within reasonable parameters and showing a modest improvement. The results for spelling were slightly improved. That means that there is a consistent baseline from which to measure the

success of the national literacy strategy from 1999 onwards.

Key Stage 2

The test results for 1998 showed only a small improvement after the major shift in 1997. 64% of pupils are now at level 4 or above, compared to 48% in 1995 and a government target of 80% by 2002. It is important to remember that this improvement has been achieved without a curriculum revamp and the correlation between the TA and the test result suggests that the measurement is reliable.

The new interim tests in year 4 presented some limited data from a self-selected group of 270 schools. 67% of pupils reached level 3 in reading, 58% in writing and 55% in spelling. The interesting fact to emerge was that 60% of the children reaching level 2 in reading at key stage 1 had moved to level 3, and 85% of the same group in writing had done the same. Carrying this forward, the government's literacy target for the end of key stage 2 could be hit sooner than expected. QCA has reported solid support for these tests from teachers and a new test paper will be available in 1998 along with more optional tests for use in years 3 and 5.

Key Stage 3

Two years ago, it seemed certain that 1998 would bring changes to this assessment after SCAA recommended the removal of the Shakespeare paper and the 1997 assessment gave rise to more appeals; after dropping to 25,000 in 1996 the number rose to 41,000. Around one-quarter of those who appeal each year see their grades rise by a full level which is significant considering the range of marks that each level encompasses. However, fearful of a right-wing backlash from proponents of high culture, David Blunkett and the DfEE have played safe and, in the meanwhile, the removal of the most popular play for study, *Romeo and Juliet*, and its replacement by *Macbeth*, the most popular GCSE text, will cause major problems for department resourcing in 2000 and 2001.

KEY STAGE 1 ENGLISH RESULTS 1996-1998 (% AT EACH LEVEL)					
Levels	Below 1 or A	1	2	3	4+
1998	3	16	63	18	0
1997	3	17	63	17	0
1996	3	18	62	17	0

KEY STAGE 2 ENGLISH RESULTS 1996-8 (% AT EACH LEVEL)										
Levels	Below 2 or A		2		3		4		5	
	TA	Test	TA	Test	TA	Test	TA	Test	TA	Test
1998	7	8	6	1	27	26	48	48	17	17
1997	2		7	11	28	26	46	47	17	16
1996	2		8	13	30	30	45	45	15	12

SCAA conducted a review of what went wrong in 1997 but similar problems resurfaced in the identification of high-achieving candidates in 1998, while the collapse of the data collection service did nothing to inspire confidence in either the testing or the results. Out of the entire range of national assessments, that at Key Stage 3 English is now the most obviously unreliable. One head of department reported that his schools submitted all of its 205 papers for remarking and 110 were reduced by one or more levels. Movement in the other direction was equally common.

This head of department had an eye on value-added measures in 2000 and, in fact, the latest dilemma for schools comes from posing the question of how well does an English department want to do in 1999? A good key stage 3 performance - more level 6s and 7s than in 1998 - could be the start of a decline in progress in 2001. At present, the test agency has difficulty in differentiating level 7 performances but appears to be pumping up the proportions at level 5 and above. If it does this and the percentages rise in English at level 7 to match, for example, those for mathematics, then the statistics will show that hard-working English departments are failing to match up.

For 1999, there are no major changes to the structure of the papers but the set Shakespeare plays have

changed and, from 1999, *Twelfth Night* replaces *A Midsummer Night's Dream*. In 2000, *Macbeth* will replace *Julius Caesar* and, in 2001, *Henry V* will replace *Romeo and Juliet*. 'It is intended' - QCA's choice of words - that *Twelfth Night*, *Macbeth* and *Henry V* will remain as the set plays for 'a number of years'.

There are some interesting issues for departments to unravel here. Book economics would suggest that *Romeo and Juliet* will have to become the common text for GCSE study but the cross-over will need to be carefully managed. The loss of *Romeo and Juliet* will also be felt in many schools as it is probably the most accessible Shakespeare play for the 14-year-old age group. *Twelfth Night* is an odd choice with its dark humour and sexual undertones (just look at the sexual innuendo in the extracts for study) but, perhaps, *Henry V* and *Macbeth* have been chosen to bolster the new emphasis on citizenship in the curriculum!

Public Examinations

GCSE

The carrying forward of standards with the introduction of new syllabuses in 1998 was carefully monitored by the examining boards. NEAB, now

SET SHAKESPEARE PLAYS AND PRESCRIBED SCENES FOR KEY STAGE 3 ENGLISH ASSESSMENT IN 1999				
	Play	Act & Scene	Line refs.	Cues
NEW	*Julius Caesar*	3: 1	1 to 275	*'With carrion men groaning for burial'*
	Julius Caesar	4: 3	1 to 238	*'Farewell every one'*
	Romeo and Juliet	2: 4	82 to end of Scene 5	*'Here's goodly gear!'*
NEW	*Romeo and Juliet*	3: 5	Line 37 to the end	*'Madam!'*
NEW	*Twelfth Night*	1: 1, 2 and 3	Complete scenes	
NEW	*Twelfth Night*	2: 5	Complete scenes	

KEY STAGE 3 ENGLISH RESULTS 1996-8 (% at each level)

Levels	3 and below		4		5		6		7 and above	
	TA	Test	TA	Test	TA	Test	TA	Test	TA	Test
1998	15	16	24	19	31	30	21	25	9	10
1997	15	16	25	26	32	33	20	19	8	6
1996	15	20	24	23	30	31	21	18	10	8

merged with SEG as the Assessment and Qualifications Alliance (AQA) is the dominant player in terms of candidate numbers. EDExcel is now a relatively small board where English is concerned. Schools can now choose to use syllabuses from the Northern Ireland examining group (CCEA).

The relaxation of the regulations by the DfEE to allow awards at grade E on the higher tier was announced after entries had closed, but avoided major problems with candidates being graded as 'unqualified'. It did not address the issue of whether a glass ceiling operated on the foundation tier and most boards reported small numbers of candidates who achieved the maximum grade C but were entitled, on the quality of their work, to a grade B.

NEAB was in trouble in the autumn of 1998 for reissuing the anthology which is the basis for its mainstream English and English Literature courses. A completely new set of materials left schools angry about the cost of re-equipping for the new course and at the way preparation work and teacher-developed materials were wasted. The previous anthology had only been in use for two years.

A Level Cores

New A Level cores for English Language, English Literature and English Language and Literature were published in 1997 and were then subsequently revised to allow the AS Level to be a subset of the full certificate, permit modular and synoptic assessment and deliver key skills in communication. From these, syllabuses are currently being developed for new courses set to commence in September 2000. The English Literature core specifies the study of a minimum of four texts for AS Level including prose, poetry, drama, a Shakespeare play and one other pre-1900 text. A Level requires four further texts covering prose, poetry and drama, one of which must be pre-1770 and another pre-1900. This means that the full course requires the study of at least four pre-1900 texts, one of which is pre-1770 and one a Shakespeare play. For English Language and Literature at AS Level, two literary or non-literary texts covering two genres (prose, poetry, drama) must be studied including one written before 1900. For the full course, two more texts must be studied and the full range of prose, poetry and drama must be covered by the course. One text must be pre-1770.

THE KEY STAGE 3 TESTS IN ENGLISH 1999

Level	Levels 4-7	Levels 4-7	Levels 8-10
Paper	*Paper One Reading & Writing*	*Paper Two Scenes from Shakespeare Plays*	*Extension Paper Comparative Reading*
Length	*90 minutes (15 minutes reading time)*	*75 minutes (set scenes provided as booklet)*	*90 minutes*
Weighting	*60%*	*40%*	*100% (only if level 7 reached on Papers 1 and 2)*
Description	*Section A: Literary comprehension (15 marks). Section B: Non-literary comprehension (10 marks). Section C: Imaginative extension - narrative or non-literary (30 marks). Presentation (5 marks).*	*One task set in response to scene from Shakespeare play. Response to text (25 marks). Writing (10 marks). Presentation (5 marks).*	*Questions on reading of two or more texts including one written before 1900 and additional writing task*
Date	*May 4th 1999 morning*	*May 4th 1999 afternoon*	*May 5th 1999*

The Curriculum

Plans for Curriculum Review

The early drafts of the new curriculum follow the secretary of state's requests that change should be minimal and that the alterations at key stags 1 and 2 should be designed to align the curriculum with literacy strategy. This means that there is probably less reduction in content than in other subjects and no changes to the attainment target structure. In particular, the key stage 3 and 4 programmes of study have not been unravelled.

There has been an attempt to improve the requirements for speaking & listening and to make some connections with key skill communications at key stages 3 and 4 but, again, in draft form this is not explicit. There are fuller requirements for ICT use, a greater highlighting of skills and there is a suggestion that the prescribed pre- and post-1900 authors might be reduced to the status of exemplification. For the most part, the impression given to teachers is that the curriculum has been rewritten rather than revised. As an indication of this, there are no changes planned that would impact on national assessment or precipitate changes in GCSE syllabuses.

The Current Curriculum

There are three attainment targets, Speaking & Listening (AT1), Reading (AT2) and Writing (AT3). Writing incorporates presentational skills, spelling and punctuation. The programmes of study for each attainment target are structured identically. They break down into three sections - Range, Key Skills and what is termed Standard English and Language Study. The Range section is used to define the scope of an attainment target at a specific key stage. For Reading, the criteria for selecting plays, novels and short stories and poetry are noted. But, with Writing, the notion of range is less applicable. Here, Writing is defined as of value for personal expression, as a means of responding to stimuli and as a way of organising ideas and impressions in particular ways. Essentially, what the curriculum writers are trying to say is that Writing can be defined by subject, purpose and audience - a matter of variety rather than range. There are separate programmes of study for key stages 1 and 2 but the key stage 3 and 4 programmes are combined.

The Programmes of Study - English

ATTAINMENT TARGET 1 - SPEAKING & LISTENING

ATTAINMENT TARGET 2 - READING

ATTAINMENT TARGET 3 - WRITING

KEY STAGE 2

ATTAINMENT TARGET 1 - SPEAKING & LISTENING

RANGE: Students should be given opportunities to:

a) talk for a range of purposes;
b) to a range of audiences ...
c) ... and people;
d) act in drama.

KEY SKILLS: The following skills should be developed:-

a) confident personal expression and listening.
b) reading with increasing accuracy and fluency.

STANDARD ENGLISH & LANGUAGE STUDY: Students should be given opportunities to develop an understanding of how vocabulary changes according to context and explore the differences between written and spoken English. They should learn about the structured vocabulary of word groups and the language used in word games.

ATTAINMENT TARGET 2 - READING

RANGE: Students should be given opportunities to:

a) develop independent reading for pleasure and information
b) ... using a wide range of sources;
c) read texts that are challenging in terms of content, structure and language and...
d) ... include modern fiction by established writers, classic and modern poetry, texts with multicultural origins and myths and traditional stories.

KEY SKILLS: *The following skills should be developed:-*

a) *the ability to read with fluency, understanding and enjoyment.*

b) *the ability to reflect, respond and evaluate what is read.*

c) *information retrieval skills.*

d) *the use of classification schemes and indexes.*

STANDARD ENGLISH & LANGUAGE STUDY:

Students should be given opportunities to explore the structural and organisational features of texts and to use their knowledge in understanding features of standard English.

ATTAINMENT TARGET 3 - WRITING

RANGE: *Students should be given opportunities to:*

a) *write for varied purposes;*

b) *write for a wider range of readers;*

c) *learn about the characteristics of different writing types and use layout and presentation for effect.*

KEY SKILLS: *The following skills should be developed:-*

a) *writing where degrees of formality, or the selection of tone or style is necessary.*

b) *the ability to plan, draft, revise, proofread and present.*

c) *the use of correct punctuation marks including full stop, question and exclamation marks, commas, inverted commas, possessive apostrophes.*

d) *the spelling of prefixed and suffixed words and dictionary retrieval.*

e) *confident and legible handwriting.*

STANDARD ENGLISH & LANGUAGE STUDY:

Students should be given opportunities to reflect on their use of language in spoken and written forms and explore the formality of standard English. They should develop understanding of the grammar of complex sentences and use paragraphs and the written forms of parts of speech.

KEY STAGE 3

ATTAINMENT TARGET 1 - SPEAKING & LISTENING

RANGE: *Students should be given opportunities to:*

a) *talk for a range of purposes including explanation, argument and analysis ...*

b) *... in a range of contexts;*

c) *listen attentively and distinguish features of presentation;*

d) *participate in scripted and unscripted dramatic activity and consider features of performance.*

KEY SKILLS: *The following skills should be developed:-*

a) *varying speech according to context and audience and taking a variety of roles in discussion.*

b) *listening for intention, tone and ambiguity and responding in discussions.*

STANDARD ENGLISH & LANGUAGE STUDY:

Students should be taught to be fluent users of standard English and to recognise its importance in public communication. They should be encouraged to adapt talk to circumstances. They should explore the development of the English language with reference to change over time, the differences between speech and writing and the grammar of dialect.

ATTAINMENT TARGET 2 - READING

RANGE: *Students should be given opportunities to:*

a) *develop their independent reading of, and their responses to, demanding texts read both for pleasure and for information;*

b) *read plays, novels, short stories and poetry that are varied in approach, extend ideas, develop emotional and moral understanding and use language in interesting ways;*

c) *read texts from other cultures and traditions;*

d) *read major works of literature from a prescribed list of pre-1900 writers (drama, fiction, poetry) and the equivalents of a recommended list of post-1900 writers;*

e) *read a range of non-fiction texts;*

f) *study a wide range of media.*

KEY SKILLS: *The following skills should be developed:-*

a) *the ability to extract textual meanings that go beyond the literal.*

b) *the ability to reflect on, respond to, appreciate and evaluate what is read at imaginative and intellectual levels.*

c) *reading to select information, synthesise it effectively in writing and evaluate presentation.*

STANDARD ENGLISH & LANGUAGE STUDY:

Students should be given opportunities to analyse and evaluate the characteristics of texts across a range of media by exploring how intentions are realised and values communicated. They should be taught the main features of literary language and their deployment in different kinds of text and genres and should explore the range of literary techniques used by writers.

ATTAINMENT TARGET 3 - WRITING

RANGE: *Students should be given opportunities to:*

a) *write with commitment and a personal style for varied purposes;*

b) *write for specified readers including a large unknown audience;*

c) *practise a range of different forms of writing.*

KEY SKILLS: The following skills should be developed:-

a) the individual use of planning, drafting and proof-reading as required. The ability to write at speed and to make full use of presentational devices where appropriate.

b) the ability to write narrative, poetry, scripts and dialogues and non-fiction.

c) the spelling of complex words.

d) neat and legible handwriting.

STANDARD ENGLISH & LANGUAGE STUDY:
Students should be given opportunities to write standard English across a range of writing types selecting the appropriate degree of formality. They should develop and practise their understanding of discourse structure, sentence structure, words and punctuation devices and consider apt and imaginative language choices made by writers.

Level Descriptions   Level 3

Attainment Target 1: Speaking & Listening: Students talk and listen confidently in different contexts, exploring and communicating ideas. In discussion, they show understanding of the main points. Through relevant comments and questions, they show they have listened carefully. They begin to adapt what they say to the needs of the listener, varying the use of vocabulary and the level of detail. They are beginning to be aware of standard English and when it is used.

Attainment Target 2: Reading: Students read a range of texts fluently and accurately. They read independently, using strategies appropriately to establish meaning. In responding to fiction and non-fiction they show understanding of the main points and express preferences. They use their knowledge of the alphabet to locate books and find information.

Attainment Target 3: Writing: Students' writing is often organised, imaginative and clear. The main features of different forms of writing are used appropriately, beginning to be adapted to different readers. Sequences of sentences extend ideas logically and words are chosen for variety and interest. The basic grammatical structure of sentences is usually correct. Spelling is usually accurate, including that of common, polysyllabic words. Punctuation to mark sentences - full stops, capital letters and question marks - is used accurately. Handwriting is joined and legible.

Level 7

Attainment Target 1: Speaking & Listening: Students are confident in matching their talk to the demands of different contexts. They use vocabulary precisely and organise their talk to communicate clearly. In discussion, students make significant contributions, evaluating others' ideas and varying how and when they participate. They show confident use of standard English in situations that require it.

Attainment Target 2: Reading: Students show understanding of the ways in which meaning and information are conveyed in a range of texts. They articulate personal and critical responses to poems, plays and novels, showing awareness of their thematic, structural and linguistic features. They select and synthesise a range of information from a variety of sources.

Attainment Target 3: Writing: Students' writing is confident and shows appropriate choices of style in a range of forms. In narrative writing, characters and settings are developed and, in non-fiction, ideas are organised and coherent. Grammatical features and vocabulary are accurately and effectively used. Spelling is correct, including that of complex irregular words. Work is legible and attractively presented. Paragraphing and correct punctuation are used to make the sequence of events or ideas coherent and clear to the reader.

Mathematics 1999

The one thing that badly affects performance in maths is letting children work on their own.

Professor David Reynolds at the launch of the NNS.

The NNS will see pupils in every primary school benefiting from a ban on the use of calculators by children up to the age of eight.

DfEE Press Release, 1998.

We're not banning calculators.

David Blunkett, Secretary of State for Education, 1998.

SUMMARY: *The current curriculum came into force at key stages 1-3 in September 1995. A revised version will be introduced in September 2000. GCSE syllabuses were introduced in September 1996 for examination in 1998. New A and AS Level cores have been published from which syllabuses will be developed by April 2000 for examinations commencing in 2000.*

Attainment Targets:	*Using and Applying Mathematics (AT1)*	*Number and Algebra (AT2)*
	Shape, Space and Measures (AT3)	*Handling Data (AT4)*
Key Stage variations:	*Key stage 1: AT1, Number, AT3 - no Algebra or Handling Data. Key stage 2: AT1, Number, AT3, AT4 - no Algebra. Key stages 3 and 4: AT1, AT2, AT3, AT4.*	
1999 Teacher Assessment:	*Key stage 1: Assessments of AT1-AT3 weighted 1:2:1. Levels are averaged and rounded upwards. Key stage 2: Assessments of AT1-AT4 weighted 1:2:1:1. Levels are averaged and rounded upwards. Key stage 3: Assessments of AT1-AT4 weighted 1:2:1:1. Levels are averaged and rounded to the nearest whole number. GCSE: 20% coursework - AT1. AT2 is double-weighted.*	
1999 Test Assessment:	*Key stage 1: Mathematics task covering level 1. Mathematics test sampling AT2 and AT3 in ratio 2:1. The 40-minute test covers levels 2-3, with A-C grading at level 2. The first five questions are oral. Able pupils may sit key stage 2 tests.*	
	Key stage 2: Two 45-minute tests (A and B) sampling AT2-AT4 in ratio 2:1:1 at levels 3-5 (10th and 11th May). Test A is non-calculator paper. 30-minute extension paper, test C, covering level 6 (12th May). 20-minute pilot mental arithmetic test (10th May).	
	Key stage 3: Two 60-minute papers (6th May) sampling AT2-AT4 set at four tiers, 3-5, 4-6, 5-7 and 6-8. 90-minute extension paper covering SEP (10th May). 20-minute pilot mental arithmetic test (5th or 6th May).	
MAJOR CHANGES:		
1999:	*National numeracy strategy to be introduced in primary schools. Training for primary teachers.*	
2000:	*New curriculum and A Level syllabuses to be introduced.*	

Update

■ The government was in trouble with the numeracy task force for putting out a press release saying that calculators would be banned from primary classrooms when the National Numeracy Strategy (NNS) was implemented. The task force wanted to convey a different message from that purveyed by the last government but the media office was stuck in old tramlines. The official position is that calculators have their place.

■ A piece of research from King's College with Margaret Brown's name on it discovered that able girls are disadvantaged by setting for GCSE in secondary schools. The researchers argued that girls - usually outnumbered in the top sets - did not get the attention they deserved. Most top set pupils - boys and girls - did not like the setting arrangements and were no happier than those in the lower sets. They claimed that the work was rushed and there was too little time given to the understanding of the subject. The main complaint in the lower set was that the teaching was poor and the work was not challenging enough. Since most secondary schools operate setting in mathematics, this is a piece of research worth following up.

■ QCA has been working on what are called 'bolt on' mathematics modules for GNVQ courses. These are intended as sixty hour courses (45 hours taught time) that will provide the mathematical skills needed, for example, by a business or an engineering GNVQ in a single module. As a way of delivering real mathematics and key skills in context, they are to be admired but their introduction will be difficult alongside the new AS Level structure and the need for key skills in a range of areas including number.

■ A few mathematicians have voiced doubts about the NNS, mostly focusing on the dangers of taking an untried curriculum and imposing it on schools. The opposition has been muted because most of the best known voices in the subject have been brought into the task force deliberations and then effectively gagged by the government's procedures. There were rumours about the draconian approach of the civil servants who were meant to service the task force and draft its reports and who were sometimes said to be following a different agenda altogether.

■ SMP mathematics is reckoned to be coming up for its twentieth birthday in 1999. Proponents of the series love the books but other see them as largely behaviour control mechanisms designed to keep pupils busy rather than learning. Foucault would certainly reckon that they were a classic example - there are many in education - of discredited bureaucratised disciplinary structures re-imposing themselves on the system.

■ With mental arithmetic now featuring prominently in the NNS and in key stage testing, Ian Thompson, a lecturer in education at the University of Newcastle, has made a useful distinction between mental recall and mental strategies, arguing that national testing seems to emphasise the latter - working in the head - at the expense of the former - working with one's brain. An example of the distinction would be using a remembered number bond and applying it (recall), as opposed to thinking through from two given two-digit numbers to find out their sum (strategy).

■ OFSTED produced a leaflet in 1998 on progress in primary mathematics. It was critical of numeracy standards and of the use made by schools of homework. Curriculum planning in mathematics and the use of assessments to inform what happens in classrooms also came in for comment. However, it was complimentary about teachers' knowledge - only one in fifteen teachers was reckoned to have an inadequate grasp of the subject.

The National Numeracy Strategy

The section on Literacy and Numeracy gives more information about this strategy and the timetable for introduction and training. Secondary teachers should note that there will be training provided in 2000 to enable them to work with children who are still below level 4 on entry to secondary school.

The strategy offers schools the same deal - training, supply cover, a whole-school mathematics audit and free materials in return for the complete implementation of the framework on set lines and external monitoring.

Local education authority appointments of advisory and specialist teachers are likely to continue throughout 1999. There have been worries that the impressive training and monitoring arrangements will take too many good teachers out of the classroom.

The framework itself, with ten minutes of direct instruction, questioning and mental arithmetic, followed by a main teaching activity together with the use of a designated vocabulary, is quite extraordinarily prescriptive about content. It will be interesting to see how publishers respond to the challenge but the preparation of schemes of work looks, at first sight at least, to be very much more guided and straightforward than the equivalent process is in the national literacy strategy.

National Assessment

Key Stage 1

The changes introduced in 1997, including the introduction of five oral questions at the start of the level 2 test, do not seem to have had any impact on performance where there is a pleasing two per cent rise year-on-year that has been sustained for three years and bodes well for the government's long-term

KEY STAGE 1 MATHEMATICS RESULTS 1996-1998 (% AT EACH LEVEL)					
Levels	Below 1 or A	1	2	3	4+
1998	2	13	65	20	0
1997	2	14	65	18	0
1996	2	16	66	16	0

targets. The teacher assessed and task components are well in line as well.

Key Stage 2

KEY STAGE 2 TEST TRENDS IN MATHEMATICS			
1995	1996	1997	1998
44%	54%	63%	59%

After four years of steady improvement, there was almost a 4% drop in the percentage of pupils achieving level 4 or above. However, the TA remained consistent suggesting that the fault probably lay with the assessment.

It is possible that the mental arithmetic test had some effect. In the pilot in 1997, the marks were depressed so that children who received level 3 on the test scored an average of nine correct answers out of twenty-eight for mental arithmetic, those on level 4 scored 17 marks on average while those on level 5 scored 23 marks. When the cohort is so large this does not mean that children are bad at mental arithmetic - they may or may not be - but simply that the test is incorrectly calibrated.

If, in 1998, the questions were pitched at the same level then the aggregated marks used to draw level boundaries would have come in at lower figures than in 1997. The likelihood, therefore, is that the awarding group misread the data in drawing their boundaries and, thinking that they were carrying forward standards, moved in the direction of severity. Of course, the result was handy ammunition for those who promote the NNS as a necessary step forward.

What is slightly worrying is that national test assessments can fluctuate like this. A shift of 4% in a cohort of half a million is simply nothing to do with standards but, carried forward as value-added data into a system of performance-related appraisal, it is a nonsense.

The other major concern should be the assessment tail. The stubborn group of pupils left on level 3 are a cause for real concern. It is slightly ironic that the NNS is intended to aim its whole class work at the top 20% of the group.

Key Stage 3

The 1998 results could suggest that the 4% increase in performance at level 5 or above achieved in 1997 and 1998 is an indication of genuine improvement. It also appears that, at key stage 3, the mental arithmetic test has had less impact but, as most teachers have noted, it is not that much more difficult than that set at key stage 2.

KEY STAGE 2 MATHEMATICS RESULTS 1996-8 (% AT EACH LEVEL)											
Levels	Below 2 or A		2		3		4		5		
	TA	Test	TA	Test	TA	Test	TA	Test	TA	Test	
1998	1	8	6	2	27	31	48	42	17	17	
1997	1		6	11	29	26	46	47	18	16	
1996	1		7	10	31	28	44	44	16	18	

KEY STAGE 3 MATHEMATICS RESULTS 1996-8 (% AT EACH LEVEL)										
Levels	3 and below		4		5		6		7 and above	
	TA	Test	TA	Test	TA	Test	TA	Test	TA	Test
1998	12	18	23	22	27	24	24	23	14	13
1997	14	17	23	22	27	23	24	25	13	12
1996	14	19	24	23	27	23	23	22	13	11

Key Stage 4 and GCSE

There was increasing disenchantment in 1998 with the tiering in mathematics. This possesses two clear weaknesses. The first is the problem of pupils falling off tiers and being ungraded in a key subject and the second is the fact that less-able, hardworking students at the foundation level are excluded from grade C which is patently a disincentive to them.

GCSE mathematics results showed a slight decline in 1998 and a reduction in the number of graded candidates almost certainly as a consequence of candidates falling off the higher tier and being ungraded.

A and AS Level

The subject cores, first published in 1997, are now guiding the syllabus development. After QCA approval, the new syllabuses will come into operation from September 2000. It seems likely that AS Level will be a subset of the full certificate so that separate A Level syllabuses can be developed in Pure Mathematics, Mechanics, Statistics, Discrete Mathematics and, in some subject combinations, Applied Mathematics. Modular syllabuses will probably be very popular if the syllabus writers can produce adequate synoptic tests.

The Curriculum

Curriculum Review

The intention, as with English, has been to maintain the pattern of the curriculum while aligning its requirements with the numeracy strategy. In draft form this has involved moving some material - fractions and proportions - from key stage 3 to key stage 2 and reducing the requirements for handling data to compensate.

One significant change concerns a proposal to integrate Using and Applying mathematics so that it becomes a subset of each of the other attainment targets and a hint that the key stage 3 and 4 programmes of study should be differentiated.

There is also a hint that some curriculum revision might make it possible to reduce the number of tiers in key stage 3 assessment - a move that would be welcomed by those who administer the assessment in schools.

The Current Curriculum

There are now three attainment targets at key stage 1: Understanding and Applying Mathematics (AT1); Number (AT2); and Shape, Space and Measures (AT3). At key stage 2, Data Handling (AT4) is introduced and, at key stages 3 and 4, Algebra is separated from Number in the programmes of study. However, they remain linked in the level descriptions, so Algebra is not a discrete attainment target. The first stages of curriculum review in mathematics will be interesting.

The Programmes of Study - Mathematics

ATTAINMENT TARGET 1 - USING AND APPLYING MATHEMATICS
ATTAINMENT TARGET 2 - NUMBER and ALGEBRA
ATTAINMENT TARGET 3 - SHAPE, SPACE AND MEASURES
ATTAINMENT TARGET 4 - HANDLING DATA

KEY STAGE 2

ATTAINMENT TARGET 1: USING AND APPLYING MATHEMATICS.

Pupils should be given opportunities to: apply mathematics in practical tasks; take responsibility for tasks; devise ways of recording and ask questions.

Making and monitoring decisions to solve problems.
Pupils should be taught to:

- *select appropriate mathematics;*
- *try different approaches;*
- *develop mathematical strategies;*
- *check results.*

Developing mathematical language and forms of communication. *Pupils should be taught to:*

- *understand and use the language of: number; shapes; measures and probability;*
- *use diagrams and graphs;*
- *present information.*

Developing mathematical reasoning. *Pupils should be taught to:*

- *investigate general statements;*
- *search for pattern;*
- *explain their reasoning.*

ATTAINMENT TARGET 2: NUMBER.

Pupils should be given opportunities to: develop effective methods of computation; use calculators and computers and develop the skills needed for appropriate use of equipment.

Developing an understanding of place value and extending the number system. *Pupils should be taught to:*

- *understand that the position of a digit signifies its values;*
- *understand negative numbers;*
- *understand fractions and percentages.*

Understanding relationships between numbers and developing methods of computation. Pupils should be taught to:

- *explore number sequences;*
- *recognise number relationship between co-ordinates;*
- *consolidate knowledge of addition and subtraction facts to 20;*
- *know the multiplication facts to 10×10;*
- *develop a variety of mental methods of computation with whole numbers up to 100;*
- *understand multiplication;*
- *use the relationships between the four operations;*
- *add and subtract with negative numbers, calculating fractions and percentages of quantities;*
- *use a basic calculator.*

Solving numerical problems. Pupils should be taught to:

- *develop their use of the four operations to solve problems;*
- *choose sequences of computation;*
- *check results.*

ATTAINMENT TARGET 3: SHAPE, SPACE AND MEASURES.

Pupils should be given opportunities to: use geometrical properties and relationships; use a wide range of materials; use computers; consider a wide range of patterns and apply their measuring skills.

Understanding and using properties of shape. *Pupils should be taught to:*

- *visualise shapes and movements;*
- *make 2-D and 3-D shapes;*
- *recognise reflective symmetries of 2-D and 3-D shapes.*

Understanding and using properties of position and movement. *Pupils should be taught to:*

- *transform 2-D shapes by translation;*
- *use co-ordinates;*
- *use right angles, fractions of a turn and, later, degrees, to measure rotation.*

Understanding and using measures. *Pupils should be taught to:*

- *choose appropriate standard units;*
- *use appropriate measuring instruments;*
- *find perimeters, circumferences, areas and volumes.*

ATTAINMENT TARGET 4: HANDLING DATA.

Pupils should be given opportunities to: formulate questions; access and collect data and use computers for representing data.

Collecting, representing and interpreting data. *Pupils should be taught to:*

- *interpret tables used in every day life;*
- *collect and represent discrete data appropriately;*
- *understand and use measures of average;*
- *draw conclusions from statistics and graphs.*

Understanding and using probability. *Pupils should be taught to:*

- *develop an understanding of probability;*
- *understand that the probability of any event lies between impossibility and certainty;*
- *recognise situations where probabilities can be based on equally likely outcomes.*

KEY STAGE 3

ATTAINMENT TARGET 1: USING AND APPLYING MATHEMATICS.

Pupils should be given opportunities to: apply mathematics in real life problems; work on problems that pose a challenge and consider different lines of mathematical argument.

Making and monitoring decisions to solve problems. *Pupils should be taught to:*

- *develop and use their own strategies;*
- *trial and evaluate a variety of possible approaches;*
- *organise mathematics and resources;*
- *review progress.*

Communicating mathematically. *Pupils should be taught to:*

- *use mathematical language and notation;*
- *use mathematical communication;*
- *present work clearly;*
- *evaluate forms of presentation;*
- *examine critically their choice of mathematical presentation.*

Developing skills of mathematical reasoning. *Pupils should be taught to:*

- *justify a solution to a problem;*
- *make conjecture and hypotheses;*
- *understand general statements;*
- *appreciate and use "if ... then ..." lines of argument;*
- *use mathematical reasoning when following a line of argument.*

ATTAINMENT TARGET 2: NUMBER.

Pupils should be given opportunities to: use calculators and computer software; develop a range of methods of computation.

Understanding place value and extending the number system. *Pupils should be taught to:*

- *use the concept of place value in whole numbers and decimals;*
- *use decimals, ratios, fractions and percentages;*
- *use index notation.*

Understanding and using relationships between numbers and developing methods of computation. *Pupils should be taught to:*

- *consolidate knowledge of multiplication to 10×10;*
- *extend mental methods of computation;*
- *calculate with negative numbers, decimals, fractions, percentages and ratio;*
- *understand how to use fractions and percentages to make proportional comparisons;*
- *use a calculator, including the use of the constant function, memory and brackets;*
- *mentally estimate solutions to numerical calculations.*

Solving numerical problems. *Pupils should be taught to:*

- *develop an understanding of the four operations and apply them to solving problems, including those that involve ratios;*
- *select suitable sequences of operations;*
- *use a variety of checking strategies;*
- *give solutions in the context of the problem.*

ALGEBRA. *Pupils should be given the opportunities to: explore a variety of relationships; consider techniques for manipulating algebraic expressions and consider how algebra can be used to solve problems.*

Understanding and using functional relationships. *Pupils should be taught to:*

- *appreciate the use of letters to represent variables;*
- *explore number patterns arising from a variety of situations;*
- *interpret graphs;*

- *explore the properties of standard mathematical functions;*

Understanding and using equations and formulae.
Pupils should be taught to:

- *appreciate the use of letters to represent unknowns;*
- *construct, interpret and evaluate formulae and expressions;*
- *manipulate algebraic expressions;*
- *solve a range of linear equations.*

ATTAINMENT TARGET 3: SHAPE, SPACE AND MEASURES.

Pupils should be given the opportunities to: use different representations; explore shape through drawing and practical work and use computers to generate graphic images.

Understanding and using properties of shape.
Pupils should be taught to:

- *visualise, describe and represent shapes;*
- *construct 2-D and 3-D shapes;*
- *understand the symmetry properties of 2-D and 3-D shapes;*
- *measure angles, and use the language associated with them;*
- *understand and use Pythagoras' theorem;*
- *understand the trigonometrical relationships in right-angled triangles.*

Understanding and using properties of position, movement and transformation.
Pupils should be taught to:

- *use co-ordinate systems to specify location;*
- *recognise and visualise transformations;*
- *use the properties of transformations;*
- *develop an understanding of scale;*
- *determine the locus of an object moving according to a given rule.*

Understanding and using measures.
Pupils should be taught to:

- *choose appropriate instruments;*
- *understand the differences between discrete and continuous measures;*
- *use compound measures;*
- *find perimeters, areas and volumes of common shapes, including circles and cylinders.*

ATTAINMENT TARGET 4: HANDLING DATA.

Pupils should be given opportunities to: formulate questions; undertake purposeful enquiries; use computers; engage in practical and experimental work and look critically at some of the ways in which representations of data can be misleading.

Processing and interpreting data.
Pupils should be taught to:

- *design and use data collection sheets;*
- *design a questionnaire;*
- *construct appropriate diagrams;*
- *calculate or estimate, and use appropriate measures of central tendency;*
- *calculate or estimate appropriate measures of spread;*
- *interpret a wide range of graphs and diagrams;*
- *evaluate results critically;*
- *recognise that inferences may suggest further questions for investigation.*

Estimating and calculating the probabilities of events.
Pupils should be taught to:

- *use the vocabulary of probability;*
- *justify estimates of probability;*
- *use relative frequency as an estimate of probability;*
- *recognise where probabilities can be based on equally likely outcomes;*
- *identify all the outcomes of a combination of two experiments;*
- *recognise when the multiplication of probabilities for two independent events apply and make appropriate calculations.*

Level Descriptions   Level 3

Attainment Target 1: Using and Applying Mathematics: Pupils try different approaches and find ways of overcoming difficulties that arise when they are solving problems. They are beginning to organise their work and check results. Pupils discuss their mathematical work and are beginning to explain their thinking. They use and interpret mathematical symbols and diagrams. Pupils show that they understand a general statement by finding particular examples that match it.

Attainment Target 2: Number and Algebra: Pupils show understanding of place value in numbers up to 1000 and use this to make approximations. They have begun to use decimal notation and to recognise negative numbers, in contexts such as money, temperature and calculator displays. Pupils use mental recall of addition and subtraction facts to 20 in solving problems involving larger numbers. They use mental recall of the 2, 5 and 10 multiplication tables, and others up to 5x5, in solving whole-number problems involving multiplication or division, including those that give rise to remainders. Pupils use calculator methods where numbers include several digits. They have begun to develop mental strategies, and use them to find methods for adding and subtracting numbers with at least two digits.

Attainment Target 3: Shape, Space and Measures: Pupils classify 3-D and 2-D shapes in various ways using mathematical properties such as reflective symmetry. They use non-standard units and standard metric units of length, capacity, mass and time, in a range of contexts.

Attainment Target 4: Handling Data: Pupils extract and interpret information presented in simple tables and lists. They construct bar charts and pictograms, where the symbol represents a group of units, to communicate information, and they interpret information presented to them in these forms.

Level 7

Attainment Target 1: Using and Applying Mathematics: Starting from problems or contexts that have been presented to them, pupils introduce questions of their own, which generate fuller solutions. They examine critically and justify their choice of mathematical presentation, considering alternative approaches and explaining improvements they have made. Pupils justify their generalisations or solutions, showing some insight into the mathematical structure of the situation being investigated. They appreciate the difference between mathematical explanation and experimental evidence.

Attainment Target 2: Number and Algebra: In making estimates, pupils round to one significant figure and multiply and divide mentally. They understand the effects of multiplying and dividing by numbers between 0 and 1. Pupils solve numerical problems involving multiplication and division with numbers of any size, using a calculator efficiently and appropriately. They understand and use proportional changes. Pupils find and describe in symbols the next term or nth term of a sequence where the rule is quadratic. Pupils use algebraic and graphical methods to solve simultaneous linear equations in two variables. They solve simple inequalities.

Attainment Target 3: Shape, Space and Measures: Pupils understand and apply Pythagoras' theorem when solving problems in two dimensions. They calculate lengths, areas and volumes in plane shapes and right prisms. Pupils enlarge shapes by a fractional scale factor. They determine the locus of an object moving according to a rule. Pupils appreciate the continuous nature of measurement and recognise that a measurement given to the nearest whole number may be inaccurate by up to one half in either direction. They understand and use compound measures, such as speed.

Attainment Target 4: Handling Data: Pupils specify hypotheses and test them by designing and using appropriate methods that take account of bias. They determine the modal class and estimate the mean, median and range of sets of grouped data, selecting the statistic most appropriate to their line of enquiry. They use measures of average and range, with associated frequency polygons, as appropriate, to compare distributions and make inferences. They draw a line of best fit on a scatter diagram, by inspection. Pupils understand relative frequency as an estimate of probability and use this to compare outcomes of experiments.

Science 1999

SUMMARY: *The current curriculum came into force at key stages 1-3 in September 1995. A revised version will be introduced in September 2000. GCSE syllabuses were introduced in September 1996 for examination in 1998. New A and AS Level cores have been published from which syllabuses will be developed by April 2000 for examinations commencing in 2000.*		
Attainment Targets: Key Stages 1-4	*Experimental and Investigative Science (AT1)*	*Life Processes and Living Things (AT2)*
	Materials and their Properties (AT3)	*Physical Processes (AT4)*
1999 Teacher Assessment:	*Key stage 1: Assessments of AT1-AT4 in ratio 3:1:1:1. Levels are averaged and rounded upwards. Key stage 2: Assessments of AT1-AT4 in ratio 2:1:1:1. Levels are averaged and rounded upwards. Key stage 3: Assessments of AT1-AT4 in ratio 1:1:1:1. Levels are averaged and rounded upwards. GCSE: Coursework - AT1.*	
1999 Test Assessment:	*Key stage 1: There is no statutory test at key stage 1 but optional assessment materials have previously been produced for schools. Teachers can make an assessment at level 4 but there is no facility for entry to key stage 2 tests.* *Key stage 2: Two 35-minute test papers (A - 11th May and B - 14th May) covering AT2-AT4 at levels 3-5. A 30-minute extension test (Test C - 14th May) is available for pupils operating at level 6.* *Key stage 3: Two tiers covering levels 3-6 and 5-7 with allowable levels 2 and 4. Two 60-minute test papers (Paper One and Paper Two) for each tier covering AT2-AT4 (7th May). 60-minute extension paper covering level 8 and SEP (10th May).*	
MAJOR CHANGES:		
1999:	*New initial training curriculum for science to be introduced in September.*	
2000:	*New curriculum and A Level syllabuses to be introduced.*	

Update

- Safety in science was back in the news in 1998 with a reaction against the over-cautious policies introduced by some schools and local authorities for fear of legislation. There is currently DfEE guidance, Safety in Science Education, and further advice is available from the Association for Science Education (ASE).

- Schemes of work for primary science are also making a comeback as the best means of sustaining the subject that has to survive in competition with the literacy and numeracy strategies. QCA's version came in for some criticism as being dull but many local education authorities have produced their own versions.

- OFSTED was reasonably impressed with primary science teaching in its 1998 review but noted more unevenness in provision than in the other core subjects. The agency felt that more should be done at the start of key stage 2 to introduce practical work and scientific methods of investigation. However, the scientific knowledge of primary teachers was rated on a par with their knowledge of English and mathematics. This finding relates interestingly to some other 1998 research which suggests that secondary school science teachers typically assume too little knowledge on the part of new pupils and ignore the schemes of work they have followed.

KEY STAGE 2 SCIENCE RESULTS 1996-8 (% AT EACH LEVEL)										
Levels	**Below 2 or A**		**2**		**3**		**4**		**5**	
	TA	Test	TA	Test	TA	Test	TA	Test	TA	Test
1998	1	6	4	1	24	23	53	53	18	16
1997	1	6	4	1	25	23	51	50	18	18
1996	1	6	6	4	28	28	50	48	15	14

■ Three children in Tasmania were reported to have shown that the archetypal classroom experiment to measure the amount of oxygen in the air by burning a candle over water was a teachers' con. Using more candles apparently increased the oxygen component indicating that the warmth of the air is also a factor (when the candles go out it cools, contracts and draws the water level upwards). Others have suggested that the burning creates water vapour and carbon dioxide as well to cloud the results.

National Assessment

Key Stage 1

Since 1993, there has been no formal test of science. However, teachers still have to record a national curriculum assessment for each child. Support materials are available to schools to make the assessments against each attainment target, which are then aggregated together in the ratio of 3:1:1:1 in favour of AT1.

Key Stage 2

It is hard to resist the impression that, despite a rather clumsy adjustment to the numbers achieving level 5 in 1996, standards are rising in primary science even though the seven percentage point increase since 1996 for level 4 and above is almost certainly an overestimate.

Key Stage 3

The current tests are based on a model that was introduced in 1994 but, in spite of refinements, it has not proved itself to be particularly reliable. There are two 60-minute papers set at two main tiers (levels 3-6 and 5-7), with an optional extension paper for level 8+. Questions in both papers are set on AT2-AT4. The attainment targets are equally weighted and the papers set in 'half-tiers' so that there is a gradient of difficulty within them.

However, while the TA is showing a clear and consistent pattern, the test papers are producing erratic outcomes. Although the proportion achieving level 5 and above remained constant from 1995 to 1998, there was a 4% downward shift in 1996 in levels 5-7 and an 8% improvement at levels 6 and 7 in 1997. In 1998, the pendulum has swung back to somewhere in the middle. Such figures have little validity where value-added measurement is concerned and underline that the swing of a pendulum is not the ideal metaphor for describing important national tests!

KEY STAGE 3 SCIENCE RESULTS 1996-8 (% AT EACH LEVEL)										
Levels	**3 and below**		**4**		**5**		**6**		**7 and above**	
	TA	Test	TA	Test	TA	Test	TA	Test	TA	Test
1998	13	19	25	25	32	29	22	20	8	7
1997	13	16	26	24	32	31	22	22	7	7
1996	14	16	26	26	32	35	21	17	7	4

GCSE

In comparison to English and mathematics, science continued to offer a wide range of courses in 1998. So, there are still syllabuses for science as single and double GCSE awards and for the three separate sciences. Also, non-curriculum subjects like human biology and rural science continue and several boards offer syllabuses under brand-name project labels. Single science differs from the double-award in that it only has to cover two of the three sections in the programme of study - in practice two of biology, chemistry and physics. In addition, the *Co-ordinated*, *Integrated* and *Modular* approaches to the curriculum are maintained with separate syllabuses for the latter option. There has been concern expressed that comparability between assessments is not well achieved in science with such a range of alternatives.

A and AS Level

The new subject cores, published in 1997, will be followed through with new syllabuses in September 1999. A major worry for some scientists is the decline of physics. The entry has declined by 25% since 1990 to just over 32,000 - about 6% of the cohort of 18-year-olds - and the rate of decline is increasing. The suggestion is that it is the introduction of double science at GCSE which has caused this to happen. While there is some evidence that pupils who do separate sciences at GCSE do better in A Level courses, that may well be because they are in selective or independent schools and science receives more curriculum time at the expense of other subjects.

Of course, one other reason is the perceived difficulty of A Level Physics, which discourages teachers who are concerned about measures of performance and puts off students who are keeping an eye on their potential A Level points. Another reason might be the nature of science itself and the question of where physics should position itself in a modern view of science that distinguishes between engaged truth (true in one context but not in another) and objective fact (traditional physics).

The Curriculum

Curriculum Review

The science curriculum has come in for criticism in 1998. It has been seen as disjointed in its approaches and preoccupied with facts, most of which seem rather stale to a generation that thinks *Tomorrow's World* is old hat! The Association for Science Education (ASE) has published a discussion document, *Beyond 2000*, which suggests a new model rooted in the history of scientific discovery and contemporary issues. However, the tension remains between providing a curriculum that aims to produce scientifically literate adults on the one hand and provide a platform for a scientific specialism on the other.

The proposals for curriculum review do not engage with these issues but are, typically, lost in points of detail. So, there is talk of moving flowering plants from key stage 3 to key stage 2 without contemplating whether teenage pregnancy rates might be affected. There is a desire to foreground what might be termed scientific enquiry and a suggestion that this should be the new label for AT1. Work at key stages 1 and 2 is designed to link to QCA's scheme of work.

The Current Curriculum

This version of the curriculum has proved more popular with teachers than the last. Experimental and Investigative Science (AT1) is seen as helpfully framing the requirements for practical science and the programme of study for single-award science is clear.

The disapplication of science at key stage 4 was allowed from September 1998. As long as appropriate criteria are met, science lessons can now be replaced with employment-orientated courses and qualifications achieved outside school. In action zones, for example, NVQ courses may replace some formal science teaching in schools.

GNVQ Science may start to make inroads at GCSE level from September 1999. The certification provides a continuous science course, running from 14-19 at intermediate and advanced level. There are two components - Knowledge & Understanding and Exploration of Science.

The Programmes of Study

ATTAINMENT TARGET 1 - EXPERIMENTAL AND INVESTIGATIVE SCIENCE

ATTAINMENT TARGET 2 - LIFE PROCESSES AND LIVING THINGS

ATTAINMENT TARGET 3 - MATERIALS AND THEIR PROPERTIES

ATTAINMENT TARGET 4 - PHYSICAL PROCESSES

KEY STAGE 2

Systematic enquiry. Pupils should be given opportunities to: ask questions; use focused exploration; use first-hand experience and secondary sources and use IT.

Science in everyday life. Pupils should be given opportunities to: use their knowledge to interpret a range of familiar phenomena; consider the part science has played in the development of things that they use; relate science to personal health and consider ways in which the environment needs protection.

The nature of scientific ideas. Pupils should be given opportunities to: obtain evidence and recognise that science provides explanations.

Communication. Pupils should be taught to use appropriate scientific vocabulary; use standard measures and use a wide range of methods.

Health and safety. Pupils should be taught to recognise and assess hazards and risks and control these risks.

ATTAINMENT TARGET 1: EXPERIMENTAL AND INVESTIGATIVE SCIENCE.

Pupils should be taught to:
- turn ideas into a form that can be investigated;
- make predictions;
- decide what evidence should be collected;
- change one factor;
- use apparatus correctly;
- make careful observations;
- check observations;
- use tables, bar charts and line graphs;
- make comparisons;
- use results to draw conclusions;
- indicate whether evidence supports any prediction;
- explain conclusions in terms of scientific knowledge.

ATTAINMENT TARGET 2: LIFE PROCESSES AND LIVING THINGS.

Pupils should be taught about:

- life processes common to animals, including humans;
- life processes common to plants;
- the functions of teeth;
- how food is needed for activity and growth;
- a simple model of the structure of the heart;
- how blood circulates;
- the effect of exercise;
- the human skeleton;
- the stages of the human life cycle;
- how drugs can have harmful effects;
- plant growth;
- how plants need light;
- how water and nutrients are taken in through the root;
- the life cycle of flowering plants;
- how locally occurring animals and plants can be identified using keys;
- that different plants and animals are found in different habitats;
- how animals and plants in two different habitats are suited to their environment;
- feeding;
- that food chains show feeding relationships in an ecosystem;
- how nearly all food chains start with green plants;
- how many micro-organisms may be helpful while others may be harmful.

ATTAINMENT TARGET 3: MATERIALS AND THEIR PROPERTIES.

Pupils should be taught:

- to compare everyday materials;
- that some materials are better thermal insulators;
- that some materials are better electrical conductors;
- to describe and group rocks and soils;
- to recognise differences between solids, liquids and gases;
- that mixing materials can cause them to change;
- that heating or cooling materials can cause them to change;

- *that some changes can be reversed;*
- *that dissolving, boiling, melting, condensing, freezing and evaporating are changes that can be reversed;*
- *about the water cycle;*
- *that the changes that occur when most materials are burned are not reversible;*
- *that solid particles of different sizes can be separated;*
- *that some solids dissolve in water;*
- *about filtering;*
- *about evaporating;*
- *that there is a limit to the mass of a solid that can dissolve in a given amount of water.*

ATTAINMENT TARGET 4: PHYSICAL PROCESSES.

Pupils should be taught:

- *that a complete circuit, including a battery or power supply, is needed to make electrical devices work;*
- *about switches;*
- *ways of varying the current in a circuit;*
- *how to represent series circuits;*
- *about forces of attraction and repulsion;*
- *about gravitational attraction;*
- *about friction;*
- *that when springs and elastic bands are stretched they exert a force;*
- *that when springs are compressed they exert a force;*
- *that forces act in directions;*
- *that forces can balance;*
- *that unbalanced forces can make things speed up;*
- *that light travels from a source;*
- *that light cannot pass through some materials;*
- *that light is reflected;*
- *that light from sources enters our eyes;*
- *that sounds are made when objects vibrate;*
- *that the pitch and loudness of a sound can be changed;*
- *that vibrations can travel through materials;*
- *that the Sun, Earth and Moon are spherical;*
- *that the position of the Sun appears to change during the day;*
- *that the Earth spins around its own axis;*
- *that the Earth orbits the Sun once each year, and that the Moon takes approximately 28 days to orbit the Earth.*

KEY STAGE 3

Systematic enquiry. *Pupils should be given opportunities to: use investigations to acquire scientific knowledge; use first-hand experience and secondary sources; work quantitatively and choose ways of using IT.*

Application of science. *Pupils should be given opportunities to: relate scientific knowledge to familiar phenomena; consider applications of science; relate scientific knowledge to the environment and consider the benefits and drawbacks of scientific developments.*

The nature of scientific ideas. *Pupils should be given opportunities to: consider the importance of evidence; consider empirical evidence and relate social and historical contexts to scientific ideas.*

Communication. *Pupils should be taught to: use a wide range of terms and symbols; use SI units and appropriate scientific and mathematical conventions.*

Health and safety. *Pupils should be taught to: take responsibility for recognising hazards; assess risks and control the risks to themselves and others.*

ATTAINMENT TARGET 1: EXPERIMENTAL AND INVESTIGATIVE SCIENCE.

Pupils should be taught to:

- *use scientific knowledge to turn ideas into a form that can be investigated;*
- *carry out trial runs;*
- *make predictions;*
- *consider key factors;*
- *isolate the effect of changing one factor;*
- *decide how many observations or measurements need to be made;*
- *consider texts;*
- *select apparatus;*
- *use a range of equipment with skill;*
- *make measurements to a degree of precision;*
- *make relevant observations;*
- *repeat measurements;*
- *record evidence clearly;*
- *present qualitative and quantitative data;*
- *use graphs;*
- *use lines of best fit;*
- *identify trends;*
- *use results to draw conclusions;*
- *decide whether results support predictions;*
- *explain conclusions;*
- *consider whether the evidence is sufficient;*
- *consider anomalies;*
- *consider improvements.*

ATTAINMENT TARGET 2: LIFE PROCESSES AND LIVING THINGS.

Pupils should be taught:

- that animals and plants have organs that enable life processes to take place;
- that animals and plants are made up of cells;
- the functions of the cell membrane;
- the functions of chloroplasts and cell walls;
- ways in which some cells are adapted to their functions;
- about balanced diets;
- some sources of the main food components;
- that food is used as fuel during respiration and for growth and repair;
- the principles of digestion;
- the products of digestion;
- how blood acts as a transport medium;
- the role of the skeleton;
- the principle of antagonistic muscle pairs;
- about the physical and emotional changes that take place during adolescence;
- the human reproductive system;
- how the foetus develops;
- lung structure;
- how smoking effects lung structure;
- aerobic respiration;
- that during aerobic respiration glucose is broken down to carbon dioxide and water;
- to summarise aerobic respiration;
- that the abuse of alcohol, solvents and other drugs affects health;
- that bacteria and viruses can affect health;
- about immunisation and medicines;
- nutrition and growth in green plants;
- how photosynthesis produces biomass and oxygen;
- that plants need carbon dioxide, water and light;
- to summarise photosynthesis in a word equation;
- that nitrogen and other elements are required for plant growth;
- that root hairs absorb water;
- how reproduction occurs in flowering plants;
- that plants carry out aerobic respiration;
- about variation within species;
- that variation can have both environmental and inherited causes;
- how keys can be used;
- to classify living things;
- about selective breeding;
- how different habitats support different plants and animals;
- how organisms are adapted to survive changes in their habitat;
- about food chains;
- about food webs;
- how toxic materials may accumulate in food chains;
- about factors affecting the size of populations;
- that organisms competing in their environment contribute relatively more offspring.

ATTAINMENT TARGET 3: MATERIALS AND THEIR PROPERTIES.

Pupils should be taught:

- to recognise differences between solids, liquids and gases;
- the arrangement and movement of particles;
- how the particle theory of matter can be used to explain the properties of solids;
- that elements consist of atoms;
- elements can be represented by symbols and the periodic table;
- how some elements combine to form compounds;
- to represent compounds by formulae;
- that mixtures contain constituents that are not combined;
- methods that can be used to separate mixtures;
- about metals and non-metals;
- about metallic elements;
- about non-metallic elements;
- to classify elements as metals or non-metals;
- that mass is conserved;
- that solutes have different solubilities;
- that materials change at different temperatures;
- how materials expand and contract;
- how rocks are weathered;
- the rock cycle;
- that rocks are classified;
- when chemical reactions take place, mass is conserved;
- that virtually all materials are made through chemical reactions;
- to represent chemical reactions;
- that there are different types of reaction;
- that products can be made from chemical reactions;
- about chemical reactions that are not useful;
- that energy transfers can be controlled;
- about the effects of burning fossil fuels;
- reactions of metals;
- about displacement reactions;
- about reactivity series of metals;
- how reactivity series can be used to make predictions;
- acids and bases pH;
- to use indicators;
- the reactions of acids with metals and bases;
- everyday applications of neutralisation;
- how acids in the atmosphere can lead to corrosion.

ATTAINMENT TARGET 4: PHYSICAL PROCESSES.

Pupils should be taught:
- that insulating material can be charged by friction;
- about forces of attraction between positive and negative charges;
- how to measure current;

- *that current depends on the number of cells and nature of other components;*
- *that current is not used up by components;*
- *that current is a flow of charge;*
- *about magnetic fields;*
- *about the field pattern produced by a magnet;*
- *that a current in a coil produces a magnetic field;*
- *how electromagnets are constructed;*
- *how to determine speed;*
- *the quantitative relationship between speed, distance and time;*
- *that unbalanced forces change the speed and/or direction;*
- *that balanced forces produce no change;*
- *ways in which frictional forces affect motion;*
- *that forces cause objects to turn;*
- *the principle of moments;*
- *the quantitative relationship between force and pressure;*
- *applications of this relationship;*
- *how light travels;*
- *how shadows are formed;*
- *that light travels much faster than sound;*
- *how non-luminous objects are seen;*
- *how light is reflected;*
- *how light is refracted;*

- *that white light can be dispersed;*
- *the effect of colour filters;*
- *how coloured objects appear;*
- *about sound waves;*
- *the effects of loud sounds on the ear;*
- *that sound waves cannot travel through a vacuum;*
- *the link between sound and amplitude;*
- *the link between pitch and frequency;*
- *that apparent movement of the Sun and other stars is caused by the movement of the Earth;*
- *the relative positions of the Earth and planets;*
- *about gravitational forces;*
- *that the Sun and other stars are light sources;*
- *about artificial satellites;*
- *that there is a variety of energy resources;*
- *that the Sun is the ultimate source of most of the Earth's energy;*
- *that electricity is generated;*
- *that some resources are renewable;*
- *the distinction between temperature and energy;*
- *that energy can be transferred and stored;*
- *that energy is conserved;*
- *that energy may be dissipated.*

Level Descriptions   Level 3

Attainment Target 1: Experimental and Investigative Science: Pupils respond to suggestions, put forward their own ideas and, where appropriate, make simple predictions. They make relevant observations and measure quantities, such as length or mass, using a range of simple equipment. With some help they carry out a fair test, recognising and explaining why it is fair. They record their observations in a variety of ways. They provide explanations for observations and, where they occur, for simple patterns in recorded measurements. They say what they have found out from their work.

Attainment Target 2: Life Processes and Living Things: Pupils use their knowledge of basic life processes, such as growth or reproduction, when they describe differences between living and non-living things. They provide simple explanations for changes in living things, such as diet affecting the health of humans or other animals, or lack of light or water altering plant growth. They identify ways in which an animal is suited to its environment, such as a fish having fins to help it swim.

Attainment Target 3: Materials and their Properties: Pupils use their knowledge and understanding of materials when they describe a variety of ways of sorting them into groups according to their properties. They explain why some materials are particularly suitable for specific purposes, such as a metal for making electrical cables. They recognise that some changes, such as the freezing of water, can be reversed and some, such as the baking of clay, cannot, and they classify changes in this way.

Attainment Target 4: Physical Processes: Pupils use their knowledge and understanding to link cause and effect in simple explanations of physical phenomena, such as a bulb failing to light because of a break in an electrical circuit, or the direction or speed of movement of an object changing because of a force applied to it. They begin to make simple generalisations about physical phenomena such as explaining that sounds they hear become fainter the further they are from the source.

Level 7

Attainment Target 1: Experimental and Investigative Science: Pupils use scientific knowledge and understanding to identify the key factors in situations involving a range of factors and, where appropriate, to make predictions. They make systematic observations and measurements with precision using a wide range of apparatus. They identify when they need to repeat measurements and observations in order to obtain reliable data. They present qualitative observations clearly and concisely. They present data in graphs, where appropriate, and use lines of best fit. They draw conclusions that are consistent with the evidence and explain these using scientific knowledge and understanding. They begin to consider whether the data they have collected are sufficient for the conclusions they have drawn.

Attainment Target 2: Life Processes and Living Things: Pupils use knowledge and understanding of life processes and living things drawn from the key stage 3 programme of study, to make links between life processes in animals and plants and the organ systems involved. They explain the processes of respiration and photosynthesis in terms of the main underlying chemical change. They use their knowledge of cell structure to explain how cells, such as the ovum, sperm or root hair, are adapted for their functions. They identify characteristic variations between individuals, including some features, such as eye colour, that are inherited and others, such as height, that can also be affected by environmental factors. They construct models, such as food webs or pyramids of numbers, to represent feeding relationships, and explain how these relationships affect population size.

Attainment Target 3: Materials and their Properties: Pupils use knowledge and understanding drawn from the key stage 3 programme of study, to make links between the nature and behaviour of materials and the particles of which they are composed. They use the particle model of matter in explanations of phenomena such as changes of state. They explain differences between elements, compounds and mixtures in terms of their constituent particles. They recognise that elements and compounds can be represented by symbols and formulae. They apply their knowledge of physical and chemical processes to explain the behaviour of materials in a variety of contexts, such as the way in which natural limestone is changed through the action of rainwater, or ways in which rocks are weathered. They use patterns of reactivity, such as those associated with a reactivity series of metals, to make predictions about other chemical reactions.

Attainment Target 4: Physical Processes: Pupils use knowledge and understanding of physical processes drawn from the key stage 3 programme of study, to make links between different phenomena. They make connections between electricity and magnetism to explain phenomena such as the strength of electromagnets. They use some quantitative definitions, such as those for speed or pressure, and perform calculations involving physical quantities, using the correct units. They apply abstract ideas in explanations of a range of physical phenomena, such as the appearance of objects in different colours of light, the relationship between the frequency of vibration and the pitch of a sound, the role of gravitational attraction in determining the motion of bodies in the solar system, or the dissipation of energy during energy transfers.

Design & Technology 1999

Curriculum Review

Design & technology has never managed to achieve a settled curriculum framework and, according to the most recent draft proposals, the next version of the subject will be changed yet again - ending considerably leaner than the existing model. One plan is to conflate the two attainment targets into one as part of an extensive reduction in the statutory content which will also see considerable simplification of some of the wordier statements in the programmes of study. The material on disassembly and investigation - a throwback to the first curriculum model - is to be replaced by a new heading for project analysis. With ICT clearly removed from design & technology, it should now be possible to define a more precise role for ICT within the subject. The review will be written to complement the QCA primary schemes of work, themselves very brief, at key stages 1 and 2. The case put forward by the design and technology professional associations for the reinstatement of food technology as a compulsory element at key stage 3 may lead to a curriculum addition in this area.

With the possibility of disapplication at key stage 4, the future for the subject is not guaranteed. Also, the opening up of GNVQ Part One alternatives may also threaten its status as a GCSE subject. It is clear that the days of technology for all are probably numbered - a big change from the early 1990s when enhanced technology teaching in schools was going to bring manufacturing industry out of the doldrums.

The Programmes of Study

ATTAINMENT TARGET 1 - DESIGNING
ATTAINMENT TARGET 2 - MAKING

KEY STAGE 2

Pupils should develop their design & technology capability through: assignments; focused practical tasks and activities. Pupils should be given opportunities to: work with a range of materials and components; work independently and in teams; apply skills, knowledge and understanding from other subjects.

Designing skills. *Pupils should be taught to:*

- *use information sources;*
- *generate ideas;*
- *clarify their ideas;*
- *consider appearance, function, safety and reliability;*
- *explore aspects of design by modelling;*
- *develop a sequence of actions;*
- *evaluate design ideas as these develop.*

Making skills. *Pupils should be taught to:*

- *select appropriate materials;*
- *measure and shape using equipment;*
- *join and combine materials and components accurately;*
- *apply finishing techniques;*
- *plan how to use materials, equipment and processes;*
- *evaluate their products;*
- *implement improvements.*

Knowledge and understanding. *Pupils should be taught:*

- *the characteristics of materials;*
- *how materials can be combined and mixed;*
- *about simple mechanisms;*
- *about electrical circuits;*
- *how structures can fail;*
- *to investigate, disassemble and evaluate simple products;*
- *to relate the way things work to their intended purpose;*
- *to distinguish between how well a product has been made and designed;*
- *to consider the effectiveness of a product;*
- *further knowledge and understanding of health and safety;*
- *to use the appropriate vocabulary.*

KEY STAGE 3

Pupils should develop their design & technology capability through assignments including the use of resistant materials, compliant materials and/or food and through focused practical tasks or activities in which they investigate, disassemble and evaluate familiar products. Pupils should be given opportunities to work independently and in teams and apply skills, knowledge and understanding from other subjects.

Designing skills. *Pupils should be taught to:*

- *identify sources of information;*
- *use design briefs;*
- *develop a specification;*
- *consider the needs and values of intended users;*
- *generate design proposals;*
- *consider the aesthetics, function, safety, reliability and cost;*
- *take account of characteristics and materials;*
- *prioritise and reconcile decisions on materials within design proposals;*
- *take account of restrictions imposed by tools and equipment;*
- *explore, develop and communicate design ideas by modelling in a variety of ways, including the use of IT;*
- *propose an outline plan, which includes alternative methods;*
- *evaluate design ideas as these develop.*

Making skills. *Pupils should be taught to:*

- *shape and form materials;*
- *select materials, tools and equipment;*
- *use methods of shaping and forming materials accurately;*
- *join and combine materials and components;*
- *use construction kits;*
- *interconnect components;*
- *apply a range of finishing techniques;*
- *make products in quantity;*
- *propose an outline plan that includes materials, equipment and processes;*
- *evaluate products;*
- *implement improvements and take on-going action.*

Knowledge and understanding. *Pupils should be taught:*

- *to consider the physical and chemical properties of materials;*
- *the major classifications within the material categories;*
- *that materials can be combined, processed and finished to create useful properties and desired effects;*
- *about heat treatment;*
- *about pressing or casting;*
- *to design, use and interconnect simple mechanical, electronic and pneumatic systems and sub-systems;*
- *how to interconnect mechanisms;*
- *to use electrical switches;*
- *to use sensors;*
- *that systems have inputs, processes and outputs;*
- *the importance of feedback;*
- *to analyse the performance of systems;*
- *to use structures;*
- *that excessive loads can cause structures to fail;*
- *to use simple tests;*
- *to devise methods to reinforce structures;*
- *to understand that forces produce different effects;*
- *pupils should be taught to investigate, disassemble and evaluate a wide range of products and applications, in order to learn how they function.*

Pupils should also be taught to distinguish between quality of design and quality of manufacture, in order to identify, and use criteria that help them judge the quality of a product. They should be taught further knowledge and understanding of health and safety as designers, makers and consumers.

Level Descriptions   Level 3

Attainment Target 1: Designing: When designing and making, pupils generate ideas, recognising that their designs will have to satisfy conflicting requirements. They make realistic suggestions about how they can achieve their intentions and suggest more ideas when asked. They draw on their knowledge and understanding of the appropriate programme of study to help them generate ideas. Labelled sketches are used to show the details of their designs.

Attainment Target 2: Making: When designing and making, pupils think ahead about the order of their work, choosing tools, materials and techniques more purposefully. They use tools with some accuracy and use simple finishing techniques to improve their products. They cut and shape materials and components, with some precision, to help assembly. Their products are similar to their original intentions and, where changes have been made, they are identified.

Level 7

Attainment Target 1: Designing: When designing and making, pupils identify the appropriate sources of information and use them to help generate ideas. They investigate the characteristics of familiar products, including form, function and production processes, in order to develop their ideas. The working characteristics of materials and components are taken into account. They recognise the different needs of a variety of users, and use appropriate evaluation techniques to identify ways forward. They use their knowledge and understanding of the key stage 3 programme of study to develop realistic intentions, which they communicate to others through a variety of media, showing how their designs will function in use.

Attainment Target 1: Making: When designing and making, pupils produce plans that predict the time needed to carry out the main stages in making, and match their choice of materials and components with tools, equipment and processes. They adapt their methods of manufacture to changing circumstances, providing a sound rationale for any deviations from the design proposal. They select appropriate techniques to evaluate how their products would perform in use and modify them to improve their performance.

I.C.T 1999

Curriculum Review

The place of information and communications technology in the curriculum has evolved rapidly. In primary schools, the subject has to be taught while even science has been disapplied and, at key stage 4, information technology is now a core subject. However, that does not appear to mean that the subject has to be taught discretely. The major influences on curriculum review have been the new Initial Teacher Training curriculum which is famously designed to be future-proof, the vocational qualification key skill requirement and the QCA schemes of work in the subject for key stages 1 and 2.

The resulting pudding is likely to mean considerable rewriting but less change of any substance. However, there is an attempt to separate out subjects where the use of ICT is integral to the teaching of the subject and those where ICT can enhance teaching and learning. But, the draft proposals show that while this sounds like a good idea in theory, the practical difficulties are considerable. It raises the question eventually of whether there is such a subject as ICT and whether, ideally, there should be a number of subjects all of which use ICT as a matter of course in a world where the computer is more familiar to pupils than the video-recorder. Of course, that position would require a fuller realignment of other subjects. English, for example, with responsibility for writing would have to teach text processing while databases might feature in geography and research skills in history.

The Programmes of Study

ATTAINMENT TARGET 1 - INFORMATION TECHNOLOGY CAPABILITY

KEY STAGE 2

Pupils should be given opportunities to: use IT to explore and solve problems; use IT to further their understanding of information retrieved; assess its value and investigate parallels with the use of IT in the wider world.

Communicating and handling information. *Pupils should be taught to:*

- *use IT equipment and software to communicate ideas and information;*
- *organise, reorganise and analyse ideas;*
- *select suitable information and media;*
- *interpret information held on IT systems.*

Controlling and handling information. *Pupils should be taught to:*

- *create, test, modify and store sequences of instructions;*
- *monitor external events;*
- *explore the effect of changing variables;*
- *recognise patterns and relationships.*

KEY STAGE 3

Pupils should be given opportunities to: use IT equipment autonomously; consider the purposes for which information is to be processed; use their understanding of IT to design information systems; investigate problems by constructing IT processes; consider the limitations of IT tools and discuss some of the issues raised by IT.

Communicating and handling information. *Pupils should be taught to:*

- *use a range of IT equipment and software efficiently;*
- *select appropriate IT equipment and software;*
- *collect and amend quantitative and qualitative information;*
- *interpret, analyse and display information.*

Controlling, measuring and modelling. *Pupils should be taught to:*

- *plan, develop, test and modify sets of instructions;*
- *use a system and explain how it makes use of feedback;*
- *measure and record physical variables;*
- *explore a given model with a number of variables;*
- *modify the rules and data of a model;*
- *evaluate a computer model.*

Level Descriptions   Level 3

Attainment Target: Information Technology Capability: Pupils use IT to generate, amend, organise and present ideas. They use IT to save data and to access stored information, following straightforward lines of enquiry. They understand how to control equipment to achieve specific outcomes by giving a series of instructions. They use IT-based models or simulations to help them make decisions, and are aware of the consequences of their choices. They describe their use of IT, and its use in the outside world.

Level 7

Attainment Target: Information Technology Capability: Pupils combine a variety of forms of electronic and other information for presentation to an unfamiliar and critical audience. They identify the advantages and limitations of different data-handling applications, and select and use suitable information systems, translating enquiries expressed in ordinary language into forms required by the system. They use IT equipment and software to measure and record physical variables. They design computer models or procedures, with variables, which meet identified needs. They consider the limitations of IT tools and information sources.

Modern Foreign Language 1999

Curriculum Review

Draft proposals for curriculum review suggest that the heavyweight four attainment target model will be retained. However, each of the attainment targets - Listening and Responding (AT1), Speaking (AT2), Reading and Responding (AT3) and Writing (AT4) - will be radically pruned. One proposal is to merge the two sections. Currently, the Part I and Part II divisions differentiate between *language skills* developed through activities in the target language and the *areas of experience* which should be explored through the language. Another idea is to keep the Part II areas of experience - Everyday Activities (A), Personal and Social Life (B), The World Around Us (C), The World of Work (D) and The International World (E) - as statutory requirements but to make the sub-topics advisory.

In addition, the much criticised list of non-EU languages is likely to disappear, there will be specific IT requirements and an attempt to link understanding of grammar and structure from English with the study of the foreign language. While the future of the subject is anything but secure with the possibility of disapplication at key stage 4, the arrival of specialist language schools and some revived interest in learning a language at key stage 2 could be helpful.

The Programmes of Study

ATTAINMENT TARGET 1 - LISTENING AND RESPONDING
ATTAINMENT TARGET 2 - SPEAKING
ATTAINMENT TARGET 3 - READING AND RESPONDING
ATTAINMENT TARGET 4 - WRITING

KEY STAGE 3

The programme of study for key stage 3 consists of two parts.

PART I: Learning and Using the Target Language. *This covers the skills and understanding that should be developed through the target language at both key stages.*

1. *Communicating in the target language.*
2. *Language skills.*
3. *Language-learning skills and knowledge of language.*
4. *Cultural awareness.*

PART II: Areas of Experience. *This sets out the broad topic areas that provide contexts for learning and using the target language at each key stage. In key stage 3, pupils should study Areas of Experience A, B and C.*

A. *Everyday activities.*

B. *Personal and social life.*

C. *The world around us.*

Level Descriptions Level 3

Attainment Target 1: Listening and Responding: Pupils show understanding of short passages, including instructions, messages and dialogues, made up of familiar language spoken at near normal speed but without interference. They identify and note main points and personal responses, such as likes, dislikes and feelings, but may need short sections to be repeated.

Attainment Target 2: Speaking: Pupils take part in brief prepared tasks of at least two or three exchanges, using visual or other cues to help them initiate and respond. They use short phrases to express personal responses, such as likes, dislikes and feelings. Although they use mainly memorised language, they occasionally substitute items of vocabulary to vary questions or statements.

Attainment Target 3: Reading and Responding: Pupils show understanding of short texts and dialogues, made up of familiar language, printed in books or word-processed. They identify and note main points, including likes, dislikes and feelings. They are beginning to read independently, selecting simple texts and using a bilingual dictionary or glossary to look up new words.

Attainment Target 4: Writing: Pupils write two or three short sentences on familiar topics, using aids such as exercise books, textbooks and wallcharts. They express personal responses, such as likes, dislikes and feelings. They write short phrases from memory and their spelling is readily understandable.

Level 7

Attainment Target 1: Listening and Responding: Pupils show understanding of a range of material that contains some complex sentences and unfamiliar language. They understand language spoken at normal speed, including brief news items and non-factual material taken from radio or television, and need little repetition.

Attainment Target 2: Speaking: Pupils give and justify opinions when discussing matters of personal or topical interest. They adapt language to deal with some unprepared situations. They speak with good pronunciation and intonation. Their accuracy is such that they are readily understood.

Attainment Target 3: Reading and Responding: Pupils show understanding of a range of material, imaginative and factual, that includes some complex sentences and unfamiliar language. They make use of new vocabulary and structures encountered in their reading to respond in speech or in writing. They use reference materials as appropriate.

Attainment Target 4: Writing: Pupils produce pieces of writing of varying lengths on real and imaginary subjects. They link sentences and paragraphs, structure ideas and adapt previously learnt language for their own purposes. They edit and redraft their work, using reference sources to achieve greater accuracy, precision and variety of expression. Although there may be occasional mistakes, the meaning is clear.

Humanities 1999

Curriculum Review

Their disapplication at key stages 1 and 2 after the removal of their programmes of study for key stage 4 in the last review has left geography and history in tatters. The proposal to cut work on the quality of the environment out of key stage 1 is an indication of where the geography curriculum is headed. The proposals for review involve cutting out details and increasing flexibility at key stages 1 and 2, largely by textual changes and the removal of subsidiary information.

The Thatcherite notion of history, that pupils would learn about a series of major events in British history in the same chronological sequence has all but evaporated leaving a vacuum in its wake. The subject proposals aimed squarely at reducing prescription have not done so by developing a new model but have, instead, set about even further mauling of the existing structure. So, the plan is to keep the study unit structure but to remove most of the specification within it. One idea is to limit the key stage 2 study units to four instead of six. There are also minor proposals to add more flexibility and choice and to link with the QCA scheme of work at key stages 1 and 2. The problem with such an approach is that any sense of coherence between study units will be lost as will the overall chronology.

The crux of the problem is that both geography and history are evidently the rumps of larger, wide-ranging subjects that have been radically pruned and, as such, the organising principles that once applied to them have disappeared. The notions that geography should prepare the literate adult of the future for living in a geographical world or that history tells you enough about the past to stop you making the same mistakes in the future have got lost along the way and have been replaced by fragmentary glimpses of the subjects.

The Programmes of Study - Geography

ATTAINMENT TARGET 1 - GEOGRAPHY

KEY STAGE 2

Pupils should be given opportunities to: investigate places and themes; undertake studies; develop the ability to recognise patterns and become aware of a wider geographical context.

Geographical Skills. Pupils should be given opportunities to: observe and ask questions; collect and record evidence and analyse the evidence.

Pupils should be taught to:
- *use geographical vocabulary;*
- *undertake fieldwork;*
- *make plans and maps;*
- *use and interpret globes, and maps and plans at a variety of scales;*
- *use secondary sources of evidence;*
- *use IT.*

Places. Three localities should be studied - the locality of the school and two contrasting localities. One should be in the United Kingdom and the other in a country in Africa, Asia (excluding Japan), South America, or Central America (including the Caribbean).

Thematic Studies. The four geographical themes to be investigated are: Rivers, Weather, Settlement and Environmental Change.

KEY STAGE 3

Pupils should be given opportunities to: investigate places and themes; undertake studies that focus on geographical questions; explain geographical patterns; consider issues and become aware of the global context within which places are set.

Geographical Skills. *Pupils should be given the opportunities to: identify geographical questions and issues; identify the evidence required and analyse and evaluate the evidence.*

Pupils should be taught to:

- *use an extended geographical vocabulary;*
- *undertake fieldwork using instruments to measure accurately;*
- *make maps and plans at a variety of scales, using symbols, keys and scales;*
- *use and interpret maps and plans at a variety of scales;*
- *make effective use of globes and atlases to find appropriate information;*
- *use appropriate techniques to present evidence;*
- *use secondary sources of evidence;*
- *use information technology.*

Places. *Two countries should be studied. They should be in significantly different states of development. One country should be selected from the areas in LIST A, the other from those in LIST B.*

LIST A - Australia and New Zealand, Europe, Japan, North America, Russian Federation.

LIST B - Africa, Asia (excluding Japan), South and Central America (including the Caribbean).

Thematic Studies. *The nine geographical themes to be studied are: Tectonic Processes, Geomorphological Processes, Weather and Climate, Ecosystems, Population, Settlement, Economic Activities, Development, and Environmental Issues.*

Level Descriptions - Geography   Level 3

Attainment Target: Geography: Pupils describe and make comparisons between the physical and human features of different localities. They offer explanations for the locations of some of those features. They show an awareness that different places may have both similar and different characteristics. They offer reasons for some of their observations and judgements about places. They use skills and sources of evidence to respond to a range of geographical questions.

Level 7

Attainment Target: Geography: Pupils show their knowledge, understanding and skills in relation to a wide range of studies of places and themes, at various scales. They describe the interactions within and between physical and human processes. They show how these interactions create geographical patterns and contribute to change in places and patterns. They show understanding that many factors influence decisions made about places, and use this to explain how places change. They appreciate that peoples' lives and environment in one place are affected by actions and events in other places. They recognise that human actions may have unintended environmental consequences and that change sometimes leads to conflict. With growing independence, pupils draw on their knowledge and understanding to identify geographical questions, establish a sequence of investigation, and select and use accurately a wide range of skills (from key stage 3 programme of study) and evidence. They are beginning to reach substantial conclusions.

The Programmes of Study - History

ATTAINMENT TARGET 1 - HISTORY

KEY STAGE 2

Pupils should be taught SIX Study Units.

1. *Romans, Anglo-Saxons and Vikings in Britain.*
2. *Life in Tudor times.*
3a. *Victorian Britain;*
OR 3b. *Britain since 1930.*
4. *Ancient Greece.*
5. *Local history.*
6. *A past non-European society.*

Key Elements. Pupils should be taught:

- *to place events within a chronological framework;*
- *to use dates and terms relating to the passing of time;*
- *about characteristic features of particular periods and societies;*
- *to describe reasons for and results of historical events;*
- *to describe links between the main events, both within and across periods;*
- *to identify and give reasons for different ways in which the past is represented;*
- *how to find out about aspects of the periods studied;*
- *to ask and answer questions;*
- *to recall, select and organise historical information;*
- *the terms necessary to describe the periods and topics studied;*
- *to communicate their knowledge in a variety of ways.*

KEY STAGE 3

Pupils should be taught SIX Study Units.

1. *Medieval realms: Britain 1066-1500.*
2. *The making of the United Kingdom: crowns, parliaments and peoples 1500-1750.*
3. *Britain 1750-circa 1900.*
4. *The twentieth-century world.*
5. *An era or turning point in European history before 1914.*
6. *A past non-European society.*

Key Elements. Pupils should be taught:

- *to place events, people and changes within a chronological framework;*
- *to use dates, terms and conventions that describe historical periods;*
- *to analyse the features of particular periods, including ideas, attitudes, experiences and social, cultural, religious and ethnic diversity;*
- *to explain reasons for historical events, situations and changes;*
- *to develop overviews;*
- *to assess significance of events;*
- *why historical events have been interpreted differently;*
- *to investigate independently aspects of the periods studied;*
- *to ask significant questions, to evaluate sources, and to collect and record information;*
- *to recall, select and organise historical information;*
- *to organise their knowledge and understanding of history through the deployment of terms;*
- *to communicate their knowledge in a variety of ways, including substantiated explanations.*

Level Descriptions - History   Level 3

Attainment Target: History: Pupils show their understanding of chronology by their increasing awareness that the past can be divided into different periods of time, their recognition of some of the similarities and differences between these periods, and their use of dates and terms. They demonstrate factual knowledge and understanding of some of the main events, people and changes drawn from the appropriate programme of study. They are beginning to give a few reasons for, and results of, the main events and changes. They identify some of the different ways in which the past is represented. They find answers to questions about the past by using sources of information in ways that go beyond simple observations.

Level 7

Attainment Target: History: Pupils make links between their outline and detailed factual knowledge and understanding of the history of Britain and other countries drawn from the key stage 3 programme of study. They use this to analyse relationships between features of a particular period or society, and to analyse reasons for, and results of, events and changes. They explain how and why different historical interpretations have been produced. Pupils are beginning to show independence in following lines of enquiry, using their knowledge and understanding to identify, evaluate and use sources of information critically. They are beginning to reach substantiated conclusions independently. They select, organise and deploy relevant information to produce well-structured narratives, descriptions and explanations, making appropriate use of dates and terms.

Art & Music 1999

Curriculum Review

It is amusing to think back to the earliest versions of the art and music curriculum documents and the names of the artists and composers whose work had to be introduced at key stages 1 and 2. If the latest curriculum review proposals are accepted, art will have almost no compulsory elements at key stage 1 and 2 and it will be possible to knock off most of the key stage 3 requirement using a computer rather than a pencil. The plan is that the specific processes detailed at key stages 1 and 2 will be made optional and the processes greatly simplified. To assist with these reductions the attainment targets should be merged and a draft eight level scale is being devised,

undoubtedly to assist with performance-related appraisal rather than to improve access to the subject.

There is a similar scale proposed for music where the cuts in the subject are equally deep. The number of statements in the programmes of study will be halved at each key stage and work on sounds - perhaps the essence of music - will disappear altogether. The two attainment targets - Performing and Composing (AT1) and Listening and Appraising (AT2) - can be merged into one.

It is ironic of course that this is happening to music just as the government is pledging itself to make a massive investment in the subject in schools after the millennium.

The Programmes of Study - Art

ATTAINMENT TARGET 1 - INVESTIGATING AND MAKING

ATTAINMENT TARGET 2 - KNOWLEDGE AND UNDERSTANDING

KEY STAGE 2

Pupils' understanding and enjoyment of art should be developed through activities that bring together requirements from both Investigating and Making and Knowledge and Understanding, wherever possible.

Investigating and Making. *Pupils should be given opportunities to:*

- *record responses, including observations of the natural and made environment;*
- *gather resources and materials, using them to stimulate and develop ideas;*
- *explore and use two and three-dimensional media, working on a variety of scales;*
- *review and modify their work as it progresses.*

Knowledge and Understanding. *Pupils should be given opportunities to:*

- *develop understanding of the work of artists, craftspeople and designers, applying knowledge to their own work;*

- *respond to and evaluate art, craft and design, including their own and others' work.*

KEY STAGE 3

Investigating and Making. *Pupils should be taught to:*

- *develop ideas from first-hand observation;*
- *organise visual evidence using a sketchbook;*
- *experiment with other source material;*
- *experiment with materials, images and ideas;*
- *select from and interpret visual elements;*
- *modify and refine their work in the light of evaluations.*

Knowledge and Understanding. *Pupils should be taught to:*

- *recognise the diverse methods and approaches;*
- *identify how visual elements are used to convey ideas;*
- *relate art, craft and design to its social, historical and cultural context;*
- *identify how and why styles and traditions change;*
- *express ideas and opinions and justify preferences.*

End-of-Key-Stage Descriptions - Art

KEY STAGE 2

Attainment Target 1: Investigating and Making: Pupils record what they have experienced and imagined, expressing ideas and feelings confidently. They represent chosen features of the world around them with increasing accuracy and attention to detail. They select relevant resources and materials and experiment with ideas that are suggested by these. They experiment with, and show increasing control over, a range of materials, tools and techniques. They choose materials and methods and visual elements appropriate to their intentions, making images and artefacts for different purposes. They reflect on and adapt their work, identifying ways in which it can be developed and improved.

Attainment Target 2: Knowledge and Understanding: Pupils compare images and artefacts, using an art, craft and design vocabulary, and identify similarities and differences in methods and approaches. They begin to recognise how works of art, craft and design are affected by their purpose, including where appropriate, the intentions of the artist, craftsperson or designer, and the time and place in which they are made. They evaluate their own and others' work in the light of what was intended.

KEY STAGE 3

Attainment Target 1: Investigating and Making: Pupils use technical and expressive skills in recording ideas and feelings. They show a developing ability to analyse and represent chosen features of the natural and made environment. They are increasingly able to research, organise and experiment with relevant resources and materials to develop their ideas. They make effective use of the characteristics of a range of materials, tools and techniques and select from and interpret visual elements. They modify and refine their work to realise their intentions, and plan and make further developments, taking account of their own and others' views.

Attainment Target 2: Knowledge and Understanding: Pupils analyse images and artefacts, using an appropriate art, craft and design vocabulary, and identify how ideas, feelings and meanings are conveyed in different styles and traditions. They compare work across time and place, recognising characteristics that stay the same and those that change. They critically appraise their own and others' work in the light of what was intended.

The Programmes of Study - Music

ATTAINMENT TARGET 1 - PERFORMING AND COMPOSING
ATTAINMENT TARGET 2 - LISTENING AND APPRAISING

KEY STAGE 2

Pupils' understanding and enjoyment of music should be developed through activities that bring together requirements from both Performing and Composing and Listening and Appraising wherever possible.

Performing and Composing. Pupils should be given opportunities to:

- *control sounds made by the voice and a range of tuned and untuned instruments;*

- *perform with others and develop awareness of audience, venue and occasion;*
- *compose in response to a variety of stimuli, and explore a range of resources;*
- *communicate musical ideas to others.*

Listening and Appraising. Pupils should be given opportunities to:

- *listen to, and develop understanding of, music from different times and places, applying knowledge to their own work;*

- *respond to, and evaluate, live performances and recorded music, including their own and others' compositions and performances.*

KEY STAGE 3

Performing and Composing. Pupils should be taught to:

- *sing and play a variety of music, developing control of subtle changes;*
- *sing and play music by ear;*
- *take part in group performances;*
- *plan, rehearse, direct and present performances;*
- *improvise and arrange;*
- *select and combine resources;*

- *use sounds and conventions to achieve a variety of styles;*
- *refine and complete compositions using notation(s) and recording equipment.*

Listening and Appraising. Pupils should be taught to:

- *identify how resources are used in different combinations;*
- *identify ways in which personal response is influenced by the environment;*
- *relate music to its social, historical and cultural context;*
- *identify how and why musical styles and traditions change over time;*
- *express and justify opinions and preferences.*

End-of-Key-Stage Descriptions - Music

KEY STAGE 2

Attainment Target 1: Performing and Composing: Pupils perform accurately and confidently, making expressive use of the musical elements and showing awareness of phrase. They sing songs and rounds that have two parts, and maintain independent instrumental lines with awareness of the other performers. They select and combine appropriate resources, use musical structures, make expressive use of musical elements and achieve a planned effect. They use symbols when performing and communicating musical ideas.

Attainment Target 2: Listening and Appraising: Pupils respond to music, identifying changes in character and mood, and recognise how musical elements and resources are used to communicate moods and ideas. They evaluate their own work, identifying ways in which it can be improved. They begin to recognise how music is affected by time and place, including, where appropriate, the intentions of the composer(s) and performer(s). They listen with attention to detail and describe and compare music from different traditions, using a musical vocabulary.

KEY STAGE 3

Attainment Target 1: Performing and Composing: Pupils perform an individual part with confidence and control, and interpret the mood or effect of the music. They show awareness of other performers and fit their own part within the whole. They develop musical ideas within structures, using different textures, including harmony, and exploit the musical elements and a variety of resources. They compose music for specific purposes and use notation(s) and, where appropriate, information technology, to explore, develop and revise musical ideas.

Attainment Target 2: Listening and Appraising: Pupils respond to music, identifying conventions used within different styles and traditions. They analyse changes in character and mood, and evaluate the effect of the music. They critically appraise their own work, taking account of their intentions and the comments of others. They compare music across time and place recognising those characteristics that stay the same and those that change. They use a musical vocabulary appropriately.

Physical Education 1999

The physical education curriculum is made up of one AT, plus six areas of activity: games; gymnastic activities; dance; athletic activities; outdoor and adventurous activities; and swimming. Key stage 1 requirements include games, gymnastic activities and dance. At key stage 2, these must be taught each year, and the other three areas must feature during the key stage. Curriculum review is going to cut an area of activity and limit the number of specific requirements within each of them. Swimming will be compulsory if it has not been taught at key stage 1. At key stage 3 the clumsy Unit A and B lists will go and games may not be compulsory at key stage 4. There is likely to be much less specificity, less emphasis on planning and evaluating and an eight level scale of performance.

The Programmes of Study

ATTAINMENT TARGET 1 - PHYSICAL EDUCATION

KEY STAGE 2

*Pupils should be taught six areas of activity. During each year of the key stage pupils should be taught **games, gymnastic activities** and **dance**. At points during the key stage pupils should be taught **athletic activities, outdoor and adventurous activities** and, unless they have already completed the programme of study for swimming during key stage 1, **swimming**. If aspects of the swimming programme have been taught during key stage 1, pupils should be taught the key stage 2 swimming programme starting at the appropriate point.*

KEY STAGE 3

*Pupils should be taught **games**, at least one other full area of activity (Units A+B), and at least two additional half areas of activity taken from different areas of activity. At least one half area of activity must be either **gymnastic activities** or **dance**. Games should be taught in each year of the key stage.*

End-of-Key-Stage Descriptions

KEY STAGE 2

Attainment Target 2: Physical Education: Pupils find solutions, sometimes responding imaginatively, to the various challenges that they encounter in the different areas of activity. They practice, improve and refine performance, and repeat series of movements they have performed previously, with increasing control and accuracy. They work safely alone, in pairs and in groups, and as members of a team. They make simple judgements about their own and others' performance, and use this information effectively to improve the accuracy, quality and variety of their own performance. They sustain energetic activity over appropriate periods of time, and demonstrate that they understand what is happening to their bodies during exercise.

KEY STAGE 3

Attainment Target 2: Physical Education: Pupils devise strategies and tactics for appropriate activities, and plan or compose more complex sequences of movements. They adapt and refine existing skills and apply these to new situations. Pupils show that they can use skills with precision, and perform sequences with greater clarity and fluency. Pupils recognise the importance of rules and apply them. They appreciate strengths and limitations in performance and use this information in co-operative team work as well as to outwit the opposition in competition. They understand the short-term and long-term effects of exercise n the body systems, and demonstrate how to prepare for particular activities and how to recover after vigorous physical activity.

Religious Education 1999

Although religious education is not one of the core or foundation subjects it is a compulsory subject with special status under the 1988 Education Act. It must be provided for all pupils, but parents have a right of withdrawal, as do teachers who would prefer not to participate. There must be a daily act of collective worship, the requirement was reaffirmed by the 1998 School Standards and Framework Act, which can be provided for separate groups at different times of the day but which should be broadly Christian in character.

Curriculum Update

■ The upsurge of interest in the spiritual and moral curriculum has done much to raise the status of religious education in secondary schools. Also, the GCSE syllabuses - both long and short courses - have made RE into a viable qualification for many more students at the same time as schools have been seeking ways to pump up the crucial performance table measure of five GCSE grades at A*-C. As long as the subject is compulsory, its future is assured. At the same time, there have been complaints. Some specialists consider the short course to be insultingly lightweight and, in a few schools, it has become the only option available.

■ The implementation of agreed syllabuses has also worked out well and, in 1998, it forced OFSTED to apologise after some of the agency's inspectors failed to keep up with local SACRE plans. In fact, OFSTED has found that well over 80% of schools meet all of the legal requirements for the teaching of RE.

■ OFSTED's 1998 comments on primary religious education noted that two out of ten primary schools still do not meet the statutory requirement to provide RE for all, but was approving of the quality of teaching in the subject. A deeper concern was expressed over assessment where schools' policies were often confused or non-existent.

■ The provision of collective worship has continued to feature in OFSTED reports as a key area for action in many schools. However, in the second cycle of inspections, many schools are jumping through the appropriate hoops rather than standing out against the requirement which was confirmed by 1998 legislation.

Sex and Drug Education

Sex education is now a compulsory subject in all schools. It should be delivered through a policy that is shared by governors, teachers and parents. Schools also have a responsibility for drug education which should be handled in a similar way through science and PSE lessons. Drug incidents and reactions to them are an increasingly difficult area for schools to negotiate.

Sex Education

There is no curriculum for sex education but, instead, every school must have a policy approved by the governors and in line with national guidelines (*DfE Circular 5/94*) published in May 1994. This policy - and its implementation in the school - is inspected by OFSTED. In primary schools, the governors have responsibility for deciding whether or not to include sex education in the curriculum. They are obliged to maintain a policy statement on the matter which must be available to parents. In secondary schools, sex education - including education about HIV, AIDS and other sexually transmitted diseases - must be provided for all registered pupils including sixth-formers. All sex education must be provided within a spiritual and moral context.

How successful is this? In 1996, there were 95,000 conceptions reported by under 20s and almost 9,000 by under 16-year-olds. The figure for births in 1997 are much lower at around 1600 for the under-16s and 46,000 for the under 20s. Either way, the figures have risen slightly during the 1990s. They relate to a total cohort in the age range of about two million so, out of a million girls, about 100,000 or - very approximately - one in ten probably become pregnant when they would have preferred not to.

The reasons why education is not that effective can be argued over endlessly. It is certainly true that the typical pregnant teenager is in the bottom half of the ability percentile range but that is not invariably the case. It is also a fact that condom use is not the norm in first sexual encounters (first time ever or with new partners) and interestingly, since so much sex

education is about getting children to talk about sex, the majority of the encounters are mute or, at least, unaccompanied by discussion.

One indication of where things go wrong was the publicity accorded to a school in Bath where the school nurse has prescribed the 'morning after pill' without any fuss for the last five years. In 1998, it became a special case and had to be visited by the Social Exclusion Unit! Another suggestion is that some primary schools have such an unhelpful attitude to menstruation that girls tend not to value the school as a source of advice on sex later on.

Drug Education

According to the 1996 British Crime survey, 50% of 16 to 24-year-olds have tried an illegal drug and 20% use one or other at least once a month. In spite of the occasional horror stories, there is very little evidence of drug experimentation before the age of thirteen. In 1998, a new publication (*Protecting Young People: Good Practice in Drug Education*, DfEE) set out Labour's plans for dealing with drugs. The new ideas concerned the need for primary schools to get to grips with the educational messages - types of drugs, their effects and associated risks - and to introduce these at an early age while secondary schools needed to cover the legal aspects more than some do at present. Sound policies, consistent messages and good relations with the local police are seen as key factors in handling drug issues in schools. Estelle Morris was in trouble with the opposition in the autumn of 1998 for reiterating the drug czar, Keith Helliwell's, advice that automatic exclusion was not the best policy.

Addresses

CURRICULUM DEVELOPMENT

Department for Education and Employment (DfEE),
Sanctuary Buildings,
Great Smith St,
Westminster,
London,
SW1P 3BT
Tel: *0171 925 5000*
Fax: *0171 925 6000*
website: *www.standards.dfee.gov.uk*

Qualifications and Curriculum Authority (QCA),
29 Bolton Street,
London,
W1Y 7PD
Tel: 0171 509 5555
Fax: 0171 509 6666
website: www.qca.org.uk

Office for Standards in Education (OFSTED),
Alexandra House,
29-33 Kingsway,
London,
WC2B 6SE
Tel: *0171 421 6800*
Fax: *0171 421 6707*
website: *www.ofsted.gov.uk*

OFSTED Complaints Adjudicator,
Elaine Rassaby,
50 Canonbury Park South,
London,
N1 2JG
Tel: 0171 354 9869

The Teacher Training Agency (TTA),
Portland House,
Stag Place,
London,
SW1E 5TT
Tel: *0171 925 3700*
Fax: *0171 421 6522*
email: *teach.tta.gov.uk*

EXAMINING BOARDS

IAASE,
29 Bolton Street,
London,
W1Y 7PD
Tel: 0171 509 5555
Fax: 0171 509 6950

Joint Council for General Qualifications,
1 Regent Street,
Cambridge,
CB2 1GG
Tel: *01223 552552*
Fax: *01223 552553*

EdExcel Foundation,
(incorporating London Examinations, BTEC)
Stewart House,
32 Russell Square,
London,
WC1B 5DN
Tel: *0171 393 4500*
Fax: *0171 393 4501*
website: *edexcel.org.uk*

OCR Oxford, Cambridge and RSA Examinations,
(incorporating MEG, RSA, OCEAC)
1 Regent Street,
Cambridge,
CB2 1GG
Tel: *01223 552552*
Fax: *01223 552553*
website: *ocr.org.uk*

AQA, The Assessment & Qualifications Alliance,
(incorporating NEAB, AEB, SEG, CGLI)
Manchester,
M15 6EX
Tel: *0161 953 1180*
Fax: *0161 273 7572*
website: *aqa.org.uk or aeb.org.uk*

The Welsh Joint Education Committee (WJEC),
245 Western Avenue,
Cardiff,
CF5 2YX
Tel: *01222 265134*
Fax: *01222 562998*
email: *wjec.co.uk*

Index

A

access to examination scripts, 18
art, 133
Assessment and Qualifications Authority, AQA, 16
Audit Commission, 16, 56, 76, 83

B

beacon schools, 16, 49, 54, 78
Bentley, Tom, 8, 24
Blunkett, David, 5, 6, 8, 11, 16, 22, 24, 25, 28, 33, 35, 53,
    59, 75, 76, 78, 84, 89, 92, 99, 100, 106
Brown, Gordon, 7, 10, 19, 59, 98, 107

C

central government, 6
Clark, Peter, 8
computers in schools, 72
Crime and Disorder Act (1988), 8
curriculum 3 - 16, 27
curriculum 14-19, 37

D

Data Protection Act, 10
design & technology, 122
devolved funding, 11

E

education action zones, EAZ, 6, 8, 9, 10, 37, 49, 52, 57, 61
Education Select Committee, 6, 16, 81
English, 99
Examination Appeals Board , EAB, 18

F

Foster, Don, 6, 75
further education, 19

G

General Teaching Council, GTC, 8, 9, 15, 62
geography, 129
Goldstein, Harvey, 20, 75, 96

H

history, 129
Hodge, Margaret, 5, 6, 7, 29, 75

I

Independent Appeals Authority, IAASE, 17
individual school budget, ISB, 12
induction years, 9, 50, 61, 80
information and communications technology, 125

L

Liberal Democrats, 6, 10, 50
literacy and numeracy, 86

M

maternity leave, 10
Mathematics, 106
Millett, Anthea, TTA, 11, 63
Modern Foreign Language, 127
Morris, Estelle, 6, 7, 25, 50, 63, 139
Mortimore, Peter, 20
music, 133

N

National Advisory Council for Education and Training,
    NACETT, 7, 94
National Grid for Learning, NGFL, 4, 6, 72
National Lottery Act (1998), 10
National Test Teacher Assessment, TA, 102

O

OFSTED, 15, 75
Oxford, Cambridge and RSA Examinations, OCR, 17, 18,
    140

P

Path Finder Scheme, 7
physical education, 136

Q

Qualifications and Curriculum Authority, QCA, 14

R

racism in schools, 5
raising standards, 92
rebuilding programme, 13
religious education, 138

S

School Standards and Framework Act (!998), 10
school system, 49
science, 114
Section 11 Funding, 13
security, school, 20
social exclusion, 7, 38, 57, 58, 83
spending on education, 10
standard spending assessment, SSA, 11
Standards and Effectiveness Unit, SEU, 6, 14, 58, 78
Standards Task Force, STF, 4, 6, 78, 93

T

Tate, Nick, QCA, 6, 11, 14, 22, 23, 27, 47
Teacher Training Agency, TTA, 4, 5, 6, 15, 62, 74, 85, 140
Teaching and Higher Education Act (1998), 8, 9
Tooley, James, 20, 55, 80
Training and Enterprise Councils, TEC, 19
truancy, 7, 9, 67, 84

U

unfair dismissal, 10
University for Industry, 19

W

Willetts, David, 5, 6, 51
Woodhead, Chris HMCI, 4, 6, 11, 15, 16, 20, 21, 27, 28, 37, 46, 59, 75, 76, 77, 78, 80, 81, 82, 85, 86, 87, 88, 93, 95

Y

Youth Music Trust, 20
youth workers, 20